The MYSTERY of the HANDSOME MAN

First published 2020 by Interventions Inc

Interventions is a not-for-profit, independent left wing book publisher. For further information:
    www.interventions.org.au
    info@interventions.org.au
    PO Box 24132
    Melbourne VIC 3001

Queer Oz Folk Series Vol 1
Series Editor: Graham Willett
Queer Oz Folk publishes in the broad field of Australian queer history, with an eye to quality, affordability and the widest possible audiences.

Design and layout by Viktoria Ivanova
Front cover photos: John Lempriere Irvine from the collection of John McCullagh; St Kilda pier and esplanade, State Library of Victoria: Accession no: H32939
Back cover: Chapel Street, Windsor, State Library of Victoria: Accession number: H11718

Author: Wayne Murdoch

Title: Mystery of the Handsome Man: The Double Life of John Lempriere Irvine
ISBN: 978-0-6487603-3-7: Paperback
         978-0-6487603-4-4: ebook

© Wayne Murdoch 2020

The moral rights of the author have been asserted.
All rights reserved. Except as permitted under the Australian Copyright Act 1968 (for example, a fair dealing for the purposes of study, research, criticism or review), no part of this book may be reproduced, stored in a retrieval system, communicated or transmitted in any form or by any means without prior written permission.

All inquiries should be made to the author.

A catalogue record for this work is available from the National Library of Australia

The MYSTERY of the HANDSOME MAN

The Double Life of John Lempriere Irvine

Wayne Murdoch

INTERVENTIONS
MELBOURNE

Interventions is produced on the land of the Wurundjeri people of the Kulin Nation. We acknowledge the Traditional Owners of country throughout Australia and recognise their continuing connection to land, waters and culture. We pay our respects to their Elders past, present and emerging. Their land was stolen, never ceded.
It always was and always will be Aboriginal land.

To Graham Willett, for making it possible.

CONTENTS

1	'Hallo; Are You Working?' – September 1897	1
2	'This Vile Country': The Irvines in Tasmania	9
3	A Young Man about Town	34
4	'Into that pleasant maelstrom, Victoria'	55
5	Intercolonial champion	71
6	'Bow your knees to the bombastic Irvine'	106
7	'A sterling oarsman and hard worker'	128
8	'I could hardly see. I felt exhausted – very much so.'	146
9	'Your obliged servant J.L. Irvine'	175
10	'An Unfortunate Gentleman'	206
11	Falling off the Face of the Earth	212
	Afterword	221
	Endnotes	225
	Picture Credits	236

CHAPTER 1
"Hallo; Are You Working?": September 1897

The sun had set over the city of Melbourne a couple of hours earlier; it was half-past eight o'clock on a Monday night in September 1897. Nineteen-year-old Ernest Smith stood outside the Carlton Bowling Club, on the corner of Grattan and Leicester Streets, having a smoke and passing the time with a mate. They wore the standard uniform of Melbourne's larrikin youth: short-waisted jackets, tight trousers and boots with a heel just a little higher than was considered respectable.

The university buildings opposite were in darkness, and not many people were abroad. Along Grattan Street, from the direction of Swanston Street, came a well-dressed, dapper middle-aged man. He was well built, rather short, but trim; he had the look of a former sportsman who had not let himself run to seed. Dark hair, just silvering at the sides, a neat moustache and a suit whose quality was maybe just a little too good for this working class neighbourhood on a Monday evening. Approaching Smith and his mate, the man looked into Smith's face and said, 'Hallo, are you working?'

Smith's mate wanted nothing to do with what might be happening. Giving a snort of disgust at the suggestion that the two might be rent boys, he walked off down the street. It was then that the man made an 'improper proposal' to Smith, offering him three shillings 'on compliance.' Smith refused and walked away, but the man followed him, caught up with him and groped his crotch. Smith broke away and ran down Leicester Street to Queensberry, where he found a police constable patrolling. Smith complained to Constable W. Stephens that he had been improperly assaulted, and the two went back up nearby Barry Street to confront the man.

Swanston Street, late nineteenth century.

Ernest Smith, mug shot, 1896.

As they approached the corner of Barry and Grattan Streets, they saw the man entering a house. Stephens knocked on the door and apprehended the man, arresting him on a charge of behaving in an insulting manner. He was taken to the Carlton watchhouse in Drummond Street, charged, and held to appear before the Carlton Magistrates' Court the next day.

The following morning, Tuesday 28 September, the accused appeared in Court. He gave his name as John Lempriere Irvine and described himself as a clerk. In fact, the 50-year-old Irvine was a mining and general legal manager, with offices in the grand, eight-storey skyscraper in the heart of the city's financial district, Norwich Union Chambers in Queen Street. A former inter-colonial rowing champion, Irvine was related to members of the Melbourne elite, the brother-in-law of a BHP Board member and brother to the Chairman of the Adelaide Steamship Company and two successful pastoralists. On the

The area south of Grattan Street, Carlton, in the late nineteenth century. Swanston Street, then called Madeline Street, runs diagonally across the picture.

day of his hearing, he was described in the press as 'a stalwart and fashionably dressed man' of respectable appearance. Irvine denied Smith's story, claiming instead that he had been walking down Grattan Street when he had been set upon by a 'push' of 'young roughs' and that he had gone into the house in order to escape them.[1]

Sub-inspector Sharp, representing the police, said that the charge against Irvine could develop into something much more serious (for example, attempted buggery, which could be punished with a prison sentence of up to two years). Sharp asked that Irvine be remanded for seven days, pending further investigations. Irvine's solicitor, A.T. Lewis, offered no objection but asked that Irvine be bailed to appear on Thursday 7 October, rather than spending a week in the watchhouse. Bail was set at £10.

Irvine fronted Carlton Court on 7 October, before magistrates Hurst, Ievers and Sheahan. The charge was read, and Ernest Smith testified. Irvine's defence barrister, Eagleson, cross-examined Smith, who admitted that he had been accused of breaking into a factory the previous year; although the theft charges had been dismissed, he had received a six-month suspended sentence for perjury, having given a false statement.

Smith then made the startling claim that he had been accosted in a laneway a couple of days earlier by two boys, one of whom he knew as Tip. The pair told him that, if he said anything against Irvine, he would be killed by the 'pugs,' a larrikin gang. Smith said that the two boys had given him money and frightened him into signing a written document, but he did not know what the document said.

On hearing Smith's extraordinary story, JPs Hurst, Ievers and Sheahan immediately, 'without any comment,' dismissed the case. In their eyes, Smith, with his previous conviction, connection to larrikin gangs and wild stories of death threats and mysterious documents, was obviously an unreliable witness, if not a fantasist. The magistrates easily formed the opinion that the middle-class Irvine was a decent, upright member of the community who had been the victim of a lower-class perjurer. Irvine was free to go.

That was not the end of the story, however. What happened next was the stuff of nightmares.

In the week that followed the court's rejection of the charges against him, Irvine's life fell apart. In a matter of days, he went from being a pillar of the community and a respected businessman to being a social pariah. Although the case against him had been dismissed, and he had been found apparently innocent of Smith's accusations, he was the topic of gossip around Melbourne. The Carlton case was the topic *du jour* in the reading rooms of gentlemen's clubs, in suburban drawing rooms and kitchens, in ballrooms in Toorak and Brighton, in the bars and taprooms of pubs in working class Fitzroy and Collingwood, in factories, shops and offices throughout the metropolis of Melbourne. On street corners and sporting fields, all Melbourne was talking about the scandal.

Irvine found himself being looked at askance by business acquaintances and avoided by members of the rowing club of which he was a life member. Fellow residents at the exclusive East Melbourne boarding house where he lived gave him a wide berth and gossiped behind his back: 'I always knew there was something about him ...' The advertising columns of the *Argus* and the *Age* bore witness to the dissolution of his successful business; company after company divested itself of his professional services. The Buffalo Hydraulic Gold Mining Company, the Barfold Gold Mining Company and the Southern Leads Gold Mines Mining Company were among many who advertised new managers and a change of registered offices: 'vice Mr John L. Irvine (resigned).'[2] Nothing more was said in the advertisements; nothing more needed to be said. Irvine was now *persona non grata* professionally and socially.

How did this happen, and why? The story of Irvine's spectacular fall from grace is one of prejudice and social ignominy, showing the damage that can be done by influential enemies with axes to grind. What happened to him after his disgrace is a true nineteenth-century mystery.

Jacobina Burn, a silhouette, c. 1830.

CHAPTER 2
"This Vile Country": The Irvines in Tasmania

Who was John Irvine? Banker, sporting champion, bon vivant, clubman, committee member and friend to the colonial elites of Tasmania and Victoria. He was also a man with a secret; a secret that would occasionally lead him into the half-light of the Victorian underworld and ultimately to his downfall, disgrace and disappearance.

John Lempriere Irvine was among the first generation of his family to be born in the Australian colonies, but the fourth generation of an exceptional family to actually live in Van Diemen's Land. This is remarkable, given that he was born within living memory of the British settlement of Australia. Only 59 years separated his birth from the arrival of the First Fleet in Port Jackson, and only 44 years from the establishment of the Tasmanian colony.

His great-grandmother, Jacobina Burn, was the first of the family to emigrate to Van Diemen's Land. Born in February 1762 at Canongate, Edinburgh, Scotland, Jacobina was the daughter of John and Robina Hunter. She married late, at the age of nearly 36, on 20 December 1797. David Burn, her husband, has been variously described as a builder, a marble cutter or an architect, of Edinburgh. Jacobina and David had at least one son, David Edmund, born in 1799.[1]

Around 1820, while the family was planning to migrate to Van Diemen's Land, a convict settlement at the bottom of the world, David Burn Senior died. Letters of introduction to the Lieutenant-Governor of the colony and other members of the colonial establishment were already in hand, and papers allowing David Burn substantial land grants had been drafted, so Jacobina, at the age of 59, decided to continue with the planned migration rather than sit at home in Edinburgh and live off her deceased husband's capital. Her son, David, said that she was 'lured to emigrate to Van Diemen's Land in consequence of the powerful temptations held out by the British Colonial Office, partly in consequence of the glowing description of the colony present in the pages of the work of Lieut. Jeffrey, R.N.' She arrived in Hobart Town in 5 May 1821 on the *Westmoreland*, accompanied by her nephew, William Patterson, son of her sister Katharine.[2]

> To get to the other side of the world in the mid-nineteenth century required a sea voyage that could take months. Those who migrated to the Antipodes in this era were almost unimaginably brave by our cosseted standards. They left behind everything familiar and ventured into the unknown on a boat that might get wrecked, might never reach its destination.[3]

Even a safe voyage would take months on a small wooden vessel in cramped conditions, living cheek by jowl with strangers, with no news of the outside world. Almost everything about the journey eventually became monotonous: the diet, the company, the amusements and activities. One day merged into another, with very little to differentiate them. Ships could drift listlessly on calm seas without a wind for weeks or might encounter terrifying storms.

Jacobina, and those of her family who later followed her to the colonies, travelled as 'Cabin' (that is, first class) passengers and would have expected a degree of comfort and privacy unknown to ordinary migrants who were lodged in communal dormitories for the voyage. However, even first class travel was cramped, uncomfortable, wearisome and potentially dangerous.

On arrival in Hobart, Jacobina found a town that had been established just 18 years earlier as a penal colony and defensive outpost of the colony of New South Wales. The first years of settlement had been difficult, with shortages of food and other supplies. A sense of geographic isolation gave rise to a feeling of dejection among the convicts and their guards. By the time Jacobina arrived, however, she was among an increasing number of free settlers, and the population of Hobart had grown to 10,000. The town was a thriving port for the export of the colony's produce, including wool, wheat, timber, seal skins and whale oil.

"THIS VILE COUNTRY": THE IRVINES IN TASMANIA   11

Hobart in the early 1820s, around the time of Jacobina Burn's arrival.

The society of Van Diemen's Land was extremely stratified, with a large underclass of convicts, ruled by a small civil establishment, and an upper class of free settlers. Free settlers 'never by any chance mixed with either the emancipists [time-expired convicts] or the prisoners,' and it was said that the social division was so 'ludicrously rigid' that 'Van Diemen's Land is perhaps best seen as a caste-based society, with an untouchable majority barred from almost all contact with their "betters."'[4] As a wealthy free settler who had been promised land, Jacobina was among the elite of the colony. Her status was confirmed and enhanced when it became known that she was an old friend of Lachlan Macquarie, Governor of New South Wales and Van Diemen's Land, who was making a rare visit to the colony when she arrived. Macquarie's Journal records Jacobina dining informally with the Macquaries at Government House in Hobart on Thursday 28 June: 'We had Major and Mrs Bell, Mrs Burn, and Mr Moodie to Dine with us in a Family way.'[5] No surprise, then, that Jacobina was readily given 500 acres in the Sorell district near Hobart and another 1,500 acres near Hamilton, which she named Ellangowan.

> She lost no time in taking possession of her land [at Hamilton], although unaccompanied by any female servant or friend, and buried herself ... with assigned servants and a free overseer only, at a distance of fifty miles in an unreclaimed and savage interior.

Fifty miles from Hobart in 1820 might as well have been 1,000 miles from anywhere. The land was uncleared, roads were non-existent, and neighbours were few. Escaped convicts who had taken to bushranging abounded in the district, but they never bothered her; 'Gentleman Brady' would occasionally ask her for 'a little tea, sugar, flour and the like' from her supplies. It is said, however, that the gully behind the stone homestead that Jacobina built was the site where, in 1817, the psychotic bushranger Mike Howe had murdered two of his Irish companions in a fit of paranoia, 'suspecting their innocent Gaelic conversation of concealing secret plotting against him.'[6]

So successful was Jacobina initially that she persuaded other members of her family to follow her to VDL. Her sisters, Katharine and Susan, with their husbands, were the first to join her. Katharine's husband, Myles Patterson, was granted land on the Shannon River, which he named Hunterston. Susan and her husband, Captain John Young, settled at Hunter's Hill, near Bothwell. Both Jacobina and her sister Katharine, who was widowed about six years after arriving in VDL, were remarked upon as 'capable farmers and business-women in their own right.'[7]

At Jacobina's urging, her son David sailed from Glasgow on the *Greenock* late in 1825, with his five-year-old daughter Jemima and infant son. He was estranged from his wife, Maria, and, as was usual with nineteenth-century law, the father was granted custody of the couple's children. The long journey of several months saw conditions on the ship deteriorate and supplies of food run short. Burn's young son died of malnutrition several days before the ship arrived at its halfway point, at Cape Town, and the boy was buried there. Father and daughter continued on to VDL, arriving in Hobart in May 1826. They were greeted by David's mother and broke the news of her grandson's death.

They settled with Jacobina at Ellangowan, and young Jemima quickly became her grandmother's favourite. When David returned to Scotland in 1829 to divorce his wife, he left Jemima in the care of her grandmother. The two grew ever closer. David was back in Hobart by November 1830, buying 500 acres near New Norfolk, a property which he named Rotherwood. In November 1832, he married Catherine Fenton, a member of another establishment family. David also took up the running of his mother's properties, but it was noted that he was 'no farmer.'

In the early days of Ellangowan, the local Aboriginal people were regarded as 'harmless and docile, trustful and playful until they were ill-treated by bushrangers and escaped convicts and became resentful, cunning and savage.'[8] However, it was the settlers and their sheep who drove the Aboriginal people from their lands, killing many in the process and creating resentment over the dispossession of their lands and the disruption of traditional ways of life. This progressed to open conflict in the so-called 'Black War' of the 1820s, and the Aboriginal people retaliated by raiding properties and murdering settlers and their families. By 1830, the relationship between the white settlers and the first inhabitants at Ellangowan had broken down completely. That year, one of Jacobina's shepherds, 'Old Tom', was said to have been 'roasted alive by aborigines'[9] in his hut; a female servant was speared to death on the estate; and another narrowly escaped. Jacobina suggested to Lieutenant-Governor Arthur that something be done to clear the colony of what she saw as a 'scourge which had not only thinned [the Colony's] population but had carried terror and distress to the hearts of her best and bravest.'[10] According to David Burn, Jacobina's suggestion to the Lieutenant-Governor was the so-called 'black line,' a human chain of soldiers, settlers and assigned convict servants who would move south over the settled districts of the colony, driving the Aboriginal people before it and corralling them on the Tasman Peninsula. From there, they would be shipped off to offshore islands, effectively ending their resistance to the Whites. Arthur agreed to the plan. On 7 October 1830, over 2,200 men, representing about 10% of the European population of the Colony, reported to seven nominated locations across the settled districts. They formed into three separate lines which slowly advanced over the countryside, hoping to drive the Aboriginal people before them. The 'black line' was an immediate, and expensive, failure; although there were sightings of Aboriginal people, almost all of them successfully evaded

Jacobina Burn's Ellangowan, in its later days as a shearing shed.

the line. Two were captured, and two were killed. However, the longer term effects of the line, in the words of a modern commentator, were that: 'the scale of the operation, along with ongoing violence and disruption from the Europeans, troubled the Tasmanian Aborigines and they began to avoid living in the settled districts.'[11] Jacobina's obituary reports: 'so startling a display of European energy effectually cowed the blacks. The atrocities of the natives were, thenceforward, stayed.'[12]

In 1836, all three generations of the family – Jacobina, David and Catherine, and young Jemima – returned to England in order to settle Jemima into boarding school. Jacobina spent three years living in London and returned to VDL in 1839. By 1841, Jemima, David and Catherine had all returned from England. The family settled briefly at Rotherwood before moving to Newtown, Hobart, offering the Rotherwood and Ellangowan estates for lease.

The agricultural depression of the early 1840s saw David and Jacobina Burn declared insolvent. Their combined estates of nearly 4,000 'splendid' acres were put up for auction in 1844. The bankruptcy proceedings were complicated by the efforts of Captain Michael Fenton to protect his sister's property entitlement.[13] and involved David in lawsuits in which the legality of his Scottish divorce was called into question. The legal battle caused considerable antagonism between Jacobina, David and Catherine, so much so that, in 1845, David and Catherine left Van Diemen's Land for New South Wales, living there for about 12 months before settling in their final home of New Zealand.[14]

Ellangowan was eventually sold in 1849, but Jacobina saw none of the proceeds, which were used to pay creditors. She was penniless and spent the last few years of her life living with relatives in Bothwell. She died on 10 January 1851, at the residence of her sister, Mrs Katharine Patterson, Clyde Villa, Bothwell, and was buried at Dennistoun.[15]

She was remembered in her obituary as: 'A woman of powerful intellect, strong affections, and considerable conversational powers.'[16]

Ellangowan passed through many hands following its sale and Jacobina's death. Over the years, the homestead was abandoned and deteriorated. By the mid-twentieth century, it was being used as a shearing shed:

> The sheep, so the story goes, were driven in through the front door, penned in the [drawing] room, and then despatched bewildered out through the kitchen door. Finally, one night in 1982, after an electrical fault developed, the old place burned and it is now a mere shell.[17]

Jacobina's son, David, may have been 'no farmer', but he had literary interests and was one of the earliest published Australian authors and playwrights. In his youth, Burn 'associated with some English playwrights and acquired some talent as an actor and a writer.' He had early success with the production of his play, *The Bushrangers*, which was performed at Edinburgh's Caledonian Theatre in September 1829. He later claimed some fame as a journalist; while in England in 1840, he wrote a number of descriptive articles on life in VDL for the *Colonial Magazine* and addressed the Colonial Society Club, arguing for representative government in the Australian colonies. That speech was developed in a pamphlet of the same year, entitled *Vindication of Van Diemen's Land in A Cursory Glance at Her Colonists as They Are, Not as They Have Been Represented to Be*. On his return to VDL, he accompanied the Governor of the colony, Sir John Franklin, and his wife Lady Jane on an extended expedition to the wild west coast of the island, publishing an account of the journey as *Narrative of the Overland Journey ... From Hobart Town to Macquarie Harbour, 1842*. Dietrich Borchardt's *Australian Dictionary of Biography* entry on David Burn considers that the account 'reveals him as an acute observer of men and countryside,' but also rather disparagingly claims that Burn's ornate language spoils his style and that his collection of *Plays, and Fugitive Pieces in Verse*, published in Hobart Town in 1842, 'was of little literary quality.'[18]

Following David and Catherine's move to New Zealand in 1847, David became the editor of the *Maori Messenger* and, later, the *New Zealand Herald*. He retired in 1865 and died in June 1875 in Auckland.

David's daughter Jemima Frances, who was to be John L.'s mother, was born in Scotland in 1821 before coming to Australia with her father and baby brother in 1826. Because of her father's rather peripatetic life, spent travelling around Van Diemen's Land, Jemima was largely raised by her grandmother at Ellangowan.

She was initially educated at home, sharing a governess with the children of Alexander Reid of Ratho, Bothwell. At the age of 15, she accompanied her grandmother, father and stepmother to England and was enrolled as a boarder at Oxford Hall, a small private school run by the Misses Rigg and Fishwick, near Warrington, Cheshire, halfway between Liverpool and Manchester. This marked the beginning of an extensive correspondence with her grandmother, which was to last until Jacobina's death in 1851. Unfortunately, only Jacobina's half of the correspondence has survived. Her letters, held by the Launceston Public Library, show the old lady to have had a generally bright, intelligent and 'no-nonsense' tone, giving her granddaughter advice on everything from the employment of servants and the necessity of women having money of their own, to appropriate behaviour to those less fortunate than oneself. She also shared a good degree of gossip about family, friends and neighbours.

The first letter which Jacobina wrote to Jemima is dated 17 October 1836. She expressed relief that Jemima's new school and the women who ran it appeared to be of a decent standard:

> I was much gratified on the return of your Aunt to find she was
> so much pleased with the ladies under whose charge she left

you – she spoke highly of the genteel and pleasing manner of both – and expressed great satisfaction with the Establishment and its rules generally – said, so far as she could judge you were left in excellent hands – and that she should consider the fault your own should you not make great improvement. ... Remember you are now far advanced and really ignorant for your years – permit me therefore to implore you not to neglect the present opportunity but endeavour to store your mind with every kind of useful knowledge.

Oxford Hall appears to have been a cut above the usual standard of girls' boarding schools in the nineteenth century. Most girls' schools' curricula offered the 'three Rs' but focused more on the fashionable accomplishments of deportment, etiquette, fancy sewing, music, singing and dancing. These were certainly on offer at Oxford Hall, although the practical Jacobina looked askance at them:

> I felt rather disappointed when your Aunt told me that she had consented to your being taught music – the study of which consumes a great deal of time which might be more profitably employed in the culture of your mind ... As for instrumental music it requires a particular talent so as to make any proficiency – and that you do not possess, likewise great perseverance – a virtue in which I also fear you will be found deficient. Should you however refute my prognostications I shall be truly delighted.

Instead, Jacobina opined that:

> The general cultivation of the mind is ... the most essential of all studies. Composition I consider as a most important piece of education, particularly that of letter-writing as it is not only a beautiful accomplishment but a great pleasure to be able to express yourself with ease and elegance. In short my dear girl my love for you is such as makes me feel an earnest desire that you may possess many valuable qualities both of head and heart.

Within 12 months of starting at Oxford Hall, Jacobina was commenting on Jemima's glowing school reports:

> I was quite delighted with the accounts your Papa gave of general improvement – among other things, he said you sung very sweetly and drew very prettily. Miss Rigg also gave a very favourable report of your increased perseverance and attention to your studies. All of which you will readily believe was matter of much pleasure and gratification to me. Should I ever again have the felicity of embracing you my dearest girl I shall hope to find your mind highly cultivated and yourself a good and dutiful girl.[19]

Oxford Hall appears to have given Jemima an entrée into things of the mind. The evidence of her future life and interests show her to have had above-average intelligence and an intellectual curiosity about the world around her, particularly the natural world. She became an avid collector of all manner of natural and historical materials, was well read and could turn a decent phrase, as is shown by newspaper articles and reminiscences she wrote later in life.

Jemima returned to Van Diemen's Land in 1841 at the age of 20 and lived with her grandmother at Ellangowan. Her life on the property was at first one of feminine accomplishments, such as sewing: 'I am delighted to observe that you are so dexterous with your needle and sheers [sic]. Nothing appears to come wrong to you. Such will prove a great comfort through life'; riding: 'You will be quite stylish with your smart riding habit and cap. Your only want you say is a saddle. Pray have you got a horse? as I should consider that a more essential want – and if so, a saddle might be easily procured'; and dancing: 'the Ball is to take place [at Shannon]. I hope all of you may be there, and experience great enjoyment.'[20]

However, Jemima also saw firsthand the effects of the pastoral depression of the early 1840s, which was to bankrupt her grandmother and father:

> I remember too, that we often used to help the men burn the wool which had been shorn from the sheep, more with the idea of making the poor creatures comfortable than of making money selling it. This

used to annoy my grandmother very much, as it was often such good wool and she could not bear to see it wasted.[21]

In late 1842 or early 1843, Jemima met Charles James Irvine, newly arrived in the colony from the north of Ireland. Irvine was the son of John Irvine, Gentleman, of Deer Park, County Tyrone. John had died in 1831, when Charles was 13. It is likely that the early death of his father left the family in straitened circumstances, and this may ultimately have led to Charles' decision to try his luck in the colonies. He sailed from Plymouth on board the *Apolline* on 2 June 1842. Among Charles' fellow passengers in first class were John King (later Warden of the municipality of Hamilton) and W. Tarleton, a future police magistrate. The ship was also carrying 222 assisted migrants in steerage. After a voyage of nearly three months, the ship arrived at Hobart on 24 September and immediately went into quarantine, because of cases of whooping cough and measles on board. By 30 September, there was only one case of measles left (that of Mr Tarleton, Charles' companion from first class), and the passengers were allowed to disembark.[22]

Exactly what Charles did for his first year in Van Diemen's Land is unknown; he obviously had some funds and some education, and he would have arrived in the colony carrying letters of introduction to influential Vandiemonians who might have been able to find him a position in government circles or in property management. What is known is that, within nine months of his arrival, he was standing in the drawing room of David Burn's Rotherwood – about to marry Burn's daughter, Jemima.

The circumstances of their meeting are unknown. Given the small circles of 'free' society in Van Diemen's Land, the two were bound to have met socially before Irvine had been in the colony too long. An introduction would have been made, and suitably chaperoned meetings and outings would have taken place. Charles would have sought David Burn's (and, more than likely, Jacobina's) permission before asking Jemima to marry him. On Thursday, 22 June 1843, 24-year-old Charles James Irvine married 21-year-old Jemima Frances Burn according to the rites of the Church of Scotland. The groom's rank was given as 'Esquire.' His witnesses were his shipmates from the *Apolline*, John King and W. Tarleton. The bride's witnesses were her friend Marianne Dickson and Leonora Fenton, who was related to her stepmother (Catherine).[23]

Charles and Jemima settled at Rotherwood, where Charles took over the management of his father-in-law's property. The house was a pleasant stone Georgian villa. There, on 25 March 1844, their first child, Charles Hamilton, was born. The baby was apparently sickly to start with; in May 1844, Jacobina wrote that she 'was sorry to hear that your poor dear baby had been so very ill and had caused you so much uneasiness – it is however a matter of great thankfulness that he has quite recovered and thriving so well.'[24] Charlie's birth was announced in the VDL newspapers in the particularly stark way of the early nineteenth century: 'Birth – At Ellangowan, on Monday, the 25 instant [ie March], the Lady of C.J. Irvine, Esq., of a son.'[25]

By 1844, Jacobina Burn may have been in dire straits financially and facing bankruptcy; but the old lady still had influence in the colony. It is said that she used her influence with Lieutenant-Governor Sir John Eardley-Wilmot to obtain a post for Charles in the colony's civil service; in a penal colony, this often meant service in the prison system. Charles was appointed to the colony's commissariat. By early 1845, Charles, Jemima and one-year-old Charlie found themselves at the Cascades prison settlement, deep in the bush of the Tasman Peninsula, 100 kilometres by road from Hobart. When they arrived at the settlement, Jemima was heavily pregnant with her second son, Richard Francis, who was born at Cascades on 4 May 1845. The birth was a difficult one, the baby being born prematurely; a fortnight later, Jacobina wrote to Charles:

> No words of mine can express the painful sensation which I experienced while perusing your letter of the 4th Inst. announcing the premature delivery and excrutiating [sic] sufferings of my poor dear girl – nor the terrific visions which perpetually haunted my troubled mind until the welcome arrival of your second letter – which thank God brought the Joyful intelligence of her preserved life – and promising recovery ... I was delighted to [hear] that ... the little stranger was so fine and good a boy – giving no trouble, sleeping night and day. I hope he may be equally peaceful when he awakes ... You say you were disappointed that it was not a girl – but in my opinion it was better ordered – boys are not such an anxious charge and more easily provided for.[26]

Cascades was a logging settlement, founded in the early 1840s. By the time Charles took his wife and infant son there, more than 200 convicts were employed, felling timber to be used to build the nearby prison settlement of Port Arthur and also new buildings in Hobart. It was the main timber site on the Peninsula, described as having 144 'apartments and other buildings of a superior class.' The settlement had a chapel capable of holding a congregation of 300, together with a mess hall for 200 men, workshops, solitary cells, and cottages for the military and prison staff and their families. Life for the prisoners was:

> tough, being locked up at night and toiling by day in damp and leech ridden gullies. By any standards Cascades, despite its idyllic setting overlooking Norfolk Bay, was not a pleasant place and nor were the occupants of its numerous buildings the most pleasant of men. They were there for a purpose and the niceties of life were not part of this isolated and disciplined existence.[27]

Food, although not in short supply, was monotonous. In a letter of 1 May 1845, Jacobina wrote of her concern that fruit, milk, butter and eggs were not available to the families at the Cascades; but, ever practical, she asked: 'You surely would be allowed to keep poultry?'[28]

After less than a year at Cascades, Charles was transferred to the main convict settlement of Port Arthur to take up the post of Assistant Superintendent of Convicts, essentially the second-in-command of what amounted to a small town with a population of over 1,300 convicts.

Established on the supposedly inescapable Tasman Peninsula as a convict logging station in 1830, Port Arthur was developed into a permanent prison settlement for repeat offenders and those convicted of serious crimes. The location was perfect for a prison: the Tasman Peninsula was joined to the Tasmanian mainland by Eaglehawk Neck, a narrow strip of land only 30 metres wide. A chain of guard dogs stretched across the Neck, and the waters on either side were rumoured to be filled with sharks.

The move from timber camp to permanent prison was made in 1833 when Charles O'Hara Booth, an army captain who had seen service in India and the West Indies, was appointed Commandant of the settlement. Approximately 1,000 convicts were moved to Port Arthur; many came from the older convict settlements at Macquarie Harbour and Sarah Island which were being closed down and abandoned. Under Booth's command, new industries based on convict labour were established, including ship-building, shoemaking, smithing, timber milling and brickmaking. The town of Port Arthur, where the civil administration of the settlement lived, was laid out 'on an extensive scale.' Other major construction projects undertaken included harbour works; a semaphore telegraph system that could send messages rapidly all the way to Hobart, 100 kilometres away; Australia's first passenger tramway system (propelled by convicts pushing the cars along the eight kilometres of track); and an industrial-sized flour mill and granary, later converted to a penitentiary.

> [Booth's] administration of the convict system was extremely efficient, his rule was impartial, never capriciously tyrannical, and, though by present standards justice then seemed merciless, he was as prompt to reward as to punish; he had patient attention for the most trivial cases and used the lash as a last resort with great reluctance.[29]

However, the system at Port Arthur was based on punishment. Prisoners regularly experienced floggings, leg irons and isolation in solitary confinement. William Champ, who succeeded Booth in January 1844, introduced a new system that relied less on corporal punishment and more on psychological punishments. Under the 'Silent System,' prisoners were isolated in solitary confinement, wore hoods when in public areas of the prison, were forced to remain silent at all times and were referred to by numbers rather than names. A new prison, the 'Separate Prison,' was built in 1848, based on a model that allowed prisoners to be kept under constant surveillance. At the time, the new system was considered to be more humane; but it soon became apparent that the psychological strain drove many convicts to insanity.

Against this background of crime, punishment and physical and mental cruelty, a civil establishment of administrators, military personnel and their wives and children made their home at the settlement:

> for the staff and their families, life at Port Arthur was similar to life in any other town, although it lacked shops, hotels and certain amenities. Because it was a penal settlement, regulations were to be

developed that must at times have been restrictive, particularly one that prevented its residents from leaving the settlement whenever they wished. To leave, everyone required the commandant's permission, and staff members were allowed leave of absence, to Hobart only, not more than once in six months unless in urgent circumstances.[30]

Many years later, Jemima recalled going to Port Arthur in 1846:

> At that time there were as many as 1,300 prisoners there, all of whom I remember, looked very clean and orderly. There has been a great deal of exaggeration about Port Arthur and the way the prisoners were treated there, but you have only to look at the numbers of them who came on and did well for themselves to realise that it was not so bad after all. Some of them were flogged, of course, but this did not happen very often. I don't remember a single case of misconduct all the time we were there, so orderly were the prisoners.[31]

Other residents of Port Arthur, however, thought differently at the time. Dr Thomas Brownell, the medical officer, 'thought [the convicts'] influence so harmful that … he wished he and his family were anywhere but Port Arthur'. The families frequently witnessed crime and punishment, he wrote, and 'the mind becomes inured and the fine feelings blunted, so that what at first appears shocking and revolting is apt to soften down to a lighter grade and sin is not seen and felt to be so exceedingly sinful as it should be.'

The families living at Port Arthur usually kept apart from the prisoners, except for those working in their homes as servants. The Reverend Robert Crooke, the settlement's chaplain, felt that even this contact blunted sensibilities: '[A]lthough certain subjects were generally avoided even among men, they were openly discussed among mothers of family who would "unreservedly speak of unnatural crime" [as sodomy was often called at the time].'[32] However, Jemima's memory of her convict servants was more favourable:

> some of them had worked in the best houses in England. You can have no idea what good work they used to do and how much we came to like some of them. They were not the depraved, nearly maniac

creatures you may have read about, at all. Some of them had been sent out for trifles, and never broke the law again.'[33]

Jemima herself was not above flouting the law occasionally:

> Sometimes when tobacco supplies were short (for the prisoners were not officially allowed to smoke or chew it), I used to hide some of the twists or plugs of it in the pocket of my dress or in my handbag. Then as I passed them at work on the roads or in the gardens, I would accidentally let a plug fall near them on the ground. They never showed even by the flicker of an eyelid that they had seen me do this, for we should both have got into trouble if it had been discovered, but the tobacco used to disappear like magic.[34]

Meanwhile, Charles was collecting responsibilities and sinecures. He became Postmaster of the settlement on 10 March 1845[35] and was the local agent for the Hobarton *Guardian* newspaper.[36] In 1847, the *Courier* noted that he had donated a pound to the Irish and Scottish relief fund, in the wake of the Irish and Scottish potato famines.[37] In March that year, Charles was appointed deputy registrar of Births, Deaths and Marriages for the Tasman Peninsula;[38] the number of births and marriages he would have registered in the predominately male world of the convict settlement were relatively few, but one of the first was that of his third son, John Lempriere Irvine, who was born at Port Arthur on 10 April, 1847. Jacobina Burn wrote to her granddaughter:

> It was with the most heartfelt pleasure I received the few lines written by yourself being an evident proof of the happy state in which you My dearest Jemima felt yourself – after the fearful apprehensions you entertained regarding the manner in which your young stranger was to make his appearance. Thank God your fears proved groundless and that you were blessed in having an easy time, your suffering being short and your recovery such as to enable you to take the pen in hand – which was no small satisfaction to me – for which kind consideration I return you my best thanks. Having heard so much of your size I was glad to hear that he came *singly* – was also much pleased that it was a

boy as such will leave you more at your liberty – girls being an anxious charge in this Vile Country. I am delighted to hear that your dear husband makes so kind and loving a nurse – long may he be spared to attend to your every comfort and happiness. No earthly blessing comparable to conjugal love.[39]

As well as expressing thanks for the new baby's safe delivery (and the fact that he 'came singly'), Jacobina also expressed bemusement with the baby's middle name, Lempriere: 'I should have been truly delighted to learn that your own and your husband's tempers had so far bended as to have given baby a difficult name.'[40] However, the difficult name was actually that of one of Charles' close friends and respected colleagues at Port Arthur. Thomas Lempriere was the assistant commissary general and worked closely with Charles. Today, he is also known as an author and artist and for his diary and published observations of life at VDL prison settlements. Unfortunately, Lempriere was not to know his young namesake very long, because he was transferred to the commissariat in Hong Kong in 1849.

Charles was to register the births of two more of his children at Port Arthur: George Darcy in January 1849[41] and Jemima Frances, their first daughter, in October 1850.[42] By the time he resigned his position as Assistant Superintendent of Convicts at Port Arthur, around March 1851, to take up the post of Superintendent of the Launceston Gaol, Charles and Jemima had five children. They ranged in age from seven-year-old Charles Hamilton down to six-month-old Jemima.

Launceston, the largest town of northern Tasmania, was founded in 1806 as a secondary convict settlement to Hobart. It grew steadily for the first few decades of its existence, developing as a port for its local pastoral industry and Bass Strait sealers and whalers during the 1820s and 1830s. By 1827, the population was 2,000. Small local industries, including breweries and local manufactories, had developed. The town was also the base for a locally quartered British regiment and a service centre for its surrounding hinterland. Launceston grew steadily, to a population of around 10,000 by 1850. The early wealth of the town displayed itself in the range of well-built Georgian and early Victorian houses, shops, and institutional buildings. The elite of Launceston clustered on Windmill Hill, to the north-east of the main streets of the town. Here, above the smells, dust and noise of the town, lived the wealthy merchants, senior members of the establishment and the local gentry. Down on the flat in front of the Hill were the main business streets of the town; across the North Esk River, on low-lying river flats, were the poorer parts of the town.

By the time Charles and Jemima Irvine arrived, in the early 1850s, the town had been hit somewhat by the general economic depression of the 1840s. Only its economic reliance on a range of government institutions, including the local barracks, hospital, convict depot and gaol, had allowed the town to ride out the economic depression to some degree and to survive a population loss to the Victorian gold rushes in the 1850s.

The Launceston Gaol was one of the most important Of the town's government institutions. Located on the corner of Bathurst and Patterson Streets, on the present site of Launceston College, it was quite close to the town centre. The gaol's earliest buildings were among the first built in the new settlement in 1803. It was rebuilt in 1827 with further extensions, including a scaffold built in the mid-1830s and capable of hanging up to ten prisoners at one time.[43] However, by the time Charles arrived to take up his duties in the 1850s, even these relatively new buildings were in a poor state of repair. At a Committee of Enquiry held in 1860, Charles reported that the buildings were 'swarming with bugs, and [had] a close atmosphere. The old walls cannot be cleared of bugs, though I tried every means – hot lime and scalding water. I never tried fumigation because of the open grates.'[44] The prison was also overcrowded; Charles considered that the accommodation was sufficient for only 42, but there were often double that number held.

The Superintendent's family did not live on site, nor did they live on the heights of Windmill Hill. Their first home in Launceston was in St John Street, a couple of blocks from the gaol, in the very centre of the town. Today, St John Street is one of the busiest streets of central Launceston, in the heart of the central business district. In the early 1850s, it was a mix of residences, shops and businesses. Soon, however, the family moved several blocks north to William Street, where Charles and Jemima's sixth child, Mervyn Frederick, was born in November or December 1853. Mervyn was to die in March 1854 at the age of 14 months.[45] His cause of death was dysentery, a relatively common gastrointestinal disease at that time, caused by drinking dirty water. Mervyn was the first of Charles and Jemima's children to die. At the time of his death, Jemima was again pregnant, with her seventh child and second daughter, who was born in November. The new baby was christened Eliza Katherine, always to be known as Kate.

By the time that Kate was born in November 1853, Charles and Jemima had noticed that their eldest son, 11-year-old Charles Hamilton, was ill with what was diagnosed as 'disease on the heart.'[46] The boy ailed over the hot summer of 1854-55 and died at the family home in William Street on 26 February 1855. Unlike the death of his younger brother Mervyn 10 months earlier, which passed without public announcement or comment, the death of the first-born Charles Hamilton was announced in the Births, Deaths & Marriages columns of a number of the colony's newspapers.

The last convict ship reached the colony in May 1853, when the *St Vincent* arrived in Hobart. It was a momentous year in Van Diemen's Land's history. Although 'old hands' (convicts serving life sentences) would remain in the prisons of the colony until the 1880s and later, the days of the convict system were numbered. Free settlers now played a much greater role in the decision-making and development of the colony than the convict establishment, and they were keen to dismantle the convict system and remove the 'stain' of convictism from the colony's reputation. Such was the infamy of the very name, Van Diemen's Land, that the colony was renamed Tasmania in 1856 in an attempt to distance itself from its dark past.

In addition to his post at the gaol, Charles had quickly become involved in the business life of the town. He became a member of the provisional committee of the newly formed Bank of Tasmania in September 1853 and acted as the secretary of the newly formed Tamar Fire and Marine Insurance Company from February 1854. By August that year, he was paid an annual salary of £300 by the company, in addition to the £434 per annum he received as Superintendent (or, as he often now styled himself, Governor) of the Gaol: a combined income that put the Irvines into the upper reaches of Launceston society.

Charles' involvement in organisations such as the Mechanics' Institute, the Northern Tasmanian Rifle Corps, the Horticultural Gardens and Holy Trinity Anglican Church (as a churchwarden) enhanced his and Jemima's social standing. He reached the apogee of his social aspirations for the 1850s in December 1857, as a member of the executive committee organising a levee at the Horticultural Gardens for the Governor, who was visiting for the Launceston Exhibition of Industry.

While Charles was building his professional and social profile, Jemima was busy with domestic concerns, supervising servants and raising her surviving children. It is difficult to trace the lives of mid-nineteenth-century women in public sources outside the home, such as the pages of newspapers, because middle and upper-class wives and daughters were practically anonymous. Their public presence is almost always referenced in terms of their husbands and fathers' lives and activities. Until the late nineteenth century, almost the only time a respectable woman's given name was published was in the announcement of her wedding. If she did anything newsworthy prior to that, she was referred to as Miss Smith; after her marriage, she was invariably referred to by her husband's name, for example, Mrs John Smith. The anonymity of respectable women was furthered by the convention of announcing the birth of a child in only the father's name. If the mother's involvement in the birth of her child was acknowledged at all, it was as the 'wife' or 'lady' of John Smith. This convention did not start to break down until the 1890s.

Conversely, working class women and those of the 'criminal classes' were often acknowledged in the press by the use of their own full names. This was hardly ever a good thing. They were usually only represented when being reported as victims or perpetrators of crimes, or drunk, or involved in fights and public altercations; reportage often carried a tone of disparaging amusement.

In common with other respectable, middle and upper-class women, Jemima was involved in a number of public activities considered suitable for a woman of her class. These included the Holy Trinity's ladies auxiliary and the Mechanics' Institute Ladies' Committee, where she was prominent in organising fund raising bazaars, fêtes and musical recitals. But Jemima also had an interest in collecting: wildflowers, ferns, geological specimens, birds' eggs, coins, medals, shells, ephemera and items of historical interest. As a boy, Tasmanian writer K.R. von Stieglitz knew her:

> She collected almost anything you can think of – walking-sticks, match-box tops, gold seals and things like that – but most outstanding was her collection of shells. She used to exchange them with people

all over the world. She also had a fine collection of stamps, which was sold for a good deal of money when she died. She used to paint really delightful little studies of various things in water colour, particularly of autumn leaves and flowers. Moreover, she had some letters written at various times by bushrangers ...'[47]

Jemima seems to have been collecting from at least her time in Port Arthur. A seaweed specimen which she later donated to Launceston's Queen Victoria Museum and Art Gallery is dated 1848. Her collection of ephemera and oddities, now held in a private collection in northern Tasmania, creates an almost overwhelming room, full of all sorts of bits and pieces: Chinese slippers, a piece of wood from the True Cross, snippets of hangman's rope, pressed flowers, autographs and miniature books.

These interests and collections were balanced with an increasing family. Another son, Charles James, was born in June 1857, and a daughter, Florence Mary, in May 1859. In August 1861, twins Robert Claude Russell and Ellen Maude completed the family. By 1861, after 18 years of marriage, Jemima had given birth to 11 children and lost two.

Young Richard Hilder, the son of one of Jemima's friends, much later recalled her appearance and manner in 1862:

> a gracious elderly [aged 41 at the time!] woman dressed in the rustling fashionable silk material of that period, with earrings of shining jet. Her hair was dressed high and decorated with glittering ornaments, surmounted by two small feathers.

> The motherly lady soon put me at my ease, for she spoke so kindly to me and made many enquiries about my brothers and sisters and my dear mother too ... During the tea time she helped in handling her fine table appointments and laughed so heartily over some of my childish queries. It was a real pleasure that I felt in the presence of this gracious lady in her beautiful home at Launceston ... Over 70 years have passed since that evening, but memories of that kind motherly face still remain with me, and come before me as I write.[48]

By December 1859, Charles had resigned as Superintendent of the Gaol and bought the business of R.D. MacEachern, wholesale and retail grocer and wine and spirit merchant, located in Brisbane Street, central Launceston. Another change of address took place; the family moved to Brisbane Street, over the business.

The business of Irvine and MacEachern prospered from the first day, and life seemed to be set on an even keel. Charles became prominent in the newly formed Launceston Chamber of Commerce and on the committee of local business leaders established to agitate for the building of a railway in northern Tasmania. However, at his office on the morning of Saturday 14 November, Charles was suddenly 'seized at ½ 11 o'clock, with an apoplectic fit and had to be conveyed to bed. The symptoms became alarming, as from the bursting of a blood vessel, he threw up large quantities of blood.' He was attended by three doctors 'who were in attendance on him, together or alternatively, all night, but their aid was of no avail.' Charles died, aged 45, on the morning of Sunday 15 November 1863; as the reporter in the *Launceston Examiner* had it, 'he was taken ill about noon on Saturday, and twenty-four hours later was a corpse.'[49]

The following day, most of the shops and other businesses of the town shuttered their windows as a mark of respect and kept them shuttered until the funeral, which was held on Wednesday 18 November. Such was the impact of Charles' death and funeral that many of those invited to a vice-regal 'At Home' at the Cornwall Assembly Rooms on the evening of Tuesday 17 November sent their apologies, 'owing to the death of Mr Irvine.'[50]

On the morning of Wednesday 18 November, a large cortege set out from the Irvines' home in Brisbane Street. It was met at Holy Trinity by a 'large assemblage of mourners [including] influential citizens and colonists, from all the Northern Districts, who knew the deceased gentleman, and who highly esteemed him, for his many excellent virtues, sterling qualities, and generous disposition.' It was reported that 'the service for the burial dead was conducted by the Reverend Francis Hales, a principal feature of which was the performance ... of Handel's sublime Dead March in Saul; a piece of solemn music, rendered with great skill and intense feeling – a befitting accompaniment to so awful a ceremony.'[51] The reporter from the *Cornwall Chronicle*, who attended the service, thought that upwards of 300 followed the coffin to the Carr Villa Cemetery on the outskirts of Launceston.

At the time of Charles' death, Jemima's nine surviving children ranged in age from the older children – Richard, John L., George and Jemima, aged 18, 16, 14, and 13 respectively – to the younger ones, nine-year-old Kate, Charles (6), Florence (4) and the two-year-old twins, Claude and Ellen. According to a later newspaper report, Jemima ran Irvine and MacEachern for eighteen months until her eldest son Richard took over the running of the shop at the age of 20. He was to continue as the senior partner of the business for nearly 60 years.

32 THE MYSTERY OF THE HANDSOME MAN

Brisbane Street, Launceston in the late 1850s. Irvine and McEachern's store is the building with a flagpole.

CHAPTER 3
A Young Man about Town

At the time of his father's death, John L. (or Jack, as he was usually known by his family and friends) was 16. He had recently completed his education at Rostella, a private boarding school on the eastern bank of the Tamar River to the north of Launceston. Rostella was built as a country homestead on a land grant of 407 acres in 1834 and was a two-storeyed, symmetrical Georgian house. The house boasted 14-inch-thick walls, built of bricks made by convicts from clay quarried on the site, and a large cellar complete with barred windows, said to have been for protection against bushrangers.

The school's headmaster, the Reverend Henry Plow Kane, first advertised for pupils in March 1860, outlining an extensive curriculum which promised to include:

> Classics, Latin, French, English grammar, orthography, composition, derivation and analysis of words, elocution, history, geography, elementary science, mathematics, common arithmetic, vulgar and decimal fractions, theory and use of logarithms, algebra, plane geometry, Euclid, mensuration of surfaces, land surveying and mapping, practical surveying of the chain, trigonometry, science of navigation, mensuration of solids, stacks railway cuttings, canals, &c; drawing in pencil and water colors, painting in oil color, bookkeeping, writing and ornamental printing.[1]

Phew!

Jack's first appearance in the public record, apart from the announcement of his birth 14 years earlier (when he was simply described as 'a son', born to 'the Lady of C.J. Irvine'), was in December 1861. He had received second place in the class lists for the school year.[2] He was obviously an able student and appears to have been popular with his school fellows, who included the sons of other prominent and wealthy Launceston and country families. He was already developing the social skills and manners that would take him far through the rest of his life.

Nearly two years later, in November 1863, aged 16, he was noted as one of the chief mourners at his father's funeral. By all accounts, he acquitted himself well on the day. At this stage, he was very probably working in the family business as a clerk or assistant, although there is no record of exactly what he was doing during business hours. What is certain is that every spare moment he had was spent on the Tamar River, following his chief interest in life – rowing.

Nowhere in nineteenth-century Launceston was very far from a river, situated as it is at the confluence of the Tamar, the North Esk and the South Esk. Shortly after Charles' death, the family moved to a new house located on the riverbank. It was a double-storey red brick villa, with wide verandahs around three sides and extensive gardens sweeping down to the water: 'although only a few minutes from the post office and town hall, it was quite secluded, as it fronted on a by-way leading to the yachting sheds, which by-way was also planted with trees.'[3] Growing up in such a location, it was no wonder that all the Irvine boys, particularly Jack and his older brother Richard (usually known as Dick), were in, and on, the water from a young age.

In nineteenth-century Australia, rowing was a far more popular sport than it is now. In the early days of the Australian colonies, waterborne transport was faster, safer and more reliable than the often non-existent roads. Many more people had experience of ships and boating, whether as passengers, sailors and oarsmen, than now. Most people in Australia, other than the colonial born, had spent months in a ship travelling to Australia; coastal shipping was the main means of getting from one coastal town to another; and light craft and rowing boats were used extensively for getting around in areas with navigable harbours, rivers and creeks. Out of this familiarity with being on the water and handling small craft grew the sport of competitive rowing. In the nineteenth century, rowing was as popular a spectator sport as the other big sports of the day – horse racing, cricket and football. Crowds of several thousand people would gather on riverbanks to watch single oarsmen or crews of two, four or eight rowers compete for prize money, trophies or glory; 'sporting events [such as rowing] became ritual spectacles in which competitors were claimed to symbolise the sporting prowess of the community they represented.'[4]

Launceston was a keen boating town, having held a formal sailing and rowing regatta since 1840. From the very first regatta, the prize money available was indicative of the popularity of the competition: a total pool of £195 was available. In the 1850s and 1860s, when Jack was growing up, several rowing clubs were clustered around the shores of the Tamar; but the Irvine boys were used to mucking around in the river with very few facilities, as a contemporary later remembered: 'Dear me, when I ... thought of the old rowing days when Jack Irvine, Fred Haymes, Fitz and many others used to strip and leave their clothes on the steps at the George Town bridge in charge of old "Otto," while they did their pull, and the discomfort, dirt and sundry annoyances attendant on dressing, to say nothing of the articles that *would* fall into the water and "walk away," I came to the conclusion ... that there was more glory in winning of old, because of the trouble and risk, than in these degenerate days.'[5] These early experiences on the Tamar gave young Irvine a love of the water and of the sport, not to mention the male camradery of the rowing crews.

Another aspect of shipping familiar to Launcestonians in the nineteenth century was the ships linking their town with the wider world. Coastal ships ran regularly to Hobart and other Tasmanian centres and further afield to Melbourne, Geelong, Adelaide, Sydney and beyond. Launceston and shipping had a long history. The town was founded by convicts arriving in the river by ship in 1803, and it was from Launceston that ships set out to the Port Phillip District to settle Melbourne in 1835. By the 1860s, fast steamers could make the crossing of Bass Strait from Launceston to Melbourne overnight, meaning that Launceston was more and more drawn into Melbourne's sphere of influence. Business and holiday travel between the two cities was common and regular. Wealthy Tasmanians would often visit Melbourne to shop and socialise, and some of the wealthiest kept houses in Melbourne for the purpose. Tasmania, with its cooler climate, became a refuge from the summer heat for wealthy Victorians who claimed that the island was a little piece of England in the antipodes.

This regular cross-strait traffic was reported in meticulous detail in the daily newspapers of both Launceston and Melbourne. Shipping arrivals and departures occupied many tightly-printed columns, usually on the front pages of the morning papers in both cities, with cargo manifests and the names of cabin class passengers prominent. The printing of lists of cargo served the purpose of informing businessmen that their awaited goods had been dispatched or had arrived, and the listing of first class passengers apprised their friends, acquaintances and business associates of their movements more quickly than a letter and more cheaply than a telegram – and reached a far wider circle than either. As members of Launceston's establishment, the Irvines travelled cabin class as a matter of course, which makes the task of tracking members of the family at 150 years' distance extremely easy.

Jack's first Bass Strait crossing was made in the winter of 1864. He and his mother crossed from Launceston to Melbourne on the almost brand-new *City of Launceston,* which began working the Bass Strait service in October the previous year. The *City of Launceston* sailed on the morning of Monday 4 July, carrying eight cabin passengers (including Mrs and Master Irvine) and 'seventeen in the steerage'[6] and arrived in Hobson's Bay, Melbourne, on the afternoon of the following day. The first and middle parts of the crossing were made in fine weather, but the ship's captain, Woods, told Melbourne's *Argus* newspaper that they ran into strong winds, rain and high seas as they neared Melbourne, delaying them slightly.

The purpose of Jemima and Jack's visit to Melbourne in 1864 is unknown. Jack, aged 17, only stayed for three weeks, arriving back in Launceston on the *Black Swan* on 27 July. Jemima remained in Melbourne for a further three weeks and arrived in Launceston, also on the *Black Swan,* on 17 August. It is possible that they were sounding out career opportunities for Jack, because, just over six months later, he was back in Melbourne seeking employment with the Union Bank.

The Union Bank was founded in London in 1837 and opened its first Australian branch in Launceston in the following year. It quickly expanded, opening branches in Melbourne (1838), Sydney (1839), New Zealand (1840), Adelaide (1850) and Brisbane (1858). By the mid-1860s, it was one of the largest banks in Australasia. Its ornate branch buildings, in most cities, towns and suburbs, reflected its importance.

Launceston, 1860s. The Launceston Gaol is the large complex of buildings on the extreme left hand side.

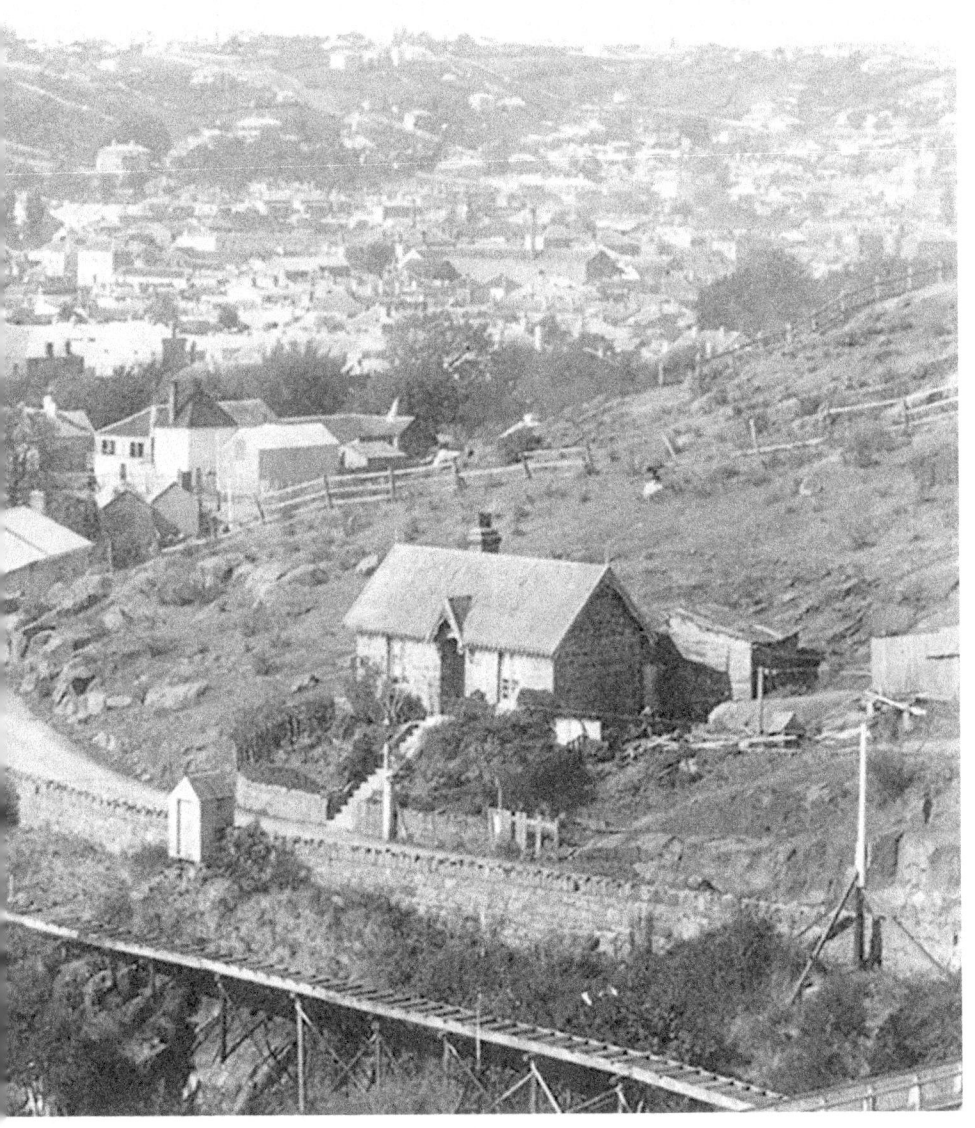

Collins Street, Melbourne, looking east in 1864. The Union Bank is on the corner at the extreme right hand side. This is the building where John Irvine undertook his entrance exam to the Bank twelve months later.

John Irvine sailed from Launceston, once again on the *City of Launceston*, on Wednesday 22 February 1865. The following day, he sat the bank's entrance exam at its main office in Collins Street. The exam encompassed arithmetic, history, geography, dictation, writing, reading and spelling, and it was followed by an interview. On 28 February, his exam results and interview having been found satisfactory, he was engaged as a junior clerk by the bank at an annual salary of £100. He undertook a month's clerical training in the Collins Street office before being transferred to the Launceston branch on 3 April. The bank's personnel ledger from 1865 notes that he was 'Sent to Launceston, where his friends reside, to fill a vacancy.'[7] The word 'friends' was often used

Launceston's Union Bank building, shortly after opening in 1866.

in the nineteenth century as a catch-all term for those with one's best interests at heart, including family.

Young clerks in the Union Bank were:

> carefully groomed to move up the [bank's] hierarchy. A typical recruit with no prior experience undertook an initial apprenticeship at the branch where he was hired, lasting 3 to 5 years. At the end of each year, the manager wrote a report on his performance and progress. The reports typically mention personal appearance, arithmetic ability, character, interpersonal skills, and enthusiasm about work.[8]

Irvine's experience in being transferred almost immediately on being appointed is unusual, but the existence of a vacancy in Launceston, where 'his friends reside' was probably grounds for a slightly unusual deployment.

After his month in Melbourne, Jack arrived home in Launceston on Wednesday 5 April. The following Monday, he commenced work at the bank. The Union was in an expansive phase at the time; just as he was starting his new post, work commenced on a grand new bank building on the corner of St John and Paterson Streets. The foundations of the new building were finished on 20 May 1865, and construction continued for the next 18 months. On 16 October 1866, the new two-storeyed, stuccoed building, with two rows of Doric columns, opened for business. Built at a cost of £7,000, it contained an eight-roomed manager's residence on the first floor and a grand banking chamber, with an ornate plaster ceiling, on the ground floor. Jack was to work here for the next nine years. His salary increased only once during his first seven years with the bank; on 1 January 1866, he received an extra £25 a year. His next pay rise was not to occur until 1 January 1873, when his salary increased to £150 a year.[9]

Living at home with the family allowed Irvine to economise, but it also released him from many of the responsibilities of day-to-day life. His weekly salary of around £2/10/- was more than many working men with families to support received. With Saturday afternoons free, he was able to cultivate the persona of a young man about town.

Sport was an important part of his life. He divided his time between football in the winter and rowing in the warmer months, with workouts at the Launceston Gymnasium in between. In September 1866, some of the town's young bucks met for a friendly football match, and Irvine was there:

> The football match on the Windmill Hill, on Saturday last, was so well contested, that after three hours healthy exercise without having made a goal on either side, the captains agreed to 'draw' and meet again on Saturday next. The game commenced at 3 o'clock and the contest was given up at 6 o'clock.[10]

Jack's teammates included some of his rowing pals, namely Fred Haymes, who was the captain of his team, his brother Richard, and one of the McEacherns from the shop.

Many of the same young men were present when a meeting was held at the Town Hall on the evening of 30 October to plan the 27th annual Tamar Regatta, to be held the following January. Jack did not attend the meeting, although Dick was there to second a motion that a silver challenge cup worth £25 be offered for a single handed sculling race.

Tuesday 22 January 1867 was declared a public holiday for the regatta:

> The weather was delightful ... The rising ground [overlooking the river] was pretty well covered with select family parties well provided with picnic requisites; but probably, owing to this being the busiest part of harvest, the class who usually make the most stir at regattas and races was not well represented. Mr Morrison, of the Launceston Hotel, was the only licensed host on the Regatta Ground, and of course his booth was well patronised throughout the day. ... The band of the artillery performed some fine spirit stirring airs remarkably well, at intervals, and the scene was, on the whole, a very lovely one. The steamship *Derwent* with ... nearly a hundred passengers on board, steamed slowly past about 11 o'clock. As she neared the Regatta Ground, the band struck up 'See the conquering hero comes'; and when she came opposite, she was hailed with hearty cheers, given spontaneously by the assembled people, and they were as heartily responded to by the ... passengers and crew on board the steamer.

Jack and Dick had entered for the third race of the day, the Mayor and Aldermen's Purse, which was for outrigger canoes crewed by 'mercantile amateurs only.' Six boats lined up at the start, including Dick's boat *Little Wonder* and Jack's *Echo*. Dick's colours were red and white, but the reporter covering the day failed to record Jack's colours in this, his first major public race.

The race was, apparently:

> really well contested ... throughout, as none of the men gave in, but pulled gallantly to the last. The *Myth* took the lead, and maintained it until within two boat lengths of home, when the *Echo* shot ahead and won ... *Little Wonder* had no chance in the race whatever.

The prize purse for this race was a very handsome £12. *Myth* received £5 for second place, and the third-place getter, *Sprig of Shillelagh*, received £2.

The reference to 'mercantile amateurs only' speaks to an ongoing controversy in nineteenth-century sport, and rowing in particular. Throughout the nineteenth century, as the sport developed from 'both rowing as an occupation and from rowing for leisure', there was tension between middle-class and working-class rowers. It was agreed by middle-class rowers that the inclusion of working men in racing crews created an unfair advantage; one nineteenth-century competitor commented: 'People confined in an office all day ... had no show against men who worked with their arms or their hands, or in the sun all day.'[11] In a town as small as Launceston, one could not be choosy; the Launceston Regatta, unlike some in other colonies, never banned working class rowers from competing, instead separating competitors into specific events.

If working class rowers were not excluded from competing in the regatta, they were definitely not among the members of its organising committee. An advertisement in the *Cornwall Chronicle* of 7 December 1867, calling on the Mayor of Launceston to convene a public meeting to appoint an organising committee for the 1868 Regatta, included the names of most of Launceston's socially prominent young businessmen: Richard and John Irvine, John Cathcart of the Launceston Savings Bank, Charles Kent, from the Customs House, and R.H. McEachern and Fred Haymes, rowing and football friends of the Irvine brothers. At the public meeting, Dick was elected a member of the organising committee, while Jack was happy to compete.

The 1868 Tamar Regatta was held on Tuesday 28 January and attracted a crowd of between 3,000 and 4,000. 'The weather was delightfully fine,'[12] said the *Launceston Examiner*, while the *Cornwall Chronicle* waxed lyrical, claiming that 'the fleecy clouds acted as a celestial awning between the bright sun and Northern Tasmania.' Jack competed in three races during the day; he came second in the second race, which was for mercantile amateurs in outriggers 18 feet and under, and last in the fifth race, which was for first class sailing boats of 30 foot length and under. It was said of this race: 'There being scarcely a breath of wind, the boats were a long time getting away ... The *Spray* [Irvine's boat] being last to leave her moorings.'

He did better in the eighth race of the day, which was the Challenge Sculls, 'to be pulled for by members of the Launceston Gymnasium.' He got off to a good start in this race and came in a long way ahead of the other two boats in the race. At the close of the race:

> The victor was borne on the shoulders of a number of his friends and companions towards the committee booth, where he was formally presented with the prize – the pair of silver challenge sculls presented for competition by Mr John Cathcart. After entering the committee

booth amidst the cheers of an enthusiastic crowd, as soon as order could be restored, Mrs George Collins, accompanied by a number of ladies, presented the prize to Mr Irvine, remarking that it afforded her much pleasure in doing so, and she hoped that Mr Irvine be as successful next year in winning the silver sculls, when they would become his actual property. Mr Irvine made a brief but suitable reply, which was drowned in the hearty cheers of the spectators.[13]

The silver sculls became Irvine's the next year, when he won the Challenge Sculls race at the 1869 Regatta. The day was very nearly called off because of stormy weather the previous night and a dark and overcast morning on Thursday 28 January. By mid-afternoon, however, the sun had broken through, and the races went ahead – although in front of a much smaller crowd than usual.

The day of the 1870 Regatta broke 'cloudy and threatening' but soon improved, and a crowd of several thousand gathered on the slopes above Stephenson's Bend to watch a program of eight races:

> The ground presented a very animated appearance. In the paddock vehicles were drawn up, and there were the usual conveniences provided for the refreshment and amusement of the public. There was a very large committee booth in charge of Mr F. Jones of the Union Inn, and Mr Mason, of the Caledonian Wine Vaults also had commodious booths upon the ground, while from several refreshment stalls were vended to those who believed in them substantial cakes, fruits, and temperance beverages ... On the hill several hundreds of persons enjoyed themselves pic-nic-ing, and there were one or two tents erected, the friendly shade of which was greatly appreciated during the afternoon.[14]

Dressed in their crew colours of white and blue, Jack and Dick were entered in the second race, the Ladies' Purse (for mercantile amateurs only), a race for four-man gigs. In their boat, *Galatea*, they were up against three other boats: *Derwent Belle* (crew colours of scarlet and gold border, with the boat's name on the shirt front), *Alabama* (red and white) and *Kearsarge* (blue). Although the reporter from the *Cornwall Chronicle* acknowledged the skill of the *Galatea*'s crew, they came in second, about a quarter of a length behind the winning boat, *Derwent Belle*. 'This contest was considered by the oldest regatta men as second to none that has ever come off on the Tamar.'

Irvine also competed in the fifth race of the day, rowing the *Vivid*, an 18 foot, 6 inch outrigger, for a prize of £10. 'This single handed race attracted much attention. A fine equal start was effected, Irvine soon going to the front … Irvine maintained the lead and came in well ahead [of the nearest boat]. Three miles in 23 minutes.'

Prizes were awarded to the winners at a meeting of the regatta committee held at the Launceston Hotel two nights later. It was announced that a general meeting would be held the following week to form a Launceston Boating Club, and:

> steps will be taken for the purpose of providing staging with movable tressels [sic] for the convenience of pullers, when getting their boats in and out of the water. The inconvenience caused by contact with the mud in launching or landing a boat, under existing circumstances at the regatta ground, is very serious and sufficient to deter many persons from submitting to it.[15]

The Launceston Boating Club was duly founded at the meeting held at the Launceston Hotel, on the evening of Thursday 17 February 1870, and Richard and John Irvine were named to the committee. It was Jack's first committee experience, and he relished it, always seeming to be on one or more committees for the next two decades.

July 1870 saw the first of the Irvine children marry. Twenty-year-old Jemima Frances, the eldest Irvine daughter, travelled with her mother to Melbourne to marry Carter Weetman, a member of a well-known Launceston business family – long-time friends and business associates of the Irvines. The young couple embarked for London shortly after the ceremony and, interestingly, the marriage was not announced in any of the Tasmanian newspapers until October.

Jack Irvine did not attend his sister's wedding in Melbourne but found other things in Launceston to keep him occupied. Just two weeks after his sister's marriage, he attended a meeting at the Brisbane Hotel to establish the

A YOUNG MAN ABOUT TOWN   47

Launceston Amateur Dramatic Club, which would give occasional performances for the 'benefit of public and charitable objects.' From the start, this was to be an exclusive group: 'admission to the club should be by consent of the members, one black ball in five to exclude.' It was agreed that no membership fees would be charged, the 'legitimate expenses of the club be[ing] defrayed by an occasional performance.'[16] The first performance of the Club would be *The Honeymoon*, a comedy in five acts which had been first performed at Drury Lane in January 1805; the plot apparently owed much to the *The Taming of the Shrew* and *Twelfth Night*.[17]

The club members eagerly threw themselves into rehearsals, and their premiere was held just six weeks later. The theatre critic of the *Cornwall Chronicle*, writing the morning after the first performance on Tuesday 14 September, commented that the:

> young club ought to be proud of the position achieved by them at their first performance, given last night at the Theatre Royal. The pieces selected for the occasion were the comedy 'The Honeymoon' and Morton's farce of 'Poor Pillicoddy' ... It was a bold experiment for amateurs to play 'The Honeymoon' in its entirety, when professionals usually ... play it in three acts. But the sterling old comedy 'went' as smoothly as though it had been curtailed, and with fewer hitches than it has been our lot to witness in an amateur performance.'

Most of the actors received commendable praise, but it was noted that:

> In the early part of the play, Mr J.L. Irvine, as the Count Montalban, was rather stiff, and wanted, in fact, that at-homeness – to coin a phrase – which is rarely acquired on the stage but by practice. Being, however, well up in his part, and ably supported by Miss Ada Hart as Volante, he soon became in accord with the rest of the *dramatis personae*.[18]

The *Launceston Examiner* considered the performance 'an unqualified success' but singled out Irvine for 'laboring under severe indisposition' in the opening scene. However, he 'showed himself so thoroughly up in the part, that the house was from the very beginning of the play relieved of that indefinite apprehension of a hitch, which so generally accompanies amateur performances.'[19]

The Honeymoon went on to play three nights a week for three weeks, with such success that, the following month, 'a drawing room theatrical entertainment' consisting of 'the amusing comedietta [a short, farcical comedy], "Hunting a Turtle" ... and the burlesque [an absurd parody, rather than a strip-tease!] "Aladdin, or the Wonderful Scamp"'[20] was given at the Mechanic's Institute. 'The amateurs put themselves to great expense and trouble in rendering the stage ... suitable for the requirements of the occasion, the stage being provided with footlights, and neatly decorated with flags and evergreens.' In the first piece, Irvine played 'Timothy Dandelion' and 'came in for deserved applause'. In the parody of *Aladdin*, he took the part of the Vizier, which was considered 'well played.'[21]

Apart from rehearsing and performing with the Amateur Dramatic Club, Irvine was also one of 'many new exhibitors' to enter the Northern Tasmanian Poultry Society's third annual show of 'poultry, pigeons, singing birds, rabbits and dairy produce' at the Launceston Town Hall in September 1870. The show was judged:

> eminently successful. It has been visited by thousands of admirers during the past two days; during the evenings of which the Rifle Band enlivened the scene, and partially silenced the cock crowing by performing fine selections of music appropriate to the occasion.

Among the 350 exhibits in the show:

> the small number of entries of cage birds is surprising in a town of ten thousand inhabitants ... [however] the most noticeable cage in the collection was one exhibited by Mr J.L. Irvine, containing a fine collection of Java sparrows, firetails, canaries, budgery gars [*sic*], doves, etc. Mr Irvine was awarded first prize.[22]

From this time, records refer to Jack mainly as 'John Irvine' or 'J.L. Irvine'. 'J.L. Irvine' seems to have been his personal preference.

Planning for the 1871 Regatta was underway in December, as usual, and the date was set for Tuesday 7 February. Rain forced the postponement of the regatta until the following day, when:

> Nature seemed to smile upon the efforts of all, and a more glorious day could not have been desired. With the break in the weather on the previous night, a strong northerly breeze swept over the town drying up the moistened ground, and when the sun shone out so brilliantly soon after daybreak, it was a charming invitation to the townsfolk to pack up their hampers for the enjoyment of a picnic on 'the hill.'

The day was declared a public holiday, and a crowd of several thousand enjoyed the amusements:

> Carriages and wagons containing happy parties were drawn up by the water's edge, while the river itself was crowded with pleasure boats and sailing craft. The vessels in harbour were gaily decorated with bunting, and all wore quite a gala aspect.

Refreshment booths offered 'a lucrative trade in the buns, pies, cake, lemonade, gingerbeer and confectionary line,' while two merry-go-rounds entertained children and adults alike. A brass band played selections of popular music all afternoon, 'but a hurdy gurdy presided over by a lady in connection with one of the merry-go-rounds deserves special mention, as it was ground with an energy that appeared to have generally a very exciting effect.'

Irvine rowed only one race at the 1871 Regatta, captaining a Launceston crew in the Ladies' Purse for mercantile amateurs in a four-man gig, against a crew from Hobart. 'The Launcestonians [in the boat *Prima Donna*] looked very gay in their blue sashes and straw hats with gilt lettering, and quite put their rivals in the shade as far as dress was concerned.' Although both boats got away evenly, the Hobart boat, *Fireflash*, soon settled into a 'long sweeping stroke' and pulled away in front. The local *Tasmanian* newspaper commended the team of the *Prima Donna* for the 'plucky manner in which they rowed a losing race, especially as they had a much slower boat, and knew it.'

Following the day's races, a dinner was held for the crews and invited dignitaries at a large store in the Quadrant, Launceston's most exclusive shopping street. Sixty gentlemen sat down to dinner in a room which was 'gaily decorated with flags, evergreens, and flowers.' Irvine's local popularity was such that, during the after dinner toasts and speeches, there were 'loud calls for Mr John Irvine' to speak as the captain of his crew. Irvine demurred, saying that as 'they had such a good "blower" as Mr Whiteford in the boat, it would be folly for him to respond. He should depute the task to him. (Cheers).'[23] Drinking, speeches and toasting went on until late in the evening.

More socialising took place a fortnight later, when an impromptu ball was held at the Town Hall on Monday 20 February in celebration of the race meeting. Tickets to this rather select event were limited to 100. Among those attending were John and Richard Irvine, their mother Jemima and their sister Eliza Katherine, who was just entering local society at the age of 17.

A visit to Melbourne followed the next month, March 1871, when Irvine sailed on the *Tamar* on Wednesday 8. He appears to have stayed in Melbourne for several weeks, returning to Launceston by Thursday 11 May. On that date, he was one of 'a number of gentlemen' who gave a 'creditable entertainment' of songs, choruses and recitations at the Invalid Depot, Launceston's home for the elderly poor:

> We trust that these gentlemen will continue in the good path that they have taken and that soon again we shall be able to mark our appreciation of their philanthropic efforts to cheer the weary lives of these poor old men.[24]

The visit to Melbourne in March 1871 was Irvine's first since he went for his entrance examination and interview with the Union Bank six years earlier. There is no mention of this 1871 visit to Melbourne in his personnel file at the bank, so it is safe to assume that he was travelling for pleasure, rather than on bank business. What he got up to in Melbourne in March 1871 is unknown; it is tempting to think that he was enjoying time away from the restrictions of life with the family in Launceston.

By this time, Irvine was 23 years old. He was popular with friends and family at home in Launceston, a steady and conscientious employee of the bank, and a young man who was earning a name for himself as an enthusiastic joiner in public life and activities. He was fast becoming a well-known local sportsman in northern Tasmania. It is likely, however, that he was harbouring a secret.

Victorian society 'preached heterosexual virtue, the ideal personified by Victoria and Albert, surrounded by their offspring. Photograph albums and family trees tell a different story: large families had many spinster aunts, many bachelor uncles. Economics might have kept some single, others might have been unlucky in love. Or did they prefer not to marry, seeking alternatives for which, given discretion, an innocent explanation existed? How many people lived at odds with the prevailing heterosexual culture is unknown,'[25] but they existed. Was Irvine one of them?

The evidence makes it seem highly likely that Irvine was homosexually inclined. He never married, never kept a mistress, nor was ever romantically linked with a woman. He inhabited a homosocial world of men's sport and men's committees and pastimes (with the exception of some mixed clubs, such as the Amateur Dramatic Club). He was always at home in the company of other men – particularly with younger men. In addition to manly sports, he also had an interest in more creative hobbies, such as amateur drama, singing and painting. Interestingly, the terms 'artistic', 'musical' and 'creative' were to become code words or synonyms for 'homosexual' in the early twentieth century. Also, rather damningly, he was twice later to be accused of making a sexual advance to another man; although both accusations were dismissed by the law.

Victorian society segregated men and women into distinct, discrete spheres. Schools, professions, sports and social spaces were all gendered, and interactions between the sexes were stringently policed by society and etiquette. This led to a high degree of homosociality in many facets of everyday life. The homosocial nature of male social life 'encouraged practices of male bonding, shared physicality, and idealized camaraderie'[26] and fostered deep bonds of affection and physical intimacy between men, including the common phenomenon of 'affectionate friendships.' Intense, non-sexual friendships between members of the same sex exhibited a degree of physical intimacy which today would be seen as suspect: hand-holding, cuddling, kissing or sharing a bed. 'Men posed for photographers holding hands, entwining limbs, or resting in the shelter of each other's accommodating bodies, innocent of the suspicion that such behavior would later arouse.'[27]

While many of those involved in these intense friendships would later go on to marry, the existence of such friendships also provided cover for those men who had no interest in the opposite sex. Sexual activities did not necessarily define one's sexuality in the nineteenth century, but, by the 1870s, sexual scientists and criminologists, with their love of classifying the world around them, were beginning to identify a particular 'type' of man who acted in specific ways and exhibited particular behaviours. The homosexual was being defined.

By the 1870s, Melbourne had the beginnings of an underground homosexual subculture, with particular meeting places and places to go to find sex with other men. These 'beats' included public toilets, parks, beaches and other places where men could loiter without attracting too much attention and strike up conversations with other interested fellows. It is possible that certain hotels and cafés were already favoured by men seeking companionship and release, and it is tempting to think that Irvine headed to Melbourne in March 1871 for new experiences, away from the watchful eyes of his family and Launceston's small, socially incestuous establishment.

Arriving back in Launceston, Irvine threw himself into the Amateur Dramatic Club's celebration of the centenary of Sir Walter Scott, performing *Rob Roy* at the Theatre Royal in August 1871:

> Mr Irvine['s] ... rapid enunciation somewhat spoiled [his] part; and his rendering of that manly passage wherein he conveys the following assurance to his commanding officer, 'I know how to die for my error without disgracing the king I serve or the country that gave me birth,' lacked that fire and animation which would naturally accompany such a noble sentiment.[28]

The following month, however, he received creditable praise for his comic role in *Benjamin Buzzard*, a farce which 'kept the audience in a roar from the rise to the fall of the curtain.'[29]

The dramatic year closed on Tuesday 25 November with a performance of *Helping Hands*, a domestic drama in two parts, and the farce *Behind Time*, both of which 'passed off well'. Irvine was said to have 'ably sustained' his roles in both.[30]

The new year of 1872 saw Irvine finish his apprenticeship as a junior clerk at the bank. His appointment as a full clerk saw no increase in his annual salary, which remained at the same £125 as for the previous six years. Never mind, it was almost Regatta Day again, and it dawned bright and breezy on Tuesday 27 February. Irvine again contested the Ladies' Purse in *Prima Donna*, wearing crew colours of blue and white. Unlike the previous year, his crew won by three lengths.

May 1872 saw the 'resuscitation' of the Launceston Gymnasium Club, which appears to have been in abeyance since 1866. Twenty-seven members were enrolled at a meeting held at the Drill Room at the Cornwall Assembly Rooms, and the monthly subscription was set at a rather high 5/-. One J. Irvine was elected to the committee of management, and it was decided that 'drill nights' were to be held on Tuesdays and Fridays from 8 to 10pm. It was also decided that the gym members would commence the 1872 football season by having a friendly game on Windmill Hill on Saturday 4 May.[31]

The remainder of the year was filled with Dramatic Club performances, including playing Duncan in a parody of *Macbeth*: 'The public evidently care more for burlesque and travestie than the legitimate drama, and the odd incongruities so heterogeneously and ingeniously mixed up in the travestie of *Macbeth* pleased them mightily.'[32]

New Year's Day 1873 brought Irvine his first pay rise since 1866, when his salary was increased to £150. Thursday 13 February saw him on the Tamar, in white and red colours, rowing an outrigger in the Mercantile Amateur's Race for an £8 prize. Although 'the pace was "pretty hot,"' Irvine came second. The winner, W.B. Jones of Hobart, acknowledged that he had 'very great pleasure in winning this race at the Launceston Regatta as he had been opposed by one of the best men he ever pulled against.'[33]

Irvine's leisure activities expanded this year. By May 1873, he was secretary of the Launceston Choral Society;[34] later in the year, he again exhibited at the Northern Tasmanian Poultry Society's show, gaining first prize for a collection of caged birds.[35] In September 1873, Irvine was responsible for the 'tastefully prepared' room at the Mechanics' Institute, where the Choral Union presented their inaugural concert:

Ferns and plants adorned the staircase and the front of the platform. Upwards of 500 ladies and gentlemen accepted invitations, which were courteously sent out to the members of the Municipal Council, and a large number of residents of Launceston and suburban districts.[36]

As well as being the Union's secretary and treasurer, he also found time to sing a leading part in Locke's music for *Macbeth*. Irvine's sister, Kate, also appeared in the programme, singing a duet with her sister Jemima's mother-in-law, Mrs Weetman.

The first of January 1874 brought another salary increase from the bank – to £200. The month saw the planning for the 1874 Regatta underway, with Irvine elected to the organising committee at a meeting at the Launceston Town Hall on Friday 9 January.[37] A further meeting at the Criterion Hotel the following Tuesday decided the date of the regatta – Thursday 5 March – and planned 'a very full' programme of events: 'There is no time to be lost, and it will need the strenuous exertions of each of the committee individually in order to present a good subscription list, and a list of events that shall be worth competing for.'[38]

However, Irvine was not to compete in the 1874 Regatta. Shortly after the meeting at the Criterion which decided the date of the regatta, Irvine received his transfer instructions from the bank; he was to report for duty on 20 February at the bank's branch in Ballarat, Victoria. Unlike his previous visits to the mainland, in 1865, 1866 and 1871, this was to be a permanent move.

CHAPTER 4
"Into that pleasant maelstrom, Victoria"

At half-past 11 o'clock on the morning of Monday 16 February 1874, the steamer *Derwent*, under the command of Captain A.T. Woods, slipped out of the docks at Launceston, bound for Melbourne. The ship carried 40 passengers in steerage and 60 in the saloon, including 'J.L. Irvine'.[1] The crossing from Launceston to Melbourne was made in fine weather, with light winds, and the passengers disembarked in Melbourne at 10am on Tuesday 17 February.

Irvine had only a day or two in Melbourne before travelling to Ballarat by train. There, on the morning of Friday 20 February, he presented himself as the new clerk in the bank's office in Lydiard Street South. The Ballarat branch was a relatively new building in a relatively new town. The town was founded in 1851 during the Victorian gold rush, and the bank was only ten years old, dating from 1864. Irvine would have found his new branch very similar in style and plan to his former office in Launceston; both buildings were built in the same style by the same architect, Leonard Terry, a prolific designer of bank buildings throughout the Australian colonies. The Ballarat branch was a two-storeyed, stuccoed brick building, with Doric and Corinthian columns on the façade. It was described as Greek Revival in style. As was common with bank buildings, there was accommodation for the branch manager on the first floor of the building, but the banks' clerks had to find their own accommodation – most usually in local boarding houses which specialised in providing room and board for professional gentlemen.[2]

The bank was located in the very heart of Ballarat, opposite Her Majesty's Theatre and adjacent to Craig's Royal Hotel, the city's leading hotel. The young men of the bank would, no doubt, have been familiar with both institutions.

Sturt Street, Ballarat, from the Town Hall tower, 1871. The white building in the lower left hand corner is the rear of the Union Bank building in Lydiard Street.

The popular English novelist Anthony Trollope, visiting Ballarat just two years earlier, had enthused that would be difficult to:

> find [a town] of the same age better built and more lavishly provided with all the appurtenances which municipalities require ... It struck me with more surprise than any other city in Australia. It is not only its youth, for Melbourne also is very young; nor it is the population of Ballaarat [sic] which amazes, for it does not exceed a quarter of that of Melbourne; but that a town so well built, so well ordered, endowed with present advantages so great in the way of schools, hospitals, libraries, hotels, public gardens, and the like, should have sprung up so quickly with no internal advantages of its own other than that of gold. The town is very pleasant to the sight, which is, perhaps, more than can be said for any other 'provincial' town in the Australian colonies.[3]

Lake Wendouree, an artificially created lake on the site of former wetlands to the north-west of the centre of town, was one of Ballarat's main sights. The stream running through the swamp had been dammed in the 1850s, creating a rather reedy lake. Several rowing clubs were established, the oldest being the Ballarat Rowing Club (BRC), formed in 1861. This club and the short-lived Alabama Rowing Club, established in 1864, were instrumental in having a rowing course cut through the lake in the mid-1860s. Small lake steamers were introduced around the same time and were an immediate hit with local day-trippers. Although the lake dried up completely in a drought in 1869, it refilled in 1870. In November that year, the Ballarat City Rowing Club (BCRC) was established. The first Ballarat Regatta was held in 1872, when the rather confusingly named BRC and BCRC competed.

After moving to Ballarat, Irvine lost no time in contacting the local rowing clubs. On Saturday 11 April, less than two months after arriving in town, he was chosen as a crew member in a BRC scratch fours[4] for a race to be held on the afternoon of Saturday 25 April. It was announced that the race would commence at 4:30pm. Before the race, the crew was referred to in the local press as being that of R.D. Williams (the stroke); but, following an easy win by three lengths, during which the 'winners did not appear to be at all pressed, as they were rowing a slow, easy stroke all the way,'[5] the press began to refer to the crew as 'Irvine's.' Clearly, the new man in town was gaining a reputation as a rower and sportsman.

The final competition for the scratch fours was held on the afternoon of Friday 8 May, and Irvine's crew (with Irvine as the stroke) won easily. Irvine hosted a dinner the following Tuesday at the Gem Hotel for about 45 rowers. 'After doing justice to the good things provided, toasts and songs were the order of the evening.'[6] After dinner:

> in response to the toast of 'The Winning Crew,' Mr R.D. Williams explained that though the original stroke, he had found a better man in his crew and altered their positions, and he therefore called on Mr Irvine to reply. Mr J.L. Irvine modestly combated the assertion that he was a better man, and said that the supper was given for the interests of boating.[7]

Winter Scene, Lake Wendouree

"INTO THAT PLEASANT MAELSTROM, VICTORIA"

Wendouree Parade, Ballarat.

Working at the Union Bank's Ballarat branch appears to have given Irvine enough time to visit Melbourne; he attended a meeting of Melbourne's Banks Rowing Club at the Freemason's Hotel in Swanston Street on 21 May, where he was accepted as a member of the Club.[8]

Rowing was not the only thing occupying his time and energy. Along with a number of other Ballarat rowers, Irvine attended a meeting of the Ballarat Athletic Club on the evening of Saturday 13 June and was elected a member of the management committee. The newly formed club decided to engage the cavalry orderly room in Bath Street, Ballarat, as a gymnasium, to open for the first time on the evening of Saturday 20 June. Apparently, about 50 newly signed-up members attended the opening session:

> Being the first meeting, only the preliminary gymnastic exercises were gone through, and were on the whole admirably done. The club intend to devote three nights a week to gymnastic and sword exercise, these departments being under the immediate supervision of Mons. Rayeux, who will be assisted by a staff of lieutenants, and the same method and order will be observed as in the large gymnasiums in England and on the Continent, and if this is enforced there is no doubt of the club's success.

A boxing tutor was also engaged to give lessons twice a week. Local newspapers considered that the club would be very popular: 'We believe that already over 100 members have joined the club, and it is probable that a larger room will be required than that in present use.'[9]

Ballarat's gain of an enthusiastic and popular young man, who was willing to join clubs and committees and get things done, was Launceston's loss; news from across Bass Strait lamented:

> The Launceston Choral Society, it seems, has passed away since the removal of its energetic secretary, Mr John Irvine, into that pleasant maelstrom, Victoria, which whirls so many of our most earnest young men – not to mention an equally large number of young ladies – away from their island home.[10]

"INTO THAT PLEASANT MAELSTROM, VICTORIA" 61

Edwards rowing sheds on the southern bank of the Yarra River, Melbourne, 1870s.

The drain of youth and talent from Tasmania to the mainland was already an accepted fact of life.

Irvine's involvement in the social and sporting life of his new town went from strength to strength. In August 1874, he was elected Secretary of the BRC at their annual general meeting, held at Lester's Hotel. At the same meeting, he was also chosen as a crew member for a race against the Geelong Banks Club, to be held on 19 September.[11] As secretary of the Club, he announced that the rowing season of 1874-75 would commence on Saturday 15 August; all members of the BRC would present to the Club House at 3pm in uniform.

As part of the 1874-75 rowing season, the race against the Geelong Banks Club came off on 19 September, when Geelong beat Ballarat on Lake Wendouree. Following the race, the BRC entertained the Geelong visitors with a dinner at Lewis' Pavilion Hotel, Eastern Oval. '[A]bout fifty gentlemen sat down to an excellent spread ... [after which the visitors were presented with] a silver cup, which had been subscribed for in addition to the £25 trophy.' It was an early night, however, for 'after three cheers for the Geelong crew, the party broke up, to allow of the visitors proceeding home by the 7.10pm train.'[12]

Irvine appears to have been a conscientious secretary for the BRC, attending to the Club's correspondence in a very thorough manner and going to bat for the rights of the club. In October 1874, he responded to the Ballarat Town Council over the club's rental of lake frontage on Lake Wendouree, saying that the club had resolved the issue with the Water Commission and refused to reopen the subject of paying rent. The Council responded that, since they had taken over responsibility for the management of the lake in June that year, they would be charging boat clubs rent for the use of lake frontage; the club would have to conform to the Council's regulations. Irvine countered the following year, applying for a remission of the rent, which Council refused.[13]

Racing continued through the 1874–75 season, with a full calendar of races almost every weekend. When not competing, Irvine trained on the lake and attended the gym three nights a week. The weekend of Saturday 5 December saw him in Melbourne, training on the Yarra near Edwards' Rowing Sheds, where the Melbourne Banks Club was based. Edwards' shed had been a fixture on the southern bank of the river since the 1860s and was located on the site of the current rowing sheds at Alexandra Gardens. In the 1870s, there were no changing rooms, secure lockers or storage provided for rowers on the riverbank, and it was during training there that Saturday afternoon that Irvine's silver fob watch was stolen: 'a silver open-face geneva watch,'[14] with a flat glass and 'J. Irvine' scratched inside the case, on a fine square-link gold chain. Irvine reported the theft to the police, but there no record of its being recovered. Irvine's weekend address was number 2 Lothian Buildings, Carlton. This is the middle house of a set of three two-storey, terraced houses, now numbered 177 Drummond Street in Carlton, located between Pelham and Grattan Streets. In 1872, Number 2 Lothian Buildings was known for offering 'Superior Board and Residence for gentlemen' and appears to have offered good conditions for 'moderate' terms.[15]

Boarding houses were a common accommodation solution for single men and women in the nineteenth century. They offered a room and meals, together with cleaning and laundry service, without the expense of renting or buying a whole house and paying the necessary domestic servants whom nineteenth-century housekeeping required. Boarding houses spanned the social scale from the most expensive and exclusive, to those that were aimed at working class residents and were little better than the 'lodging houses' that rented rooms only, by the night. The best provided commodious and well-appointed public rooms for their guests, perhaps with gardens, sometimes with tennis courts and other recreational facilities. Given its inner city location and small size, Lothian Buildings could not supply these luxuries; nonetheless, it was a substantial house, with not too many rooms and, therefore, not many residents. One disadvantage of boarding house life was that boarding house keepers, who were stereotypically spinsters or widows, tended to have a reputation for protecting their investment by keeping a close eye on the activities going on in their houses. Rules about such things as smoking, drinking, church attendance, religious affiliation and visitors (especially those of the opposite sex) in residents' rooms were strictly policed, and many boarding house residents, particularly young men, found it easier to socialise outside of the landladies' view – in pubs, clubs, sporting venues, on the streets and in the city's parks. Interestingly, Lothian Buildings was only a block from the Carlton Gardens, which had long had the reputation of a night-time cruising ground for men looking for a particular type of company from other men.

Melbourne in the mid-1870s was beginning to become aware of homosexuality, largely because of press reportage of several Australian and international scandals involving homosexuality and cross-dressing. The reporting of extraordinary cases – including that of John Wilson, arrested in Victoria Parade, Fitzroy in October 1863, dressed in women's clothes and working as a prostitute (quite successfully as it turned out) and the 1870s Boulton and Park scandal involving two young men who regularly impersonated a pair of racy girls and flirted with gentlemen in London theatres – had increased public awareness of men who did not act as men were supposed to. Although the men involved in such scandals were initially seen as individuals who were acting in an unusual and sinful manner, the increase in reported cases in the 1860s and 1870s saw the press begin to identify them as members of a group of men who were not 'normal' and who behaved in these outrageous ways as a mark of the type of men they were.

By the 1870s, most men about town in Melbourne knew of the high-profile prosecutions of men who were arrested in the street dressed in women's clothing, or otherwise acting in compromising positions. They would also have been aware of places that should be avoided, unless one was looking for male companionship of a particular kind. The Melbourne Town Council introduced the first of several two-man street urinals in the late 1850s, and

Advertisement for the Ballarat Turkish Bath, 1875.

they very quickly became known as places where men could make contact. Likewise, the men-only sea baths around the bayside suburbs, the freshwater baths in both central Melbourne and most suburbs and the more exclusive Turkish baths in Bourke Street and Russell Street gave men the opportunity to socialise 'in a state of nature.' Promenading the footpaths of the central city, such as along the fashionable 'Block' in Collins Street, allowed men to linger along the pavements, and the shining plate glass windows of shops allowed the subtle study of the reflections of fellow dawdlers: a different sort of window shopping, if you like. And the city's parks and gardens, which surround the central business district in an arc on all sides, provided nooks and shady corners for discreet encounters. Any place where men had a reason for congregating and could linger without attracting attention could lend itself to being used as a homosexual trysting place; those like the various baths, which allowed for the added excitement of nudity, were even more likely to be rewarding.

Even quiet Ballarat had its meeting places. The Turkish baths opposite the city markets had a reputation from the day they opened in 1864, and the *Ballarat Star* had drawn the public's attention to 'disgusting practices' which were said to take place in the laneway at the rear of the new Court House: 'This seems to be a matter which should be looked to at once.'[16] One wonders whether Irvine had made use of either location; given his interest in aquatic sports and gym work, he probably would have been a regular user of the baths, but we will probably never know whether he took an evening stroll behind the Court House. Of course, Ballarat was a small city, with a population of 48,156 in 1871,[17] so regular trips to Melbourne would have given Irvine the opportunity to pursue adventures with a great deal more anonymity than in a town where he was known to all. And the Lothian Buildings in Carlton were located perfectly.

Races for the Ballarat rowing season continued into the first part of 1875, with Irvine travelling to Geelong to compete in the Geelong Regatta's eight oar race in mid-March.[18] The season culminated in the Ballarat Easter Saturday Regatta, held on 17 March, when he again competed in the eight oar race against the BCRC: 'This was the event of the day, and was a capital race. The distance was about two miles, and both crews seemed to be in good form, though the Ballarat men had never rowed together until Saturday [the day of

Roller skating in Sydney in 1875. A scene very similar to that enjoyed in Ballarat the same year.

the race].' Ballarat City got away in front, with a 'splendid swinging stroke,' but disaster loomed near the race's end:

> As the boats neared the winning flag, the most intense excitement prevailed, and it was increased by an unfortunate accident, which nearly lost the City men the race. The little steamer *The Fairy* had got stuck right across the City course, and the coxswain, thinking that the steamer would clear, steered straight at her. The boat just went under her stern, and the bow men had to unship their oars, and one was broken. The boat was nearly brought to a standstill but once the steamer was cleared, the crew laid out again, and came in a length ahead. 'Kick,' the coxswain of Ballarat, seeing what had happened, encouraged his crew in a characteristic manner, and a spurt was put on; but the City had secured too much of a lead for them to do anything. After the victors passed the flag they were lustily cheered, and almost lifted from the boat by their comrades who thronged the City jetty.[19]

Late May saw Irvine back in Geelong to compete as the stroke of a four-man crew representing Ballarat banks in the Challenge Cup on the Barwon River (Geelong won by three boat lengths).[20]

A change of pace took place in June. Irvine was part of a group of young people who decided to start a rollerskating club in Ballarat. An application to use a room at the Academy of Music was unsuccessful, 'in view of the damage likely to be done to the building if such a request were granted,'[21] but an approach to the Good Templars Hall was more successful: 'The hon. Secretary Mr J.L. Irvine, has written to Melbourne for a dozen pairs of skates to begin the season with. As members join, more skates will be obtained for their use.'[22] The season was to commence at 3pm on Thursday 1 July, but the season was delayed one day by the non-arrival of the skates from Melbourne.[23] A week later, the *Ballarat Courier*'s reporter visited the skating rink and noted that the previous evening had seen a 'large number of skaters assembled ... many of marked proficiency, including several ladies, some of whom, however, required the assistance of attendant cavaliers to make their gliding evolutions appear graceful.' The skates that were used were the familiar four-wheeled skates, but 'though easy enough to look at, the operation of skating ... requires some amount of practice and dexterity.' The man from the *Courier* commented that the most modern and advanced skates were two-wheeled, and the position of the wheels, 'being down the centre of the skate (instead of two at the toes and two at the heel, as used by beginners) requires of course a greater exhibition of skill in their use. No doubt the two-wheelers will be in vogue amongst our Ballarat skaters by and bye.'[24]

The modern rollerskate was invented in the USA in 1864, and the first skating rinks opened in New York City in 1866. The first British rinks were opened in the early 1870s. By 1875, there were rinks in St Kilda, Geelong and Ballarat. The sport became a great craze in the 1880s; from the start, it was seen as 'an invigorating amusement in which both sexes can engage.'[25] In August 1875, skating was described as 'quite a fashionable amusement in Ballarat,' and a skating ball was held on the evening of Friday 13 August. About 40 guests, 'the majority being ladies', executed quadrilles, gallops and round dances 'with very creditable precision, while those who were not quite equal to the terpsichorean trial, enjoyed themselves by gliding about at their ease.' The men's skating outfits consisted of dark jackets and knickerbockers with coloured hose, while 'the ladies who were skating wore pretty turban hats of bright silk or satin, and dresses suitable for the occasion.' The evening was judged a great success. It was decided that a fancy dress skating ball would be a novelty worth witnessing 'and may yet be an accomplished fact in Ballarat.'[26] The skating club was so successful that, two months after its establishment, there were about 200 members. Members of a football team from Hamilton, visiting Ballarat in late August, were treated to an exhibition of skating as one of the city's notable sights:

> a pleasant hour was spent in admiration of a couple of hundred skaters, male and female, gliding gracefully to and fro. It was elicited that this organisation was a club composed of the *elite* of the city, which of course added a charm to the invite.[27]

The BRC annual general meeting, held at Lester's Hotel on 4 August 1875, elected Irvine for a second term as Club secretary; but, less than a month later, he had to resign. The bank had transferred him to the Melbourne branch in

Collins Street, where he had started his banking career 10 years previously. Before leaving Ballarat, he was given a complimentary dinner at the Pavilion Hotel, Eastern Oval, on the night of Friday 3 September:

> A large number of Mr Irvine's personal friends and companions attended, and after partaking of the good things provided ... many eulogistic speeches in praise of the guest were made. Much merriment was infused into the gathering by the numerous comic and serio-comic songs which were given by those present. Mr Irvine's health was drunk in bumpers of champagne, and the guest responded to the toast with considerable warmth and feeling.[28]

Although Irvine had only been in Ballarat for just over a year and a half, he had obviously made many friends and was well regarded in the community. On the night he left town (Wednesday 8 September 1875), a number of friends from the BRC, the bank and the skating club gathered at the Western railway station to bid him an enthusiastic farewell as he boarded the last train for Melbourne.

Next morning, he presented himself at the bank's Collins Street office. He was 28 and would spend the next six years in Melbourne. They were to be years which would see his greatest sporting achievements.

CHAPTER 5
Intercolonial champion

When Irvine arrived in Melbourne, the colony of Victoria was in the midst of a 40-year period of economic growth, the so-called 'Long Boom' from the 1850s to the early 1890s; by the mid-1870s, the capital was recognised as 'the metropolis of the Southern Hemisphere.' Collins Street, where the Union Bank's headquarters were located, was at the heart of Melbourne's financial and commercial district. There, in the words of a commentator of the time:

> [t]he headquarters of nearly all the large commercial institutions which extend their operation beyond the limits of any one colony are to be found ... If you wish to transact business well and quickly, to organize a new enterprise – in short, to estimate and understand the trade of Australia, you must go to Melbourne.[1]

The city was one of the wonder cities of the nineteenth century. In just 40 years, it had grown to a population of approximately 210,000. Although the site of the city was considered flat and dull, without the natural beauty of other colonial cities such as Hobart and Sydney, the 'internal appearance of the city is certainly magnificent.'[2] This magnificence was considered to rest mainly in the width of the city's main streets and in the ring of parks and public gardens that surrounded the central city and dotted its suburbs. The city possessed gas street lighting and a plentiful piped water supply, but there was no underground sewerage system:

all the sewage is carried away in huge open gutters, which run all
through the town, and are at their worst and widest in the most central
part, where all the principal shops and business places are situated.[3]

The town also presented 'rather a higgledy-piggledy look ... There are
no building laws, and every man has built as seemed best in his own eyes.'[4]
English author Anthony Trollope, who visited in the early 1870s, wrote: 'Even
in Collins Street the houses stand in gaps. Here and there are grand edifices ...
[but] between the palaces there are mean little houses.'

Among the wonders of Melbourne were counted its more impressive
buildings, including its shops, churches and grand public buildings such
as the Post Office, the Town Hall, the Public Library and the Houses of
Parliament. However, Trollope considered that the most impressive buildings
of Melbourne were:

> in the first place [its] banks, as to which it seems that in these
> days grandeur pays as in old days did that quiet, almost funereal,
> deportment which was the characteristic of Lombard Street, and
> is still maintained by one or two highly respectable London firms.
> The banks in Melbourne are pre-eminent.[5]

When Irvine started work in 1875 at the Union Bank's branch on the corner of Collins and Queen Streets, it was a solid example of architect Leonard Terry's work, similar in style to the branches he had designed in Launceston and Ballarat. Nonetheless, the Union had plans to rebuild its main Melbourne branch on a much more impressive scale; plans were already being considered for a new head office, further east along the Collins Street block.

Irvine's £200 salary from the bank was sufficient for a single man, living in rooms (possibly at Lothian Buildings in Carlton, or a similar address). His working day at the bank apparently was not too strenuous or lengthy, giving him ample free time and opportunity to follow his true passion, rowing, and to make occasional visits across Bass Strait to take part in family events, such as the wedding of his brother Dick to Miss Frances Beatrice Lette on 23 November 1875. By the time he married, Dick was an established member of Launceston's commercial world, senior partner in the family business of

Irvine and McEachern. The responsibilities placed on him at an early age by the death of his father had caused Dick to delay marriage until the age of 30; his bride, the daughter of a local member of the Tasmanian parliament and gentleman farmer, was only 18. They were married in the family's church, Holy Trinity Church of England.[6] Dick's marriage established him as the head of the family, and his later home, *Lebrina* in Patterson Street, was to be the centre of Irvine family life in Launceston for the next 50 years. John L. was to become a regular, although not particularly frequent, visitor.

Back in Melbourne, Irvine's first public outing in the city's rowing circles seems to have been in April 1876. He took part in several races for the Melbourne Rowing Club in the Melbourne Annual Regatta, although he had been a member of the Banks Rowing Club for the past two years. The Junior Eight race, which was widely reported in Victorian newspapers, included three teams: Melbourne, Civil Service and Warehousemen. It was 'one of the prettiest races of the whole meeting, although won easily by the Melbourne crew'.[7] The Melbourne crew, in their new uniform of blue jerseys with blue and crimson caps, also did well in the Challenge Eight Oar race, easily winning against crews from the Civil Service and Ballarat City clubs.

However, Irvine's affiliation with the Banks Club was his strongest. The following month, on 19 May 1876, he was appointed club captain at a general meeting of members. He was to hold the position of club captain for the next five years, not resigning until September 1881.

The Banks Club, which was an amateur club with the stated objective of 'the encouragement of amateur rowing on the River Yarra among bank officers', was founded in August 1866. It was socially exclusive from the start; membership was open only to those employed in the banking industry and capable of paying the rather steep membership fee of £1/1/- and annual subscriptions of two guineas (£2/2/-), well over a week's wages for most working men.

The Club held regular training and competitions on the 'upper Yarra course', the stretch of the river from Princes Bridge and upstream beyond the Botanical Gardens. The Club had no clubhouse in those days, using Edwards' boatshed. The river, well before major works of widening and straightening the river's course were carried out in the 1890s, looked very different to now. One former rower remembered in 1919 that the river 'was practically in the same state as when the blackfellows roamed its banks. It was much narrower than at present. Steep banks rose on the north side some eight or ten feet above water level. On the south side there were lagoons and swamps.'

Rowing was a popular sport, because:

> the athletic amusements were confined practically to Cricket, Football, and Rowing ... The men were keen and devoted to the sport ... [they] used to work all the year round, so that a crew, when it came to training, had fallen into each other's stroke and swing, and the rowing ... was of a high order.[8]

October 1876 saw Irvine present at the founding of the Victorian Rowing Association, the world's oldest rowing association, predating the New South Wales Association by two years and the English Amateur Rowing Association by six. Representatives of 18 Victorian clubs met at Edwards' boatshed and agreed to form an association to organise the Melbourne Regatta (which had previously been organised by an informal committee) and to manage Victorian rowing affairs generally. The first meeting, held on 7 October, agreed that membership would consist of 10 elected members, and a representative from each club, who would each pay an annual subscription of £10. Irvine was selected by the Banks Club to be its representative on the new Association. He was to hold the position for the next five years.

Although the VRA initially met at Edwards' boatshed, meetings soon shifted to Young and Jackson's Princes Bridge Hotel, on the corner of Flinders and Swanston streets at the northern end of Princes Bridge. This was the nearest hotel to the boatsheds at the southern end of the bridge, had long been a favourite with rowers and was the obvious place for the VRA and other rowing clubs to meet. Meetings took place in the large first-floor room which overlooked the intersection of Flinders and Swanston Streets, with St Paul's Church (the forerunner of St Paul's Cathedral) on one corner and the Hobson's Bay railway station (the precursor of Flinders Street railway station) on the other. The hotel was established as the Princes Bridge Hotel in July 1861, in a three-storey building originally built as a butcher's shop in 1853. It was renamed Young & Jackson's when new owners, cousins Henry Figsby Young and Thomas Joshua Jackson, bought it in 1875. At a VRA meeting held on the evening of Monday 11 December 1876, Irvine was made secretary for a two-month period while the usual secretary, Thomas Young, was absent from Melbourne.

Irvine's rowing commitments continued in the new year of 1877, with regular races on the Yarra and a place in the Barwon Regatta at Geelong in March. On this occasion, the Hobart *Tribune* noted his involvement and commented that he 'was looked upon as one of the best amateur oarsmen that Launceston had ever produced.'[9] Winter that year saw him crossing Bass Strait on a visit to family and renewing acquaintance with old rowing friends in northern Tasmania. While in Launceston, as a guest of the Northern Tasmanian Rowing Club, Irvine suggested that they amalgamate with the newly formed, struggling Tamar Boating Club to form the Tamar Rowing Club. The Club continues to flourish, 143 years later.[10]

Once Irvine was back in Melbourne, the VRA proposed that an annual eight-oared competition be established against New South Wales. A letter of challenge was sent by the VRA to the Sydney Rowing Club on 13 August:

> The conditions proposed for the race are – 1st Eight-oared best boats to be used; 2nd coxswains, catch weights; 3rd, bona fide amateurs only to be members of the crews; 4th, the course to be ... about 3½ miles.[11]
>
> [T]he matter was taken up rather favourably at first by the Port Jackson men, but afterwards a public meeting was called in Sydney, at which a rowing association was formed, and it was agreed to make this eight-oared race an intercolonial and representative one.[12]

Excitement about the forthcoming competition grew in both colonies through the latter part of 1877. Irvine was present at many meetings of the VRA to choose a Victorian team and make arrangements for the race which, it was agreed, would take place on a course on the lower reaches of the Yarra River in March 1878.

A special meeting of the VRA committee was held at Edwards' boatshed on the evening of Tuesday 3 December to choose the Victorian crew. It was agreed that 'Messrs G. Fairbairn, T. H. Young, J. Irvine, W.H. Tuckett, J. Stout, J. Booth, Johnson and R. Ward' would form the crew, with Messrs Nichols, McKie, Haines and Cole 'as emergency men.'[13] In the months leading up to the race, however, Stout and Johnson were replaced by W.C. Bray and J.M. Simpson. The crew were mostly members of the Melbourne Rowing Club, with the exception of Bray and Ward, who were members of the Warehousemen's Club. Even Irvine deserted the Banks Club on this occasion and rowed for Melbourne, although his reasons for doing so are not obvious. Half of the crew were bank clerks: Simpson, Tuckett, Booth and Irvine; Fairbairn was a recent arrival from England, where he had rowed for Oxford in the university boat race against Cambridge.

Excitement continued to build through December, January and February, with regular reports of the Victorian crew's practice sessions on the Yarra appearing in the Melbourne press. All Melbourne held its breath on New Year's Day 1878, when it was reported that George Fairbairn, the crew's stroke, had suffered a 'rather serious accident ... during the [Christmas] holidays. Whilst riding he was thrown from his horse and has so injured the muscles of his left arm that he will not regain the use of the limb for some time.'[14] Writing several days later, 'Charon', the *Weekly Times*' contributor to 'Rowing Notes', observed:

> Bad luck seems to attend the formation of the Victorian eight oared crew for the intercolonial race. This week the great stronghold of the crew, Mr Fairbairn, has met with a nasty accident by falling off his horse, thereby severely injuring his shoulder, and it is doubtful if he will recover in time to row in the race; at all events, he will not be able to take part in practice for some weeks ... Altogether, the crew are decidedly in 'Queer Street.'[15]

The VRA looked around for a replacement for Fairbairn; but, by the middle of February, with little more than three weeks to go to the big day, it was reported that Fairbairn had recovered sufficiently to row.

The Victorian Eight were local celebrities and, literally, pin-up boys, with a full-page illustration of the crew appearing in the *Illustrated Australian News* on 20 February. Unusually, portrait heads drawn from studio photographs have been superimposed onto the crew's bodies, with varying degrees of success and naturalness. Irvine, Young and Tuckett look normal, but the heads of at least three of the crew seem to be almost detached from their bodies. However, it is the first, and one of the few, portraits of Irvine that I have been able to find.

In this image, he stands with his back to the viewer, his face in profile. He wears the striped jersey, rolled-up trousers and striped socks of the crews' uniform; a jaunty striped cap is on his head. He has a luxuriant moustache – which would be a handlebar if it were waxed – an aquiline nose, and rather deep-set, hooded eyes. At 31 years of age, he has rather a young face and is quite handsome. Unfortunately, the *News* did not identify the individual members of the crew in the illustration, so determining who is who calls for some deduction and guesswork. Comparing illustrations of later intercolonial teams, it is possible to identify Irvine and also Thomas Henry Young (tall, with a luxuriant, hipsterish beard) and 23-year-old William Henry Tuckett (also tall, cleanshaven, with a scarf knotted around his neck). The names of the rest of the crew are not easily deduced. Who is the man with the disembodied head and the magnificent dundrearies? Or the rather weaselish chap sitting in the scull in front, with a full set of mutton-chops? And the dapper gent with the silk hat, double-breasted coat and cane? He is clearly someone important, who was probably recognisable to the newspaper-reading public of 1878; today, who can tell?

Preparations for the race proceeded apace, with the Sydney crew arriving by steamer *City of Melbourne* on the afternoon of Thursday 14 February. Several representatives of the VRA met them at the Sandridge (Port Melbourne) pier in a four-horse drag (light wagon) and took them to Young and Jackson's Hotel. Their health was drunk in champagne and 'a hearty welcome accorded them by a large number of rowing men present. They bring with them an eight-oared outrigger belonging to the Sydney Rowing Club, ... the [boat's] chief peculiarity ... is her extreme sharpness fore and aft, and the extraordinarily long sides.'

With the day of the intercolonial race set for 6 March, a little more than three weeks away, the Sydney crew took to the Yarra for their first practice row on the afternoon of Friday 15 February:

> At first they were not quite in unison in getting away, but as they came down again they considerably improved and to a great extent belied the underrated view which has been taken of them. No time could be taken of them yesterday, as the men had only just come

The 1878 Victorian Eight crew outside Edwards boat sheds.
Irvine is standing third from the left, in profile in the striped cap.

off a sea voyage, but sufficient could be seen that there are several first-class oarsmen in the crew. ... The crew proceed to Footscray to-day, where they take up their quarters at the Exchange Hotel. We understand that the VRA committee have secured the right of *entrée* to all the places of amusement in Melbourne to our Sydney visitors, and there is no doubt but their stay in Melbourne will be made in every way pleasurable.[16]

It was hoped that the government would declare a public holiday for day of the race:

> as the young men in Melbourne who are engaged in the Government and mercantile offices and banks are ardent lovers of rowing, it was fully expected that, on the occasion of inaugurating the annual Intercolonial Eight-oar Race, a public half-holiday would have been proclaimed. The banks and most of the leading mercantile firms were understood to be favourable to the holiday, but the Government declined to make the concession, and the holiday was not proclaimed, to the great disappointment of a large number of rowing men.[17]

The day itself, Wednesday 6 March, dawned grey and clouded; poor weather and the lack of a public half-holiday notwithstanding, 'crowds of spectators [and] numberless carriages and horsemen occup[ied] every point of vantage.'[18] Two steamers, the *Rescue* and the *Albatross*, had been chartered in order to allow around 300 VIPs, including the Governor, to follow the race on the river. However, the *Rescue*, which was carrying the Governor, stuck fast on a mudbank right at the beginning of the race, and the *Albatross* turned out not to be fast enough to keep up with the rowers, 'so that those who went down the river saw even less of the race than those who stayed near the finish.'[19]

Both crews wore white singlets and blue caps, with the Sydney crew in a lighter blue. The starter's gun was sounded at '16½ minutes past 3 o'clock', and the Melbourne crew got away to a good start, which they held for the whole 24 minutes 30 seconds it took them to cover the four-mile course down the lower Yarra towards the Maribyrnong River:

> The style in which the race was conducted reflects the greatest credit upon both crews. Each endeavoured to their utmost to win the coveted honour in a fair and manly way. There was no paltry trickery employed on either side, and the race was won on its merits.[20]

As winners, the Victorian crew members were each presented with a gold medallion in the shape of a Maltese cross 'embellished with a circle overlay, engraved on the obverse, with crossed flags and oars, Australia Coat of Arms inside circular overlay and inscription "Intercolonial Eight Oar Race 1878,'"[21] with the names of the crew on the reverse.

That evening, both crews were treated to a complimentary dinner at the Melbourne Town Hall. The Mayor presided, with the Sydney crew as the guests of honour. The following evening, Thursday 7 March, both crews attended the Theatre Royal in Bourke Street for a performance of *The Shaughraun*, a play which seemed to be 'as attractive as ever ... judging by the audience.'[22]

The Theatre Royal, located near the corner of Bourke and Swanston Streets in the heart of Melbourne, was one of Melbourne's most popular and luxurious theatres. Originally built at a cost of £60,000 in 1855 to seat 3,300 patrons, it was considered one of the finest theatres in the southern hemisphere and the equivalent of London's Covent Garden and Theatre Royal, Drury Lane. The theatre which Irvine and the Intercolonial eights visited, however, was the second on the site, built in 1872 after the original theatre burned down. The Theatre Royal which Irvine knew seated over 4,000 theatregoers and was part of the heart of Melbourne's fashionable and popular theatre district. It was also the home of the 'saddling paddock', the theatre's bar, which overlooked Bourke Street from upstairs on the first floor – named as the haunt of some of Melbourne's most expensive prostitutes and members of the *demimonde*. Given Irvine's interest in the company of other men, he was probably not often seen in the upstairs bar, unless it was in company with a group of fellows out for a night on the town.

The Shaughraun was a melodramatic play by Irish playwright Dion Boucicault. It was first performed in New York in 1874, then in London, Sydney and Melbourne in 1875. Its plot, involving a convict returned to Ireland after serving his sentence in Australia and a Fenian conspiracy, including plenty of drama, pathos, suspense and some moments of light humour, was a great success in the United States, Britain and the Australian colonies. The 1878 season at the Theatre Royal, which played to packed houses from March to July that year, was the second time the play had appeared there – the first being its Australian debut in 1875.

Four days after attending the theatre, and after another weekend of enjoying the hospitality of Melbourne, the Sydney crew sailed on the *City of Melbourne* on Monday 11 March:

The visitors left our shores well pleased with the manner in which they had been treated, and mutual congratulations were exchanged, and a wish expressed that a better race would take place in Port Jackson next year. When the vessel moved off, hearty cheers were given to the crew.[23]

Following the excitement of the intercolonial competition, Irvine settled back into work at Collins Street and regular training, practice and competition with the Banks Club. As a recognised sporting hero, one of the Victorian Eight, his name was often in the papers; his appearances at the Melbourne Regatta in April and a scratch eights competition in June that year were widely reported.

By the middle of 1878, Irvine was probably living in East Melbourne, a well-to-do suburb. East Melbourne, separated from the central business district only by the bulk of Parliament House and the Fitzroy Gardens. It was the home of some of Melbourne's mercantile elite, politicians and consulates and held the town houses of some of Australia's wealthiest pastoralists and graziers. Of all of the inner suburbs of Melbourne, East Melbourne was the only one never to really slide down the social scale from upper-class wealth and middle-class respectability to being a working-class neighbourhood or slum, as was the fate of other inner city suburbs such as North Melbourne, Fitzroy, Collingwood and Abbotsford. The proximity of Parliament and the Anglican Bishop of Melbourne's residence in Clarendon Street, and the presence of the Fitzroy Gardens, buffering the suburb from the central district, gave East Melbourne an air of rather splendid isolation. Its wide streets and large, well-built houses were keenly sought by members of Melbourne society, so preserving the suburb's cachet.

East Melbourne was also home to a number of exclusive boarding houses, offering 'elegant' and 'superior' accommodation to gentlemen, usually those working in the offices and banks of the city. A 'select' room, perhaps with access to a verandah overlooking the street, could be had for a guinea a week in East Melbourne; in the adjoining working class, although still respectable, suburb of Fitzroy, to the north of Victoria Parade, a single room might cost less than half that.[24] Number 8 Canterbury Terrace, Powlett Street (now number 98 Powlett Street) was one such 'commodious and well-appointed' terrace house. The house, one of a terrace of 16 Italianate houses, was built

The finish of the 1878 intercolonial eight-oared race on the Yarra River, 6 March 1878.

in 1877 and was used as a boarding house from the time it was first occupied. Irvine was one of the earliest lodgers and appears to have moved into the new house early in 1878.

We can gain a good idea of the taste and style of number 8 from an inventory of furnishings completed for an auction of the house's 'Really First-class household furniture and effects' in February 1881. The drawing room featured the usual complement of furniture thought necessary to furnish an elegant home:

> Rich tapestry carpet, 16ft x 15ft, and hearthrug to match, Bronze fender, Handsome oval gilt frame pier-glass, Sup. Rosewood card table, covered in blue cloth, Rosewood four-tier whatnot, Set Three Very Elegant PARIAN and ALABASTER FIGURES, 'The THREE GRACES', first-class drawing room suite, 9 pieces, in blue rep, Inlaid card table, Crystal four-light gasolier, Choice ornaments.

INTERCOLONIAL CHAMPION   83

The main banking chamber of the Union Bank's new Collins Street branch, where Irvine worked when it first opened in 1880.

Also mentioned were the prints and engravings on the walls: 'The Sanctuary', 'The Challenge', 'The Afternoon Nap' and the enormously popular example of Victorian genre painting, Landseer's 'The Stag at Bay.'[25]

In front of the engraving of 'Stag at Bay', in the drawing room with the nine-piece rosewood suite, Irvine's 23-year-old sister Kate married a distant cousin, Daniel Whittle Harvey Patterson, on 21 August 1878. Harvey, as he was known, was the 29-year-old son of 'the late John Hunter Patterson,' a member of the Patterson grazing dynasty, descended from Katharine, the sister of old Jacobina Burn. The witnesses at the wedding were J.L. Irvine and his recently

Looking toward East Melbourne from the Carlton Gardens in 1880. St Patrick's Cathedral is on the horizon on the extreme left - without towers and spires - and the bulk of the rear of Parliament House occupies the central distance. Spring Street runs diagonally on the extreme right hand side of the picture.

widowed sister, Jemima Weetman, back from London after eight years and about to head to New Zealand.

Harvey gave his address as 'Ulonga Station, Hay, New South Wales', while Kate gave her address as East Melbourne, although it is possible that she had only been in Melbourne for a few weeks. She and her mother, Jemima, had travelled together from Launceston for the wedding. Jemima would have used the visit to Melbourne to catch up with acquaintances in the city, particularly Baron von Mueller, the Victorian Government Botanist and the first director of the Melbourne Botanical Gardens, for whom she was now collecting plant specimens. Following the death of her husband Charles nearly 15 years earlier, she had gained a reputation, not only for her collections of shells and other miscellanea, but also for her extensive collection of pressed flowers, plant cuttings and seeds. This was to be a vocation which would ultimately take her to Broken Hill and the far reaches of Western Australia. At the time of Kate's wedding, she was a hearty and healthy 56, a wealthy widow with a grown family and an interest in everything going on around her.

Patterson had been born in 1848 at Tooboorac station near Heathcote, Victoria. When he turned 21 in 1869, he and his brother, John Hunter Patterson, used an inheritance from their father (who had died when Harvey was 11) to begin the acquisition of a portfolio of grazing properties in the Riverina district of southern New South Wales. Harvey owned Ulonga in partnership with his brother; in 1870, he bought Tchelery station, near Hay. In 1875, he bought Menamurtree, near Wilcannia in western New South Wales, and Corona, near Broken Hill. He then purchased Ulonga outright from John in 1876. By the time he married, he was the owner of thousands of acres, running sheep and cattle over four immense properties. He was known for having a keen interest in horse breeding and racing and was a member of Melbourne's social scene, attending the many balls, race meetings, fêtes, parties and picnics that made up the Melbourne Season – centred on the spring months either side of November's Melbourne Cup. On her marriage, Kate entered the rarefied air of upper-class Victorian society, which revolved around the colony's Government House and a number of other large houses in Toorak, Hawthorn, Brighton and St Kilda. Following the ceremony, however, the newlyweds almost immediately left for Ulonga and would not be seen back in Melbourne until the 1878 Season began in October.

Life in East Melbourne suited Irvine very well. Canterbury Terrace offered large, airy, well-furnished rooms in a quiet street, with the company of other professionally employed single men. Work was a half-hour walk away, through the leafy paths of Fitzroy Gardens and Treasury Gardens, and then along the length of Collins Street East – in those days still the preserve of the houses and rooms of Melbourne's leading medical men and exclusive clubs, including the Melbourne Club. Edwards' boatshed, on the south bank of the Yarra, was a similar distance from home. Young and Jackson's Hotel, where he spent many evenings at VRA meetings and socialising with other rowing men, was even nearer.

Crossing the Fitzroy Gardens, however, was not without its dangers, and also temptations, particularly when walking home after a night at Young and Jackson's. Robberies were regularly reported in the Gardens, and, in 1876, a young domestic servant, Eliza Brown, was raped while walking through the Gardens around 11pm one evening.[26] The Gardens were also known as the haunt of the 'depraved of both sexes.' As early as 1870, it was claimed that 'the scenes witnessed [in the Gardens] are sometimes of such a character as simply to be a disgrace to the city.' It was common knowledge that male-to-male sexual activity regularly took place in the Gardens late at night, although the press claimed that, when an offender was apprehended, they were 'so leniently dealt with by the bench [the magistrates' courts] that it is just a question whether he will not be discharged altogether. Cases of gross indecency, which are unfortunately numerous, are invariably dealt with in a spirit of leniency which seems misplaced.'[27]

There were repeated calls throughout the 1870s to shut the Gardens at night to protect public morality, but the darkened paths remained open, providing opportunities for men seeking the company of other men or quick sexual release to make connections in the shrubberies. Perhaps one of them was Irvine; he walked home through the Gardens every evening. In winter, it was dark by the time he left the bank at 5:30pm. On those nights when he attended the monthly VRA meetings or the fortnightly Banks Club meetings, which often did not end until 10 or 11pm, he had ample opportunity to stray off the paths of the Gardens. There was no doubt about it; East Melbourne was a good place to live.

As the journalist quoted above wrote in the *Leader* newspaper in 1870, the Melbourne police and magistrates' courts were not particularly interested

The 1879 Victorian Eight crew practicing near Edwards boat sheds on the Yarra. Irvine is second from the left.

VICTORIAN EIGHT—"HALF FORWARD."

in prosecuting cases of male-to-male sexual activity in the late nineteenth century. The offence of gross indecency was not brought into the Victorian statutes until 1919. In the 1870s and 1880s, the only male sexual offences that could be prosecuted were sodomy, attempted sodomy and indecent assault on a male person. All three offences were difficult to prove, particularly sodomy, which required the offenders to be actually caught in the act; attempted sodomy was used to prosecute a number of cases when actual sodomy could not be proven. Indecent assault in the 1870s and 1880s generally required a 'victim' to make a complaint. The police were not particularly vigilant about patrolling the darkened paths of the Gardens; nor did they inquire too closely into individuals' private lives, unless a concerned member of the public made a complaint. Consequently, the men of 1870s Melbourne who enjoyed male-to-male sex were left largely alone.

Throughout the second half of 1878, Irvine kept himself busy with work, VRA and Banks Club meetings, and competitions, regularly competing on the Yarra. In December that year, the rowing correspondent for the *Leader* opined that J.L. was one of the best oarsman on the river: 'Irvine's rowing last Saturday, when he was behind and his crew beaten, was the best piece of rowing I have seen for an immense time.'[28] This reputation for determination and sportsmanship made him a popular figure among Melbourne's rowers and with the public in general. No one was surprised when, at the monthly meeting of the VRA held at Young and Jackson's on the evening of 1 April, he was nominated as a member of the Victorian eight-oared crew to compete in the 1879 intercolonial competition. Of the crew who raced New South Wales on the Yarra in 1878, only four – Irvine, Tuckett, Young and Booth, with F.J. Edwards remaining as cox – would be going to Sydney to defend their championship on the Parramatta River. The crew was chosen with only eight weeks to train before the race, which was set for 31 May.

Irvine, with a weight of 10 stone 10 pounds (64 kg), was the lightest member of the crew. The rest of the crew ranged from 11 stone 1 pound to 12 stone 4 pounds (70.4kg to 78.7kg). Judging by the illustration of the 1878 crew in the *Australasian Sketcher*, Irvine was also the shortest member of the crew, a wiry little bantam of a man. At 32, he was also one of the oldest crew members; common opinion at the time held that:

rowing races should be discontinued as a rule, at twenty-five years of age. In a few cases it can be continued till thirty, but after that there is always danger to health. Youth is ever apt to overestimate its powers, and training and racing are very strenuous exercises.

That writer was also of the opinion that, although 'rowing as an exercise is one of the best for those whose constitutions are sound, ... if there is a weak spot the hard work is apt to develop it.'[29]

Notwithstanding Irvine's supposedly advanced age, short stature and light weight, the crew trained hard during April and May 1879. On Saturday 10 May, they left Spencer Street on the 2:55pm train to Sydney:

> It is their intention to travel right through to their destination, excepting a few hours' rest at Wagga. They will, therefore, arrive in Sydney at 7 o'clock on Monday morning. The boat in which the crew will row the race goes by the steamer to-day, under the charge of Sydney Edwards, who will act as coach.

The crew were listed as Messrs Tunbridge (bow), J.L. Irvine, J. McKie, W. Loughnan, W.H. Tuckett, W. Kemp, T.H. Young, J. Booth (stroke). Fred Edwards was selected as cox, although, 'owing to the coxswain's engagements in the Public Schools race, he will join the crew afterwards in Sydney.' It was noted that the crew had made good progress during the previous week and had been doing 'excellent and strong work.' The Melbourne press considered that the Sydney crew had been disrupted by the resignation of one of its most effective members, and the remainder of the crew were seen to have a 'defective and irregular'[30] technique. Things were looking good for the Victorian crew.

Two days later, the crew arrived in Sydney. Melbourne's *Illustrated Australian News* carried a full-page illustration of the Victorian crew at practice, rowing under Princes Bridge on the Yarra, with Edwards' boatshed in the background. Again, the crew's faces had been drawn from photographs (mainly taken by F. Hasler's studio in Elizabeth Street) and superimposed on their bodies in the boat. The *News* noted that Irvine was a member of the Banks Club and 'besides some races in Tasmania, won the Junior Eight in 1876, Challenge Plate in 1876, 1877 and 1878, Barwon Plate in 1877 and Intercolonial Eight 1878.'[31]

The crew took up residence at Jordan's Hotel, Ryde, near the river. They began training in earnest, but the weather on Saturday 31 May:

> broke unfavourably to the chances of the Melbourne men, who are, from the force of circumstances, smooth-water rowers, and who had not an opportunity of practicing in rough water during their stay on the Parramatta. A strong southerly wind blew across the river, rendering the water very broken and rough in places. The starting point, being more sheltered, was comparatively smooth. The crews were started from boats moored in the stream, making the starter's duty light and easy, as the racing boats are held till the signal to go is given. [32]

The Victorian crew made a false start and had to be called back, but the race was underway at 4:40pm precisely. The light blue of the Victorian uniforms and the dark blue of the NSW men were seen to take off from the starting position, and the Victorian boat pulled ahead at first. A gap between the two boats quickly opened up, with about 'half a length of daylight to [the Victorians'] credit' being viewed by spectators on the riverbanks. However, away from the comparatively smooth water of the sheltered starting point, the Victorian crew found the going steadily rougher in the choppy water, and 'the Sydney crew commenced to creep up gradually.' Although 'Irvine's rowing was much admired', the Sydney eight drew up steadily and eventually gained a slight lead. This increased over the remainder of the four-mile course, and New South Wales won by four lengths in 20 minutes, 3 seconds.

> Winners and losers having been loudly cheered, a move was made for Sydney. The arrangements made by the [New South Wales] Rowing Association for the race were excellent no hitch having occurred throughout ... Both crews were entertained at dinner in the evening at the Exchange Hotel, Mr George Thornton, M.P., presiding. The toasts of the winners and losers were hailed with great enthusiasm, and everything passed off most pleasantly.

INTERCOLONIAL CHAMPION   93

The remainder of 1879 passed steadily enough with work and competitions, including a scratch eights competition between the University, Banks and Civil Service clubs held on 26 July:

> The best race of the day was between Irvine and [the other] crews, in the fourth heat. The race was a very close one throughout, and Irvine's crew only succeeded in proving themselves victors on the winning post.

Irvine was also becoming more involved in the committee work of the VRA and of the Banks Club. At a committee meeting in October 1879 at Young and Jackson's, he was elected captain of the Banks Club for the following year. As always, these events were of a decidedly social nature: 'Business over, the proceedings took a convivial turn, toasts and songs alternated, and a most enjoyable evening was spent.'[33]

The same year, construction began on the Union Bank's new head office, a few doors from the bank's existing branch. By August, the ground storey of the façade was complete enough for the public to appreciate the 'very bold and handsome appearance, [which] will form an harmonious contrast to the chaste character of the [planned] upper story [sic].'[34] Built to impress and to reassure customers of its stability, wealth and financial soundness, the bank's ground floor was to be built of grey granite, with arcaded colonnades of New Zealand freestone on the upper level. Despite having only two storeys, the building's lofty ceilings would give it the height of a four-storeyed building and put it among the most impressive of all the Melbourne banks.

On 20 September, Irvine attended the VRA's annual general meeting at the boat sheds on the banks of the Yarra. The key controversy of this meeting was whether competitive races should be rowed on the traditional fixed seats or the newly introduced sliding seats. The *Leader*'s rowing correspondent, 'Melbourne', reported:

> all the experienced oarsmen, with the exception of Mr T.H. Young and Mr J.L. Irvine, were in favour of the fixed seats, and indeed Messrs Young and Irvine admitted the wisdom of teaching our young oarsmen to row on the fixed seats before they attempted the slide, but considered that the matter should be left to the various clubs.

'Melbourne' continued:

> If it be left to the clubs to induce their new members to learn on the fixed seats, I am quite sure we shall see the 'form' of our oarsmen getting worse and worse each year, for so long as the maiden races are to be rowed in boats with sliding seats few, if any, of the clubs will keep boats with fixed seats, and even those clubs that did could never induce their new rowing members to go out on the fixed seats while they saw other members using the slides.

Melbourne concluded, rather contemptuously:

> Messrs Young and Irvine appeared to attach more importance to the mere convenience of the various clubs, than to the general interests of rowing. Of course, it will be inconvenient for 'some' clubs, but the mere inconvenience of these should not stand in the way of the committee of the V.R.A. finally determining that the maiden races should be rowed for in boats with the fixed seats.[35]

This was the first occasion on which the rowing correspondents of the *Leader* exhibited a spirit of spitefulness when writing about Irvine; the *Leader*'s digs at Irvine continued over the next two years, finally erupting in a full-blown public attack on him in the pages of the paper in January 1881. It was common practice in the nineteenth century for newspaper journalists and contributors to be anonymous, or to use pseudonyms, so it is impossible to know who 'Melbourne', or any of the other rowing contributors such as 'Clinker' and 'Cloanthus', were; but, as a contributor, he was likely to have been a fellow rower and, apparently, no friend or supporter of Irvine.

The new year of 1880 opened with plans to hold the third intercolonial eights race on the Yarra in early April, but the first major competition of the year was the annual Melbourne Regatta, rowed on the lower Yarra and Saltwater (Maribyrnong) rivers on Saturday 21 February. Irvine competed in the Banks crew for the Clarke Challenge Cup, against crews from Footscray, Corio, and Melbourne. Although he put up a decent effort, he came in third, trailing Footscray and Corio. Irvine attended the prize giving, held at Young and Jackson's on the evening of Thursday 26 February and presided over by the Hon. W.J. Clarke. It was reported that the hotel's large upstairs room was 'filled to overflowing.'[36]

The following month, on 10 March, Irvine was selected as Number Three in the Victorian crew for the 1880 intercolonial eights. The crew practised regularly on the Yarra. Once again, Melbourne's newspaper readers were treated to regular updates on their performance, times and condition. The New South Wales crew arrived by train at Spencer Street station on the afternoon of Saturday 27 March. A large crowd of rowing men, Irvine included, greeted them and conveyed them in a public procession to Young and Jackson's Hotel, where they were officially welcomed before being driven to their lodgings at St Kilda.

The intercolonial race 'came off' on the afternoon of Saturday 10 April on the Lower Yarra course:

> The wharves and banks of the river were densely crowded, and the ships lying in the river were also invaded by spectators, whilst their crews were perched on the masts and yardarms. There was likewise a fine display of bunting which added to the gaiety of the scene.

The Victorians led from the beginning of the race and finished the four-mile course three and a half lengths in front of New South Wales:

> Their victory was warmly cheered by the onlookers. In the evening the crews were entertained at a banquet in Gunsler's Café, Collins-street. There were about 80 gentlemen present, and the Hon. W. J. Clarke, M. L. C., the president of the Victorian Rowing Association, occupied the chair. The toast of 'The Winning Crew' was proposed by the chairman and responded to by Mr. G. Upward, whilst 'The Losing Side' was given by Mr. R. Murray Smith, M. L. A., and responded to by Mr. W. G. Anslow.[37]

May 1880 saw the scaffolding on the Union Bank's new headquarters removed: 'The beauty of its front elevation can now be fully appreciated. It is the most conspicuous object in Collins street.'[38] The bank staff moved in soon after, occupying the 62 foot square banking chamber with its glass dome, cedar counters and bluestone paved floor. The bank provided some accommodation for clerks, who had their own conservatory at the rear of the first floor.[39]

Irvine's year was taken up with work and committee work for both the Banks Club and VRA, as well as regular practice and competition on the Yarra. In July, he represented the Banks Club at a VRA meeting held at the Athenaeum in Collins Street, convened to discuss the continuing subject of manual labourers competing in amateur rowing competitions. Rowing in the nineteenth century was a predominantly middle and upper-class sport; the high cost of memberships, boats and equipment barred the involvement of working men in the sport. Further, most manual labourers were required to work on Saturdays and thus had less time to train and compete. Indeed, unless employers were prepared to grant them some Saturdays off work, the competitive rowing of many manual labourers was restricted to those regattas held on public holidays. Despite these obstacles:

> a considerable manual labour interest did emerge in the 1860s and 1870s. This was no doubt aided by the 30 years of economic boom in Victoria prior to the 1890s depression, and by the relatively early achievement of the eight-hour day. By the late 1880s up to two-thirds of urban wage earners in Melbourne had won the 48-hour working week, generally arranged so as to provide a half-holiday on Saturdays. This compared favourably with the rest of Australia where longer hours of work were the norm for most people.[40]

By the early 1880s, amateur teams, overwhelmingly composed of middle-class office workers and professional men, were becoming concerned that they were operating at an unfair advantage to manual workers – who, because of their employment, were stronger and more resilient. Something had to be done. The Banks Club reported in 1880 that 'the club's Senior Eight had rowed creditably for a second at Colac behind Corio Bay and a third at the Melbourne Regatta behind both Footscray and Corio'. The report goes on to say: 'on both occasions your club Senior Eight has been beaten by crews composed essentially of what has now become known as the manual labour elements, and ... of the clubs whose members are of our class, we head the river.'

The Athenaeum meeting voted to support a motion which would have had the effect of:

> definitely distinguishing the 'manual labour rower' and the less hardened and muscular subject of office life, and ultimately confining to each, a set of competitions on a more equitable basis than at present exists. 'The thin edge of the wedge has been inserted and no doubt it will cleave the log entirely.'

The matter was adjourned for a period of twelve months and appears to have lapsed. Records, however do show the Melbourne Regatta provided for Junior Eight and Senior Eight races for *'non-Manual Labourer Amateurs'* during the years 1882 and 1883.'[41]

Irvine's membership of the VRA committee, as the representative of the Banks Club, was bringing him into contact with some of the wealthiest and most important men in the colony. W.J. Clarke, the VRA President, was a man wealthy enough to have almost considered Sunbury railway station to be his personal stop, and to have another, Clarkefield, named after him. There is a story that he arrived on the platform at Spencer Street one afternoon to see the Sunbury train just pulling out: 'Stop that train,' he bellowed, and such was his authority, it did stop! Irvine was well able to mix in such exalted circles; he was always known for having an engaging personality and a knack of getting along with others. His social background and training among Launceston's elite fitted him well to perform in the bigger pool of Melbourne society. His sister Kate's marriage into the Victorian squattocracy also led to invitations to social events at which he would have met the colony's leaders.

Irvine may have been popular in social circles, but his high profile gained him enemies in the sporting press. In January 1881, the *Leader*'s rowing contributor 'Clinker' launched an attack on Irvine and two other members of the Banks Rowing Club, Tuckett and Nichols, for apparently abandoning Banks to row for the Melbourne R.C. crew:

> anyone who takes an interest in rowing is well acquainted with
> the action of several prominent members of the Banks Club who
> have lately sought shelter under the wings of the Melbourne Club.
> Those acquainted with the facts are no doubt thoroughly disgusted
> with the action of such prominent oarsmen as Messrs A. Nichols,
> J.L. Irvine and W.H. Tuckett. There has probably never been, I
> may safely assert, a more miserable exhibition on the river of such
> pusillanimity. Probably these fortune's champions may have some
> weighty reasons for their conduct, but I feel perfectly convinced
> that they have no stronger than the desire to obtain honours (?) for
> themselves and electroplated ware for their sideboards. The Banks
> Club have reason to no longer congratulate themselves on their
> possessing such chivalrous office-bearers as their vice-president
> and captain.[42]

A week later, 'Cloanthus,' the rowing contributor for the rival *Australasian*, responded:

> A very uncalled-for attack has been made by a fellow-contributor in
> a weekly contemporary on certain members of the Banks Rowing
> Club, for having joined the Melbourne senior eight. I am aware it is
> not in accordance with usage for one scribe to take up the cudgel
> in the cause of persons who may feel they have been unfairly or
> unjustly attacked by another; but I think the facts of this case will
> justify me in at least offering an explanation of the circumstances
> under which Messrs. Nichols, Tuckett, and Irvine are said to have
> sold themselves to the MRC.[43]

'Cloanthus' went on to explain that Nichols was a long-standing member of the MRC and that Tuckett and Irvine had previously rowed for the Club's junior and senior eights, back in April 1876. The race for which 'Clinker' had accused the three of deserting Banks was one in which the Banks Club was not competing; Irvine and Tuckett had offered their services to MRC with the full awareness and blessing of Banks.

INTERCOLONIAL CHAMPION   99

The same day, the *Weekly Times*' rowing correspondent 'Aquarius' weighed in with further information:

> I have seldom or ever read a more mendacious misrepresentation than the one which appeared in the aquatic columns of the *Leader* last week, in which the writer imputed the basest motives to three prominent oarsmen, who have exercised a privilege they are surely entitled to, namely, that of rowing with either the Melbourne or Banks clubs. So much indignation was felt in the matter that on Monday last, meetings of the Melbourne and Banks clubs' committees were held to consider the article referred to. Much surprise was expressed that such a scandalous as well as unfounded charge against three well-known oarsmen should have been made, and both committees decided to support them in any action they might be advised to take.

Irvine, Tuckett and two other representatives of both Clubs called on the manager of the *Leader*, read the article to him and asked that a full apology should be given and 'Clinker's' identity revealed. The *Leader*'s manager offered to print a letter from the two Clubs; that was considered insufficient, the two Clubs' representatives 'pointing out that the assertions of the contributor reflected on the committee and the oarsmen without a shadow of justification.'[44] The newspaper's manager then fobbed Irvine and Tuckett off with a promise to consider the matter and to provide them with his answer in writing. When the paper's response was received, it revealed that all the *Leader* was willing to do was restate its offer to print a rebuttal from the Clubs, not to offer a retraction or to disclose 'Clinker's' identity.

Hiding behind the protection of the *Leader* and the anonymity of his pseudonym, 'Clinker' responded to the *Australasian* and the *Weekly Times* in his column of 22 January, crowing: 'The comments which I have at various times made in these columns concerning the want of proper spirit shown by Messrs Nichols, Irvine and Tuckett in running about from one club to another have, it appears, given dissatisfaction to those chivalrous gentlemen.' Referring to the three rowers as 'chameleons' for changing their club loyalties, 'Clinker' denounced Irvine and Tuckett as 'failures at the Melbourne Club'[45] who had originally gone to Banks because it offered a better chance of success, and then swapped back to MRC when Banks did not suit them. The matter came to a head a fortnight later. A meeting of the VRA on Thursday 3 February:

> unanimously decided that ['Clinker's'] accusation had no foundation in fact, and a great deal of sympathy was expressed for the three gentlemen who had been so unwarrantably and unfairly attacked. 'Aquarius' commented that 'Clinker's' comments were actuated by 'the black bile of personal malignity'[46] and hoped that this would be the last that would be heard of an 'unpleasant subject, which would not have attracted so much attention had it not been for the gross personalities indulged in by a person for whom, however, some excuse can be made, as he is yet a young and inexperienced writer on the Press.'

It is obvious that, by now, 'Aquarius' was aware of the identity of 'Clinker'; unfortunately, we probably never will be.

'Clinker' was obviously stung by the response to the controversy that he had stirred up. Reporting on a practice session which took place on the Yarra in the week before the 'Aquarius' comments were published, he referred to Irvine as rowing in a very 'slouching manner' and commented that 'Nichols, of course, never does row well, although I suppose it is treason to say so.'[47] Sour grapes indeed!

In the midst of this controversy, the date of the 1881 Intercolonial eights competition was announced. The date would be 9 April, and the Victorian crew would travel to Sydney to compete once more on the Parramatta River. 'Clinker' continued to be bitter about his treatment in the Banks/MRC controversy; reporting on a March training session of the Victorian crew, he said:

> I saw the crew out several times this week, but I cannot say that I am deeply impressed with their style, swing or *personnel* ['Clinker's' emphasis]. Their rowing is yet very ragged ... Mr C. Vickers is entrusted with the coaching of them, and I don't envy his task. He will have to use more firmness with them than ordinary, as some of the crew no doubt imagine themselves perfection already.

After casting aspersions at the unpreparedness and lack of strength and technique of several of the crew, he noted: 'Irvine also has no right to a seat. He seems done up, and with more work I expect to see him train too fine, as was the case when the Victorians last visited Sydney.' A week later, 'Clinker' complained that Irvine 'seems to me absolutely stale, rowing without the least vigor whatever, and his form is the worst in the [crew].'[48]

All carping aside, the Victorian Eight left Spencer Street railway station early on the morning of Friday 25 March and arrived in Sydney the following day. Representatives of the NSW Rowing Association greeted them and hosted them at a breakfast. Following their official welcome, the crew took their boat, which had been shipped to Sydney via the coastal steamer *Wotonga*, to Gladesville, to hold their practice sessions. They then went on to Ryde and lodged with Captain and Mrs Drury, 'where Mrs Drury and her family made them as comfortable as it was possible to be.' Sydney correspondents considered the Victorian crew to be 'very strong indeed'[49] – although, leading up to the big day, the New South Wales crew were considered the favourites.

The weather on Saturday 9 April was fine, with a light, warm breeze 'ruffling the water'. The race was underway at high tide at 4:30pm. NSW Rowing Association members volunteered as signalmen along the course, waving red or white flags, depending on whether Victoria or New South Wales was in the lead at that point.

> At 4 o'clock the starting point at Ryde was a busy scene. The [steamers] *Commodore*, the *Prince of Wales*, the *Telephone*, the Government steamer *Achilles*, the police launch, the *Ena*, and the Governor's launch *Nea*, were assembled there. The *Nea* carried Lord and Lady Augustus Loftus, Lieutenant A.D. Loftus, A.D.C.; Mr Reginald Bloxsome, private secretary. A boat, manned by patients from the Gladesville Asylum, attracted some attention, but their demeanour was quiet, indeed apathetic, and the only lunatic behaviour displayed was upon the steamers later on.

New South Wales got away first, 'but, collectively and individually, their form was very bad ... they splashed about a good deal, and ... [were] most uneven.' The Victorians shot forward and gradually forged further and further ahead of the New South Wales boat. Victoria won the race in 18 minutes and 12 seconds, and New South Wales trailed in half a minute after. The Sydney press opined:

> there is no getting away from the fact that the Victorians were a better crew, and, moreover they have shown us that our oarsmen have not yet accomplished the art of outrigger rowing. The style of [the Victorian crew] on Saturday, comes as near perfection as we can hope to find it away from Oxford and Cambridge.[50]

To add insult to injury, the New South Wales crew were capsized into the Parramatta River by the wash of a passing steamer but were quickly retrieved from the water and taken to their quarters. The day concluded with a dinner at Aaron's Exchange Hotel in Gresham Street. Seventy men sat down to a formal dinner with a long list of speeches, all of which were reported verbatim in the Sydney press.

Following the crew's return to Victoria, Irvine took the train to Geelong on Wednesday 20 April, to attend a dinner at Mack's Hotel. Hosted by the Mayor of Geelong, the dinner was held to honour three of the intercolonial crew who came from that city: George Upward, R. Brown and I. Hodges, all of the Corio Bay Club. '[An] excellent repast was provided, ... but the dinner which should have commenced at eight o'clock, did not begin before a quarter to nine, owing to the non-arrival of the Melbourne representatives of the crew.' During the after dinner speeches, which were always a feature of these rowing club events, Irvine 'complimented the stroke on having brought the crew in the pink of condition to the scratch. The stroke had taken the utmost interest in the crew's welfare. They had astonished the New South Wales men.'[51]

The 1881 race was the fourth intercolonial in which Irvine had competed, and it would be his last. The day after the race was his 34th birthday; he was among the oldest, if not the oldest, of the crew. He was still in good condition, fit and active, notwithstanding 'Clinker's' carping comments in the *Leader*, and he continued to compete in Banks' races throughout the remainder of 1881. He also remained very busy with both Club committee work and with his role representing the Club on the VRA committee, with its monthly meetings.

Flinders Lane, around the time that Irvine and Henry Beaumont lived there. Their house would have been similar to the two-storey house on the left.

Irvine's home life also changed in 1881. Number 8 Canterbury Terrace, East Melbourne, was sold in February, along with all its furnishings. Irvine had to find somewhere else to live. For the first time in his adult life, he decided not to move to another boarding house, but to set up home in his own, rented, house. His new address was a small, single-storeyed cottage in Flinders Lane East, just two doors from the corner of Spring Street. The location was ideal for access to work, the rowing sheds and the river, and was only three city blocks from Young and Jacksons.

Irvine shared the house with 18-year-old Henry Stewart Beaumont, another bank clerk, who worked for the Bank of New South Wales. Henry had only been in the colony for a few months and was probably grateful for the advice and friendship of the older Irvine. Their cosy bachelor establishment was looked after by a general servant who acted as cook and cleaner. Whether or not Irvine and Henry were a couple, they were obviously close friends. As always, Irvine was attracted to, and comfortable with, the company of younger men; Henry was 16 years his junior.

Their quiet existence was disturbed in September 1881, when they were burgled. The thief was 20-year-old Albert Revel. Among the items stolen were small items of jewellery belonging to Irvine, including 'a single stone diamond pin, star setting; a gold maltese cross' (Irvine's 1878 intercolonial medal); a rowing trophy inscribed 'Won by J.L. Irvine, Footscray Plate, Melbourne Annual Regatta 1877'; and six old silver coins. Henry lost more, including 'a Russian leather dressing case with his initials on it, a small black leather travelling bag containing papers, clothing, a plaid rug, two blankets, and two sheets.'[52]

Revel was described as 5 feet 6 inches tall, with a fresh complexion, brown hair and hazel eyes; he was a labourer, a Roman Catholic and a native of Geelong. Russell Street police arrested Revel very soon after the robbery was reported and found some of the items on him. He very quickly appeared before the Melbourne Petty Sessions Court, on 19 September, just a fortnight after the robbery; he was sentenced to 12 months' hard labour. He served the full term of his sentence in the Geelong Gaol, where he was a fairly well-behaved prisoner. He must have learned his lesson; he was never again in trouble with the law. Although Irvine's diamond pin was restored to him, the fate of the Footscray Plate trophy is unknown.

September 1881 was a busy month for Irvine. As well as being burgled and dealing with the police, he was active in VRA business. He chaired a number of committee meetings to organise a regatta on the Yarra, to be held in December, and attended the annual general meeting at Young and Jacksons on 16 September, where the impact of the rebuilding of Princes Bridge on the boatsheds was a topic of keen discussion:

> There is ... no doubt, that a great amount of inconvenience will have to be submitted to ... during the building of the new bridge and making the necessary excavations, but that cannot be avoided; and when it is remembered that the sites now granted [for the boat sheds] will in all probability be for all time, it is quite certain it will not be grumbled about.[53]

However, towards the end of the month, Irvine received word from the Union Bank that he was to be transferred to the Sandhurst [now Bendigo] branch, effective the second week of October. His new role was to be the bank's accountant, with a salary of £225. The next few weeks were a flurry of tying up loose ends in Melbourne before heading to the gold mining city of Sandhurst, 150 kilometres to the north. Irvine resigned as Captain of the Banks Club on 30 September, having served since 19 May 1876, and also gave up his position on the VRA Committee. The Banks Club's annual meeting, held at Young and Jacksons on the evening of Wednesday 19 October, noted: 'Special mention was made of the great loss sustained by the removal to other spheres of ... J.L. Irvine ... who had evinced the most active interest in the welfare of the Club.'[54]

The fact that Sandhurst was easily reached by train from Melbourne in around three hours meant that Irvine was able to continue to compete in VRA and Banks races; his involvement in the Banks Club, in particular, was to be long felt. He was honoured as the Club's first life member in 1884.[55]

Irvine packed his belongings, said farewell to Henry Beaumont and left their cottage in Flinders Lane. He took the train from Spencer Street to Sandhurst and reported for duty at the bank's View Street office on the morning of Monday 10 October.

CHAPTER 6
"Bow your knees to the bombastic Irvine"

When Irvine arrived in Sandhurst on the weekend of 8 and 9 October 1881, the city was Victoria's second largest inland city, trailing Ballarat by only a few thousand people. Growing out of a string of mining camps dotted along the course of the seasonal Bendigo Creek during the gold rush of the 1850s, by 1881 it boasted a busy shopping district, well-built churches, an elaborate town hall, a large hospital and a benevolent asylum. The main street, Pall Mall, lined on one side with large shops and banking chambers and on the other by Rosalind Park, led down to the town's main intersection, Charing Cross, with its ornate Alexandra Fountain as the centrepiece of the town.

The Bendigo field was the wealthiest goldfield in the world at the time, and the city's surroundings were dominated by the poppet heads of gold mines and 'heaps of upturned dry soil, ... dislocated whims, rows of humble houses built just as they were wanted, shops with gewgaw fronts put up at a moment's notice, [and] drinking bars in abundance.' The mines' stamping batteries, used to crush the quartz rock to extract gold, worked 24 hours a day, six days a week, only stopping on the Sabbath. The noise of this heavy machinery could be heard all over town, and it was said that the residents were so used to the sound that they only noticed it by its absence, when the machines fell silent on Sunday.

Anthony Trollope, visiting Sandhurst ten years before Irvine arrived, noted that, although the town had few 'attempt[s] at architecture,' those that it had were 'made almost invariably by some banking company eager to push itself into large operations.'[1] The Union Bank's View Street premises were such an example.

Sandhurst in the 1880s, looking from Rosalind Park across Pall Mall. The Bank of Australasia is the white building on the right hand side of the street corner in the centre of the image.

Irvine would have stepped off the train at the city's railway station, built when the train line reached the city from Melbourne in 1862, and walked down Mitchell Street, through Charing Cross, past the Alexandra Fountain and up View Street to reach the bank's Italianate building, built four years earlier in 1876. The bank still stands but is now a wine bar. It is possible to sit and drink in the former banking chamber, under the ornate plaster ceiling that Irvine knew so well. The strong room is used for storing wine, the manager's office on the first floor is a large private dining room, and the accountant's office, just inside the front door on the ground floor, is a small, semi-private room where it is possible to relax with a glass of local wine.

The Sandhurst branch of the Union Bank was unusual in providing live-in accommodation for unmarried bank staff, in a wing at the rear of the building. Today, this has been refurbished as tourist accommodation, with a pleasant courtyard garden overlooked by the bank's own smelter building, complete with imposing chimney.

Irvine quickly became involved in local activities, including joining the choir of All Saints Anglican church and the Sandhurst Rowing Club, who eagerly accepted a former intercolonial champion. Within a month of arriving in Sandhurst, on Wednesday 30 November, he competed in a Senior Fours race at the Sandhurst Regatta, held on the city's Lake Weeroona.

Lake Weeroona was, and still is, the centre of operations for rowing in Bendigo. In the 1880s, the city had two rowing clubs, the Sandhurst R.C. and the Bendigo R.C. The Sandhurst Club was the older, having been founded in April 1873, with the Bendigo Club just a month younger. Membership of the two clubs was said to fall into sectarian camps; the Bendigo R.C. consisted of mainly Catholic members, and the Sandhurst R.C. was mostly Protestant.

Much of the impetus for establishing rowing as a sport in Bendigo came from the town's bank employees – particularly John Godfrey of the Bank of Australasia, who was associated with the Sandhurst Club from its beginnings until his death over 50 years later. Initially, the two clubs rowed at the Upper Grassy Flat Reservoir, about an hour's ride from town; however, in 1877, the

wall of the reservoir failed, and the reservoir had to be drained in the interests of public safety. Fortunately, the previous year, the Sandhurst City Council had been granted 45 acres of swampy land to the north of the town for the purposes of 'building or forming a lake for boating and recreational purposes.'

Work on excavating the new site took three years. The lake was opened on Tuesday 21 October 1879. The surrounds were landscaped with European trees, picnic shelters and pathways spread around the lake, and both rowing clubs erected their boatsheds at the northern end of the lake. The name, Weeroona, is said to be a local Aboriginal word meaning 'We Rest.'[2]

By the early 1880s, the Bendigo and Sandhurst R.C.s were thriving, holding an annual regatta each November and a range of competitions in a rowing season extending from September to April. Irvine's first outing in Bendigo rowing circles was the 1881 Regatta, which the *Bendigo Advertiser* reported as 'a great success in every respect. The weather was most enjoyable, and as it was a business half-holiday and also a special school half-holiday there was a great concourse of people, it being estimated that over three thousand persons were present.' The 'animated' scene featured gaily decorated boatsheds and marquees for important invited guests, including the mayor of Sandhurst, and

a brass band played tunes which 'greatly enlivened the day's proceedings.' The rowing was considered to be 'far above average'; however, the lake was 'very bumpy' because of a strong breeze which kept up for most of the day. Only the first few heats were rowed, and the final races were held over to the following week. Irvine's involvement drew particular attention:

> The greatest amount of interest was taken in this race, and Irvine's crew were the favorites. This was because of the fact that Irvine has represented the colony in intercolonial contests, and it was thought that his own rowing, and the training his experience would enable him to give his men would put him in the premier place.[3]

The popular expectation that Irvine would do well was justified; his boat won the race by nearly six lengths.

The weather on the regatta's second day, the following Wednesday, was even worse than that of the first day:

> A strong and gusty wind blew from the upper end of the Lake ... so that it caused a very unpleasant cross ripple on the water, which at times seriously inconvenienced the oarsmen. The sun shone with a fierce heat early in the afternoon, but the sky soon became overclouded, and at about 5 o'clock rain fell, causing a cessation of rowing for a time, and also a general stampede from the grounds of the spectators.

The poor weather was blamed for a much lower turn-out of spectators, with only around 500 showing up.

Despite the bad weather and poor conditions, the rowing was considered to be pretty good. Irvine's crew in the Senior Fours (the regatta's principal race) rowed with 'regularity and style,'[4] winning by two lengths. That evening, the competing clubs (Sandhurst R.C. and Bendigo R.C.), together with invited guests 'numbering altogether about a hundred, sat down to an excellent light repast at the Beehive Exchange [in Pall Mall].' As Club champion, Irvine sat on the head table and was presented with a silver medal. At the dinner, local bookmaker and financier, Alfred Joseph, announced that he would present a trophy to the winner of a four-oared race to be held in February.

The Bendigo and Sandhurst clubs trained steadily over the Christmas and New Year period of 1881–82 and met at Lake Weeroona on Wednesday 22 February:

> The weather ... was hot and dusty, and to a certain extent prevented a large number of persons from visiting the lake, although in the afternoon the dust subsided somewhat. About 1,000 persons were present. At half-past three o'clock Whitlam's Sandhurst Brass Band marched from Charing Cross to the lake, and played several musical selections in excellent style. The clubs displayed flags over their boat-houses, and with the steam launch and several pleasure boats on the water the scene was rather animated.'

Irvine was stroke for the Sandhurst crew, which got away from the start quickly and won easily, covering the course, which was three times around the lake, in about 27 minutes. 'After the race the two crews, and several members of the clubs assembled on the platform of the Sandhurst Club, where light refreshments were provided.' Joseph presented the cup to Irvine, saying 'his only object in giving the cup was with a view of stimulating one of the most invigorating and pleasant of out-of-door sports.' Accepting the cup, Irvine said it gave him great pleasure to 'receive such a handsome trophy, and, in a neat speech, proceeded to compliment Mr Joseph on his liberality in support of rowing.'

Further speechifying took place that evening at separate club dinners, held at the Black Swan Hotel (Bendigo R.C.) and the City Family Hotel (Sandhurst R.C.). Irvine invited Joseph to attend the Sandhurst dinner, where he was toasted and responded by saying that 'he felt proud at the excellent race they had witnessed that day. His efforts were always to stimulate rowing. As long as he held the position of a public man he would always do his best to fill his position with honor.'[5] Other toasts followed, including 'The Defeated Crew,' and finished with 'The Health of Mr Irvine.' News of the Joseph Trophy race reached the ears of Irvine's old foe Clinker, of Melbourne's *Leader* newspaper:

> Our old Intercolonial rowing man, J.L. Irvine, rowed stroke of the winning crew – the Sandhurst. The race was won pretty easily at the

finish. Two spreads, one in the afternoon and another in the evening, followed, at which J.L. Irvine made 'neat speeches,' and everybody's health was drunk. It is to be hoped that he favored the company with some of his soul-inspiring ear-splitting songs which some of the Melbourne oarsmen have endured.[6]

Ouch!

The City Family Hotel was the Sandhurst Rowing Club's hotel, resorted to for Club meetings and functions, just as the Melbourne Banks Club used Young and Jackson's. The 'splendid' three-storeyed building was built in 1872 and was considered at the time to be the finest and most impressive building in Bendigo 'excepting only the city's Mining Exchange.' Surmounted by a 66 foot high tower, the Hotel was built in the 'modern Italian style of architecture'[7] on a triangular site overlooking the Charing Cross intersection The ground floor of the hotel boasted a large bar, billiard room, bar parlour, an 'elegant private entrance hall ... and the handsomest ornamental circular staircase in the colony.' A 'back building' contained the kitchen, scullery and servants' staircase. Upstairs on the first floor were a large drawing room, dining room, parlours, nine bedrooms and a large 'commercial room' used by commercial travellers and salesmen for displaying their product lines. The top floor had 22 bedrooms, as well as further drawing rooms. Each floor had two plunge and shower baths for the use of guests. A two-storey verandah draped in cast-iron lace marched along the long street side of the building. The City Family still stands at the southern end of Charing Cross, although stripped of its verandah and much of its internal splendour.

Three weeks after winning the Joseph Trophy, the Sandhurst crew were off to Geelong to row in the Maiden Fours at the Barwon Regatta on Wednesday 15 March 1882. Over 3,000 people lined the banks of the Barwon River to watch crews from Ballarat, Barwon, Sandhurst, Melbourne and Footscray compete in a programme of heats. Barwon and Sandhurst ended the day in competition with each other, with Sandhurst winning by half a length: 'the victory is all more creditable to the crew, as they rowed in a strange boat, lent by one of the local clubs.' Irvine, vice-captain of the Club, did not compete but was noted as the coach responsible for training the winning crew. The Club was commended for 'displaying considerable energy in sending teams to compete outside the district,'[8] something which may have sprung from the enthusiasm injected into the club by their new vice-captain.

Three days later, on Saturday 18 March, Sandhurst entered crews in several races in the annual Melbourne Regatta, but they were unsuccessful in every race. Choosing to concentrate on their win at Geelong, the Sandhurst men were back at the City Family the following Tuesday for a celebratory dinner. About 50 Club members and friends sat down to an 'excellent repast'[9] and toasted each other. Irvine responded to a toast 'Success in Rowing' which was directed at him. The Melbourne losses were laughed off.

Rowing was not the only Sandhurst activity with which Irvine became involved. A week after the City Family dinner, he was back in the hotel's commercial room, attending the annual meeting of the Sandhurst Football Club. A month shy of his 35th birthday, Irvine was too old to play, but he happily stood for a committee position and was elected one of four vice-presidents of the Club.[10] The following month, he was publicly thanked for donating a guinea to the Club's fundraising appeal.[11]

The 1881–82 rowing season closed with a scratch race competition on the afternoon of Wednesday 27 April. Irvine acted as starter and judge for two races (sculls and scratch fours) which were raced in the chilly air of an autumn afternoon. The Club awarded gold medals to the winners. The closing of the rowing season and the drawing in of winter 1882 meant that Irvine was present at a number of other social events. On the evening of Wednesday 28 June, he joined 500 other guests at the city's Corn Exchange at the Town Hall in Hargreaves Street as a guest of the Mayor and Mayoress of Sandhurst, Councillor and Mrs W.G. Jackson. The Corn Exchange, usually the scene of produce markets, was transformed into a scene of:

> beauty, a miniature sea of light and life of color of which only the brush of a talented painter could give an adequate conception ... The ballroom was prettily and neatly decorated, perhaps more tastefully than on any previous occasion. Banners, bannerets, and bunting covered the walls, evergreens festooned the corinthian columns, and ferns and exotics gave a cool and pleasing appearance to the recesses. The arrangements in the supper-room were equally tasteful in more

senses than one; and altogether the art of decoration did not appear to have been overlooked in any respect.[12]

The front page of the next morning's *Bendigo Advertiser* was given over to four and a half closely printed columns listing the guests and, most importantly, 'THE DRESSES' of the ladies of the social and commercial elite of Sandhurst. Guests attended from as far afield as Melbourne, Ballarat and Echuca, and a special invitation had been extended to four of the principal officers of a Japanese man-of-war, *Tsukuba*, then docked at Melbourne. Captain Kasama and his officers presented a very fine spectacle in full dress uniform.[13]

Irvine filled the remainder of the winter of 1882 with football club meetings, dances, church socials and rowing club meetings. The town was full of excitement about the proposal to open a telephone exchange, just a year after Melbourne's exchange opened. The *Bendigo Advertiser* commented that Ballarat already had an exchange; Sandhurst could not be seen to be lagging. Among the first businesses to be connected would be the banks. Irvine, as one of the more senior members of the Union Bank's staff, would be one of the first people in Sandhurst to use the new contraption when it became available in September 1882.[14]

The City Family was the venue for the Sandhurst R.C. annual meeting on the evening of Tuesday 10 August. Forty members attended. Irvine was singled out for thanks for his work in coaching the Club's crews for the Barwon and Melbourne regattas: 'at Melbourne, though our representatives did not score a victory, they proved themselves worthy competitors.'[15] He was then elected captain of the Club for the following year. As Club captain, he was a member of a committee which met on 8 September to plan the festivities for the opening of the 1882–83 rowing season. It was decided that, 'in addition to the usual procession of boats and scratch events there will be a State-School competition in pleasure boats, a pair-oared race, the competitors to be under 18.'[16]

Three weeks later, the 1882–83 season opened on Wednesday 27 September:

> The weather was all that could be desired. About 1,500 persons visited the lake. Shortly after three o'clock the procession of boats

was formed. Butler's Bendigo Brass Band, after marching around the streets were accommodated in two boats and headed the procession. Mr J.L. Irvine acted as commodore. Following the band came five four oared boats, one pair oar, seven outriggers, and a large number of pleasure boats. The band played inspiring music, and after going twice around the lake Mr Alfred Joseph, one of the patrons of the Sandhurst Club, declared the rowing season opened. Cheers were given, after which hearty cheers were given for the Queen. Butler's Band played 'God Save the Queen.' Cheers were then given for the commodore.

A programme of races followed, including the State School Boys' Race, which was won by 'two very big "boys," each aged about 19 years'!

The festivities at Lake Weeroona continued in October, with the Club holding an 'Electric Light and Fireworks Festival' at the lake on the evening of Wednesday 25 October. Sandhurst residents were promised that the 'Lake will be illuminated from end to end with the ELECTRIC LIGHT of 8,000 candlepower. A resplendent display of fireworks &c. consisting of Set Pieces and Devices, Rockets, Bombshells, Colored Fires Etc. A GRAND INSTRUMENTAL CONCERT and a PROCESSION OF ILLUMINATED BOATS.' Tickets (adults 1/-, children 6d.) were available from members of the Sandhurst Rowing Club and 'all the leading business houses in the city,' according to an advertisement placed in the *Bendigo Advertiser* by 'Manager, J.L. Irvine.'[17] The *Advertiser* informed its readers that the electrical 'apparatus will be worked by a 10-horse power engine, brought specially from Melbourne, and the light will be displayed from the top of a mast 70 feet high, so that it will be visible over the greater part of the district.'[18]

Over 1,000 tickets were sold before the event, and over 2,000 people paid at the gate on the evening of the 25 October:

> About eight o'clock a flotilla of boats with Chinese lanterns, and manned by the members of the Sandhurst Rowing Club and Whitlam's Band were safely landed on one of the islands, and at this juncture the electric light was arranged with its '8,000 candlepower' to shed forth a light eclipsing the moon.

Unfortunately, the belt attached to the generator broke. Although desperate attempts were made to repair it, 'the visitors to the lake were disappointed, and many returned [to town] early ... after witnessing several ineffectual efforts to show the light.' The Rowing Club persevered with their programme of illuminated boats, races and aquatic sports, 'which were fairly successful.' In a show of good faith, the Rowing Club offered a free electric light show the following night, 'if the electric light can be got to work.'[19]

Unfortunately, the following night was as disastrous as the first. The lights failed, and the generator was held to be 'old and unsuitable, and to this alone the failure must be attributed.' It was agreed that it was 'unfortunate that the promoters of the light were unsuccessful, as a considerable number of people had assembled on the ground.' It was generally felt, however, that 'a fine moonlight night and a pleasant row upon the lake, which was crowded to an unusual extent with pleasure boats, recompensed visitors for any disappointment which they may have felt.'[20]

Letters to the editor of the *Advertiser* over the next few days told a different story. Captain Thomas Sanders of the Fire Brigade, writing on the following Saturday, accused the Sandhurst Rowing Club of 'gulling' the citizens of Sandhurst, while 'To Port' commented that the S.R.C. had proven that:

> it only requires a good front, large promises, ... a defiance of authorities, an apology for an electric light, a half-dozen pounds of tallow candles with paper lanterns, a few damaged Roman candles, sixpennyworth of crackers and the wind can be raised to the tune of £150.

He concluded: 'Put that in your pipe and smoke it, you drowsy members of the Bendigo Rowing Club. Don't get savage and envious, but profit by the example.'[21]

Several weeks later, the Electric Light festival was still being referred to as a *fiasco*,[22] and the S.R.C.'s charging of an admission price to enter a public park ignited a local controversy as to whether it constituted a precedent that could be used by other sporting clubs, thereby locking the public out of public parks and reserves. The argument rumbled on in Council meetings and letters to the editor for several weeks before quietly dying.

Friday 1 December saw Irvine at St James the Less Anglican Church, in the Melbourne suburb of Brighton, for the wedding of his sister Florence to Edward Wrixon Duncan Longden. Florence was 23, and her new husband, known as 'Toppy', was a 26-year-old mining agent with offices in Collins Street, Melbourne. He was also a well-known amateur footballer, playing for Melbourne Football Club in the Victorian Football Association, the forerunner of the VFL and today's AFL. The pair married quietly, without the usual press announcements, and the Irvine family were represented by J.L., sister Kate Patterson and her husband Harvey, and the bride's mother, Jemima, who was one of the witnesses who signed the wedding register.[23] Following the wedding, the couple settled in the fashionable bayside suburb of St Kilda, where their first child was born late the following year.

The new year of 1883 brought several changes for Irvine; the most momentous personally was his resignation from the Union Bank after 18 years. He finished up at View Street on Thursday 19 April. The following Tuesday, 24 April, he started as a clerk at the Bank of Australasia's offices on the corner of Pall Mall and Williamson Street, five minutes' walk away. His new appointment was on the understanding that he would 'presently take the accountant's position.'[24]

The same month, he was elected vice-president of the Sandhurst Football Club.[25] He also became embroiled in a public spat between the Sandhurst Rowing Club and the Bendigo Rowing Club over a challenge to row for Maiden and Junior fours. The BRC published an advertisement on Monday 16 April, challenging the SRC to a race – and the *Advertiser*'s editorial that day drew the public's attention to it. The challenge was the result of ill feeling between the two clubs, with BRC accusing the SRC of refusing to row competitively for cups presented by Messrs Bradley and Moody:

> the Sandhurst Club refus[ed] to row for these cups under equitable conditions ... The Bendigo Club could not procure a coxswain of less weight than nine or ten stone, and the Sandhurst refused to carry any coxswain but one who weighed only about four or five stone ... [I]n all boat races, the coxswains are of equal weights, or made so before they start, but this the Sandhurst Club refused to do.

As a result of this argument, 'negotiations between the clubs ceased, and it was for the purpose of placing the matter before the public'[26] that the challenge was issued and the advertisement placed.

In response to the challenge, Irvine sent £5 to the editor of the *Bendigo Advertiser*, saying:

> Not having heard anything further re the challenge accepted by the Sandhurst Rowing Club to row the Bendigo Club for a trophy value £25, which appeared in your paper this week, I beg to enclose you herewith a first deposit of £5, on behalf of the Sandhurst Club, if you will kindly consent to act as stakeholder until further arrangements are made. If the Bendigo Club do not deposit in your hands a similar sum by Wednesday next, all negotiations will then be at an end.

A week later, he wrote again to the *Advertiser*:

> It is well known that the challenge published by the Bendigo Club was not a *bona fide* one, and … no response has been made to the offer of my club to row its maiden crew against the best crew the Bendigo club can produce, maiden or otherwise.

Irvine's second letter to the editor brought a speedy response from T.J. Symes of the BRC, explaining the background to the argument and, not very convincingly, apologising 'for trespassing.'

The argument ground on for several months; at the S.R.C. annual meeting in August, Irvine moved that the newly formed Eaglehawk Rowing Club be invited to take part in the procession for the opening of the 1883–84 rowing season:

> Last year the Bendigo Rowing Club assisted at the opening, but as they had treated the Sandhurst Club with such scant courtesy he had considered that they had broken the bonds of friendship, and the Sandhurst Club could not be expected to regard the Bendigo as possessing a friendly feeling towards them.

A member of the BRC responded in a letter to the newspaper a few days later, saying that the fault lay with the S.R.C.:

> I think it is only right that I should endeavour to throw a little light as to the reason why a contest did not come off for the cups generously offered by Messrs. Bradley and Moody. Mr Irvine was deputed to meet our club, and make arrangements [for the contest]. Mr Irvine proposed that gold medals should also be rowed for at the expense of the clubs which lost the race. This we declined to do. The question of boats arose. Mr Irvine insisted that we should row in an old boat of ours, which was a little leaky, and would not consent to allow us to row in a new boat which we have, a by no means fast boat. We offered to allow their crew to row in an outrigger which they have, a much faster boat than ours. The public will, I think, see who made the vexatious conditions.

A further letter published the same day carried on in a mock histrionic tone:

> Take notice you plebeian members of the Bendigo Rowing Club, and henceforth and forever hide your diminished heads. Has it not been declared by the pseudo-aristocratic Sandhurst Rowing Club that you shall no longer enjoy the honor of their friendship? ... Cry aloud for forgiveness, and bow your knees to the bombastic Irvine, and then perhaps in the plenitude of their condescension they will admit you to the enjoyment of their most honorable companionship, and raise you from the dust in which they are dragging you.

It took the annual meeting of the Bendigo Club, held in September, to mend fences and 'emphatically disclaim' any feeling of ill will between the clubs.

At the same time, the S.R.C. was very proudly showing off new extensions to its clubhouse at Lake Weeroona. They had spent £260/10/- on making the boat house 'one of the best in Victoria.' The new extension included a large dressing room, two shower baths, ample storage for all the Club's boats and 'an excellent balcony for the use of visitors.'[27] The building's 'handsome' appearance made it one of the most noticeable adornments of Lake Weeroona.

The handsome clubhouse made a fitting backdrop to the 1883 S.R.C. Regatta, held on Wednesday 15 November. This was the Club's fourth annual regatta since its first in 1880. Although the day's programme was reportedly 'first-class', the number of spectators was quite small – estimated at only about 1,000 – partly due to very 'boisterous' weather. 'Amongst those present were a large number of the fair sex, who appeared to take a great interest in the sports provided.' The boatsheds were decked with bunting, Whitlam's band played through the afternoon, and, in the opinion of the *Advertiser*, the races 'were, perhaps, the best that have been witnessed on Lake Weeroona, the contests in some cases being keen and exciting.'[28] Irvine was stroke in the Senior Fours. His crew was acknowledged as putting up a good show in a 'magnificent' race, losing only by a matter of a few inches. He rowed later in the afternoon in the Senior Pairs, winning by two lengths against the nearest rival.

As always, the regatta featured a number of novelty events, including a 'tub race', with competitors rowing across the lake to one of the islands in barrels, and a 'water polo' match:

> This event caused considerable amusement. One side was captained by Mr Irving [*sic*] and the other by Mr Godfrey. The match resulted in a draw. The competitors rode on barrels, to which were affixed representations of horses' heads and tails. As it may be imagined, it was difficult to preserve the balance, and spills were frequent.

As usual, the Club adjourned after the regatta to the City Family, where a 'dejeuner' was held. Successful competitors received prizes, 'and sentiments [were] indulged in which are usual on such occasions.'[29] As captain of the Club, Irvine donated a gold medal for the winners of the Maiden Sculls race and, in addition, was thanked by the *Advertiser* for doing 'all in his power to make the regatta a success.' The acrimony of the fight with the BRC seemed to have been forgotten, with Irvine mentioning in his after dinner speech that 'the relationship between the Sandhurst and Bendigo Clubs was much more cordial at present than hitherto.'[30]

The specific reference to the presence of ladies at the regatta speaks to a frequently noticed phenomenon in nineteenth-century rowing: the attraction of rowers for the 'fair sex'. Newspaper reports of regattas and rowing competitions routinely noted the presence of 'many ladies' among the spectators; it was an accepted fact that the sight of strong, manly men, with well-developed bodies in skimpy rowing uniforms, was something that ladies were interested in. Rowers also enjoyed showing off. An unidentified newspaper clipping from a Sydney newspaper of the 1880s, in the collection of the Mitchell Library, refers to the 'Calf and Breast-Bone Brigade' and features a full-page cartoon of sporting boatmen deliberately stripping off in front of boatloads of women: 'Hallo, I say! Here comes the steamer, and full of people – mostly ladies. Hooray! Now boys, quick, off with your duds and get on to the pier!!' And: 'A hint to some enterprising showman' – charge admission to a tent-show featuring the 'C&BB.' Interestingly, the cartoon also includes a hint that not only ladies enjoyed seeing rowers and boating types in a state of undress. One vignette features two suited boating types chatting: '1st boating person – "I say Tom, the next time we go out I'd like to bring my friend Brown – awfully nice fellow – perfect gentleman." 2nd ditto – "Oh that be hanged! The question is, how does he strip?" meaning, what does he look like with his gear off.'[31]

Irvine returned to his early interest in the theatre and dramatic performance. In December 1883, he took the role of organising secretary for a 'Soirée Musicale' to be held at Sandhurst's imposing Masonic Hall (now the Capitol Theatre), a grand Corinthian-columned temple in View Street. The soirée, scheduled for the evening of Tuesday 11, was in aid of All Saints' Anglican Church's choir library fund. Described in the press as 'indefatigable', Irvine was a key driver behind the 'original' and 'novel' entertainment, although he was not to appear on stage:

> The entertainment is exciting some interested on account of an original idea which the promoters intend to adopt. Between the two parts into which the soirée is divided, fruit and refreshments of various acceptable kinds, iced if desired, will be served by attendants. The hall will be arranged on quite a novel plan; there will be about fifty small tables, around which the audience may gather, and the room will be profusely decorated with ferns, ornamental wreathes and bouquets of flowers. The programme which has been issued is a very good one.

Admission prices were a substantial half a crown – 2/6.

The *Advertiser* reported that the soirée was a great success:

> The popular taste was hit at the Masonic Hall last night in the most unmistakeable manner. The musical programme was of that high order of merit which we would expect from the performers, and the refreshments sent round during the conversazione were of the best quality procurable, and delicately served.

'Some hundreds' of ticket holders enjoyed a programme consisting of a number of instrumental and vocal performances, all of which were accorded high praise. Special mention was reserved for visiting soprano Miss Bennett, who sang 'The Jewel Song' from *Faust*; then the 'famous duet from *Lucia* was given by Miss Bennett and Mr F. Morton.' Irvine was 'deserving of all the credit which [his] indefatigable [that word again!] exertions merit in the promotion and execution of the entertainment. As there was a capital house, All Saint's choir library fund should be extensively benefitted.'[32] It was a far cry from the disastrous Electric Light festival of the previous year!

A week later, Irvine's cup seemed to overflow when Sandhurst won the Maiden Gig Fours in the Richmond Regatta, held on the Upper Yarra course in Melbourne. A reporter for the *Age* and the *Bendigo Advertiser* singled out Sandhurst and Irvine for praise:

> The Sandhurst men well deserved their success, which is chiefly due to the excellent preparation they underwent at the hands of Mr Irvine, one time one of the best Intercolonial oarsmen in the colony.[33]

High praise, however, attracts its detractors. Two days later, on 19 December, two correspondents wrote letters to the editor of the *Advertiser* decrying the praise given to Irvine. 'Weeroona' wrote that, although Irvine picked the crew, the coaching of them fell to John Godfrey, while 'A Member' [supposedly of the S.R.C.] agreed that Godfrey was the man who should get the credit and that 'Irvine has not been out with the crew ever once.' In closing, 'A Member' thought: 'Honor should be given to whom honor is due.'[34]

Interestingly, the *Advertiser's* regular sports reporter 'Rufus' used exactly the same phrase elsewhere in the same day's paper, when reporting on the Irvine/Godfrey situation:

> In justice to Mr Godfrey I must mention that one of my favorite maxims is 'Honor to whom it is due' ... More than one paper speaks in glowing terms of the success they [the Sandhurst crew] met with, but in addition they wrongly give Mr Irvine all the praise for having brought them to perfection, for the training of the crew was entirely in the hands of *our* [my emphasis] vice-captain Mr Godfrey, senior, and he is the only one who deserves special mention for the coaching the crew underwent.[35]

It is obvious that 'A Member' and 'Rufus' are one and the same and that there was at least one member of the S.R.C. who was not a fan of Irvine.

Was the criticism, and possible dissension, in the ranks of the S.R.C. the reason Irvine submitted his registration as Club captain in early January 1884? 'Rufus' reported, with some crocodile tears:

> It is my painful duty to record the retirement of Mr J.L. Irvine from the captainship of the Sandhurst Club. His resignation is now in the hands of the committee, and from what I can ascertain they intend to accept it at a meeting to be held this evening [Wednesday 9 January].[36]

Although Irvine's resignation as captain was officially noted and regretted by the Club committee at a complimentary banquet held at the City Club Hotel on the evening of Thursday 25 January, Godfrey was the man of the hour, and speaker after speaker heaped praise on him. This would have been particularly galling for Irvine: to sit and listen to the praises sung of a man from whom Irvine had supposedly tried to steal glory, no matter how innocent Irvine was in the case. To add insult to injury, several mentions of the rift with BRC were made over the course of the evening, with the chairman of the evening specifically stating that:

any members of the Sandhurst Club who had offended the Bendigo Club members had never represented the spirit and feeling of the Sandhurst Club towards them. It was never the wish of the sensible and well-meaning members of the Sandhurst Club to offend the Bendigo Club.[37]

This was very much a back-handed slap to Irvine, whose name was at the forefront of the S.R.C./BRC spat the year before.

Having resigned from the captainship, Irvine took a back seat in S.R.C. activities, although he was asked to present the prizes to the winners of the 1884 Club's annual regatta in late March and early April.[38] With his role in the S.R.C. reduced, Irvine began to devote more time to activities outside the Club. On 15 April, he joined the Bendigo chapter of the Golden and Corinthian Masonic Lodge, based at View Street's grand Masonic Hall. He passed into the Lodge as a full member on 13 May and was then raised into the Lodge on 10 June.[39]

He would also have had plenty of opportunity around this time to visit his mother, Jemima, who had taken a substantial brick villa at 13 Patterson Street, West Beach, St Kilda to use as her Melbourne base while she visited family and friends in Melbourne.[40] Jemima was also conducting regular interviews with Baron Ferdinand von Mueller, the Victorian Government Botanist (and founding director of the Melbourne Botanic Gardens), who had commissioned her to collect specimens for the National Herbarium of Victoria. She was also curating a collection of pressed ferns and seaweeds for entry into the 1884 intercolonial exhibition, to be held at the Melbourne Exhibition Building in Carlton Gardens. The collection which Jemima presented in the Exhibition was 'not entered for competition, but being such a splendid collection the jury could not pass it without special mention,' granting it a special certificate of merit.[41]

On 12 June, Irvine was transferred from the Pall Mall branch of the Bank of Australasia to the Eaglehawk branch, finally being made accountant 12 months after being promised the role. Eaglehawk was another mining town, adjacent to Bendigo but very conscious of its status as a borough separate to the City of Bendigo. His salary was raised to £250, and he also received an accommodation allowance of £50 per year. His file in the bank's archive states that he 'is well known in the district.'[42]

"BOW YOUR KNEES TO THE BOMBASTIC IRVINE"   125

Perhaps in order to atone for the bad feeling which existed between Irvine and some members of the S.R.C., Irvine was instrumental in attracting a visit from the great Canadian rowing star, Ned Hanlan, to the Bendigo district in July 1884.

Hanlan, the son of a Toronto fisherman, had developed his rowing skills as a boy, rowing his father's catch across Toronto harbour to the city's fish markets. As a youth, he competed in amateur events. In 1873, at the age of 18, he became amateur champion of Toronto Bay. He turned professional the following year and became champion sculler of Canada in 1877 and of the United States in 1878. After competing in England in 1879, he became the acknowledged world sculling champion for five years in a row, from 1880 to 1884. His Australian visit was made in order to compete in a world championship challenge on the Nepean River in New South Wales. Hanlan arrived in Sydney in mid-March 1884 to a tumultuous welcome. Crowds lined the street as he was driven to a mayoral reception at the Oxford Hotel, and 12,000 gathered in King Street to hear him speak from the hotel's balcony.

The adulation accorded to Hanlan by the Australian public was akin to that given to the Beatles 80 years later. Newspapers in all parts of the colonies reported closely his visit to Sydney, his progress around the country areas of New South Wales and trips further afield to Queensland, Victoria and South Australia.

Hanlan spent three days in Sandhurst as the guest of the Sandhurst Rowing Club. He arrived by train from Melbourne at 10:45am on Tuesday 9 July and was met by a reception committee, which included Irvine. He was driven to the Sandhurst Town Hall for a mayoral reception and attended an official lunch at the Shamrock Hotel. The afternoon was occupied by a full programme of exhibition races at Lake Weeroona, including 'Hanlan v. Four-oared Crew, Hanlan v. Local Scullers, Hanlan v. Time, Hanlan Walking on the Water [which was accomplished by Hanlan's 'water shoes', a form of floating, raft-like paddles], and other Wonderful Aquatic Feats.'[43] The day concluded with Hanlan appearing at a variety performance at the Royal Princess Theatre in View Street.

The following day, Hanlan toured a gold mine, saw the mine machinery at work and accepted some samples of gold. He then toured Lake Neangar, the home of the Eaglehawk Rowing Club, and attended an official lunch at Eaglehawk's Park Hotel, where Irvine had the honour of being toasted as the man responsible for bringing Hanlan to Sandhurst. Following lunch, Hanlan had a practice session on Lake Weeroona, where he 'went the whole length of the Lake in 81 strokes and afterwards had some practice in running, going around the lake in four minutes.'[44] Following the practice session, a number of the S.R.C.'s committee members, including Irvine, saw him off on the evening train to Melbourne.

After the success of Hanlan's visit, Irvine was transferred again. He must have been rather confused and, at the same time, buoyed by the decision of the Bank of Australasia to close the Eaglehawk branch. He had been at work there only a month, but now he was to move to Melbourne. It was obvious that he was being groomed for bigger things – although the sudden shifts and short-term transfers showed poor timing; he received notification of his transfer to Melbourne on 15 July. Once again, Irvine began to tie up his loose ends prior to moving. On 22 July, he attended the citizens' 'Return Ball' for the Mayor of Bendigo, held at the Masonic Hall in View Street. His name was listed in the *Bendigo Advertiser* as one of a crowd of several hundred well-dressed dancers who thronged the decorated hall, danced to the music of Monaghan's Band and sat down to a first-class supper after midnight.[45]

The same edition of the *Advertiser* that reported on the ball also announced:

> Mr Irvine, of the Bank of Australasia, is about to leave Sandhurst for Melbourne and a meeting of his friends is to be held at the Commercial Bank this evening to make arrangements for recognising his departure in some suitable manner. Mr Irvine was a prominent member of the Sandhurst Rowing Club and both professionally and socially has made himself very popular, so that he is not likely to be allowed to depart without some special mark of the esteem in which he is held.

Irvine's official farewell from Bendigo took the form of a banquet, held at the City Family on Saturday 26 July. Representatives from the Sandhurst Rowing Club offered fulsome speeches of praise, including:

> When Mr. Irvine first came to Sandhurst he found the rowing club in a sickly condition, but now by his persistent efforts it occupied a

position not held by any other club in the colony. He had the highest admiration for Mr Irvine's honest and generally excellent conduct. Steps were being taken to present Mr. Irvine with a suitable souvenir, which would be forwarded to him in the course of a few days.

Mr. Irvine, in reply, said he had received nothing but kindness and consideration at the hands of the many acquaintances who had gathered around him during his residence in Sandhurst, and it was with feelings of deep regret that he had to say good-bye to them. He heartily thanked those gentlemen who had expressed such kindly remarks during the afternoon. A vote of thanks having been accorded the chairman, the proceedings terminated. Mr. Irvine left Sandhurst by the evening train for Melbourne, a large number of his friends meeting on the platform to see him off.[46]

No sooner had Irvine arrived in Melbourne, on the evening of Saturday 28 July, than he received word that he would instead be transferring to the bank's Sydney head office. His personnel register, held in the bank's archives, calls him: 'A good officer.'[47]

CHAPTER 7
"A sterling oarsman and hard worker"

Irvine spent the second half of 1884 in Sydney. This six-month period is the first time in Irvine's adult life that his name is absent from the newspapers, so how he spent his time in Sydney, apart from working at the bank's Pitt Street office, is not known. No doubt, he enjoyed his time in a city he knew from his visits with the intercolonial crews in 1879 and 1881. He would have been out on the water, visited Manly to see the Sydney Calf and Breast-Bone Brigade, joined a local Church of England congregation and found some 'clubbable chaps' to socialise with. He also probably explored Sydney's seamier side; although the city was smaller than Melbourne in the 1880s and considered something of a sleepy hollow, it was known to have a busy homosexual scene, mostly centred around the darkened paths of night-time Hyde Park and the Domain.

Irvine left Sydney on Friday 5 December, sailing from Circular Quay on board the coastal steamer *Buninyong*.[1] Arriving in Melbourne two days later, he spent just over a week there before sailing on the *Flinders* on 18 December to spend Christmas in Launceston with his brother Richard's family.[2] Dick was the principal of the family's business of Irvine and McEachern, which had long since branched out from the wine and spirit business established by his father to become northern Tasmania's largest and most successful grocery wholesaler. Dick and Frances and their three children – seven-year-old Richard, six-year-old May and five-year-old John – lived above the firm's premises in Brisbane Street. Irvine's other siblings were scattered to the corners of the antipodes: sister Jemima Adams was in New Zealand, while brothers Charles and Claude were respectively commander of the Adelaide Steamship Company and a station manager in the Riverina district of New

South Wales. Of the remaining Irvine sisters, Kate Patterson and Florence Longden were in Melbourne, while 23-year-old Nellie (Ellen Maud) was her mother's companion, assisting the always energetic Jemima in her collecting and curatorial pursuits.

After a fortnight in Launceston, catching up with friends and renewing acquaintances, Irvine sailed for Melbourne on board the *Flinders*, arriving in Melbourne on 31 December.[3] The city was enjoying the giddy heights of the boom of the 1880s. The economic good times dating from the gold rushes of the 1850s had now been going for three decades, and the results were there for all to see. Historian Michael Cannon explains:

> On a time lapse camera, it would appear as if Melbourne sprang into being as one of the great cities of the world overnight. Everywhere there was a flurry of construction, the establishment of large companies and important new industries, the building of extravagant mansions, the golden tentacles reaching out into adjacent fields and valleys. Powered trams appeared; suddenly – whole new suburbs sprang into being; suddenly – electric light flared in the streets ... Astonishing new applications of science; frightening new ideas of man's evolution from the jungle; colossal schemes of making fortunes from speculation; dangerous ideas of women's place in the new society – all these things thrilled, alarmed and astonished.[4]

The face of the city changed constantly during the 1880s, as the head offices of banks, insurance companies and manufacturers competed to see who could have the largest and most impressive headquarters, shops and factories. The General Post Office, the Law Courts, the Victorian Railways administration building, wholesale and retail markets, the Working Men's College, University colleges, schools, hotels and theatres were built or enlarged in a range of florid and ornate architectural styles. Skyscrapers of up to 12 storeys sprang up, made possible by Otis' new 'ascending rooms', manufactured at the company's South Melbourne factory. New suburbs were built along new railway lines which stretched to a distance of up to ten miles from the centre of the city. Plans to build the first line of a modern cable tram system, from Spencer Street to Richmond, were well advanced. Greater Melbourne's population doubled within 10 years, reaching a total of half a million by 1890. The increase came from the children of the gold rush generation marrying and starting families, from people moving to the city from Victoria's country cities and towns, and from a never-ending wave of migrants arriving from Britain.

Melbourne's banks and building societies were recipients of the money to be made through speculation, land development, construction and real estate, and the Bank of Australasia was one of the most successful of all of the banks. Throughout the 1880s, the bank opened a range of new branches in Melbourne's suburbs; so it was that, on Tuesday 27 January 1885, Irvine was appointed to his first managerial post, in charge of a new branch at Prahran. As manager, he was to receive a salary of £250, with an additional annual allowance of £50.

Prahran, about seven kilometres south of central Melbourne, was a mainly middle-class suburb of detached brick or weatherboard villas, but with some working-class areas of terraced housing nearer to the railway stations at Prahran and Windsor. The district's main street, Chapel Street, was a busy thoroughfare, running south from the Yarra for about three kilometres and lined with single and two-storeyed shop buildings.

The new branch opened for business on Wednesday 3 February in a temporary office at 96 Chapel Street. This was a double-storeyed shop, with residence above it – one of a set of three recently built by local grocer J.F. Pfeil. Pfeil's name still appears on the parapet of the central shop in the trio, together with the proud boast that his business was established in 1858. The shops are of a type common in Melbourne's nineteenth-century suburban shopping streets; single fronted, with a 16 foot frontage. The ground floor shop fronts have been modernised several times since the 1880s; however, upstairs on the first floor, the arched front windows of what would have been Irvine's drawing room look out over the street. The buildings are fairly plain for 1880s Melbourne, but a cornice of ornate acanthus brackets runs along the top of the first floor under the building's parapet, relieving an otherwise unadorned façade.

The shop is three doors from the corner of James Street and only a five-minute walk to Windsor railway station. From there, it was, and is, merely four stations to Flinders Street and Young and Jackson's, giving Irvine easy access to the centre of Melbourne. And now that he was back in Melbourne, Irvine threw himself back into competition on the Yarra, rowing stroke in a crew competing in a Trial Fours race for the Melbourne Rowing Club's captain's trophies on 31 January.

He also joined the St Kilda Swimming Club, based at Hegarty's Baths on the St Kilda foreshore, and appeared as 'The Multitude' in a farce entitled *The Weatherbound Island*, which was performed at a 'grand aquatic entertainment' on Saturday 24 January in aid of Club funds. Over 2,500 people, 'the majority of whom were ladies,' crammed the baths to watch the Club members parade into the baths 'attired in football and approved fancy costumes' and then demonstrate various methods of entering the water: 'diving from the springboards, platform, roof, and cistern, running headers, drop, front, and back somersaults, etc.' Various other novelty swimming events were held. Then, the:

> original moral and domestic drama 'The Weatherbound Island' was ... presented, and was ludicrous in the extreme. ... Each of the characters appeared in the costume suited to his part, and the progress of the drama was watched with much interest, and everything passed off swimmingly. The programme concluded with a race in which the competitors swam with umbrellas opened above their heads.'[5]

Hegarty's baths was one of a number of bathing establishments set around the seaside resorts and suburbs of Port Phillip Bay. St Kilda, as the most popular and fashionable of the seaside suburbs, had several baths which offered both safety and privacy for swimming. Bathing in the open sea was prohibited, so the sexes were segregated into separate bathing establishments. Ladies wore voluminous bathing dresses to take to the water, whereas men usually swam naked in the baths, away from public view. By the early 1900s, the baths had gained a reputation for being places where homosexual pickups were possible – given the opportunity for men to relax and loiter in the nude – though perhaps not common. It is more than likely that they offered just the same opportunities, 20 years earlier, in Irvine's time.

In March 1885, Irvine travelled to Geelong to take part in the Barwon Rowing Club's trial four-oared races on the Barwon River.[6] The same month, he was named vice-captain of the Melbourne Rowing Club:

The corner of Fitzroy and Grey Streets, St Kilda c. 1885 shortly after the four-storey extension to the George Hotel was opened. The Bank of Australasia's branch was located on the ground floor, facing into Fitzroy Street, and is obscured by the wagon.

> Mr Irvine is one of our oldest oarsmen, and in the Banks Club made the high reputation which he bears. For some time past he has been unable to take any very active interest in rowing. The members of the Melbourne Club are to be congratulated on the appointment of such a sterling oarsman and hard worker as Mr Irvine has long since proved himself to be.[7]

At the time, Irvine was a month off his 38th birthday, quite old for a nineteenth-century rower. Irvine was elected captain of the Club three months later at the 1885 annual meeting of the MRC, held at Young and Jackson's Hotel and attended by over 100 members.[8]

The room in which the annual meeting was held at Young and Jackson's was draped in black, 'and the proceedings were conducted in a very quiet manner, out of respect to the late W.H. Tuckett, who was a member of the club since 1878.'[9] Bill Tuckett, who had rowed with Irvine in every intercolonial race from 1878 to 1881, had died the previous month at the age of 31, of 'paralysis of the heart.' Irvine was among the members of the Melbourne Rowing Club who mustered at the St Kilda railway station on the day of his funeral in July to follow his coffin to the St Kilda cemetery.[10]

Irvine once more became active in the Victorian Rowing Association. In September 1885, he was nominated for a place on the Association's committee,[11] in time for the late September opening of the 1885–86 rowing season on the Yarra. The arrangements for the opening ceremonies and races of the season were placed in the hands of an organising committee, which included Irvine. He also began to chair meetings of the VRA.

After just 12 months running the Prahran branch of the Bank of Australasia, Irvine was entrusted with the opening of another new branch – in St Kilda, Melbourne's premier seaside suburb. This was undoubtedly a step up the career ladder; St Kilda was a much more fashionable locale than Prahran. It was also the home of two of his sisters, Kate Patterson and Florence Longden.

Established in the 1840s, St Kilda began as a select residential suburb favoured by Melbourne's elite; they built substantial mansions on the hill overlooking Port Phillip Bay and on the slopes leading down to the foreshore. When the village was linked to central Melbourne by the railway in May 1857, it became a popular resort for Melbourne's middle classes, and the large houses of the elite were joined by spacious villas, double and triple-storeyed terrace houses and comfortable hotels and boarding houses catering to visitors. A number of sea baths dotted the foreshore, a jetty promenade had been opened, and the suburb offered well-established cricket, lawn bowling and horse racing facilities.

One of the sights of St Kilda was the George Hotel, on the corner of Fitzroy and Grey Streets. First established in October 1857 as the Terminus Hotel, it was designed to take advantage of the visitors to St Kilda who arrived via the newly opened railway station directly opposite. The popular hotel was given the more genteel name, the George, during the 1860s and extended several times along Fitzroy Street. In May 1885, the foundation stone was laid for a new four-storey building on the corner of Fitzroy and Grey Streets:

> The elevation shows a façade to Fitzroy-street of 46ft, and to Grey-street of 100ft, to be executed in the decorative Italian style of architecture. The bar, with parlor attached, is situated at the corner of the above streets, having a handsome entrance portico executed in polished Harcourt granite. On either side of this, on the ground floor, are arranged large and commodious shops. Above this, on the other three floors, are arranged suites of rooms, with private dining and drawing rooms, opening into colonnades, which form a pleasing feature of the building; also spacious corridors well lighted and ventilated, with large bedrooms on either side. Baths and other conveniences of ample space are conveniently situated throughout the different floors, fitted with all the latest improvements. The whole of this is surmounted by a neat and picturesque tower, affording a grand view of the Bay in all directions, Albert Park Lake, city and suburbs.[12]

The new building was ready for occupation by 16 January the following year, when St Kilda's *Telegraph* newspaper advertised that the Bank of Australasia would open a new branch in one of the hotel's shops, under the management of J.L. Irvine.

Irvine took up his post on Thursday 28 January 1886, on the same salary and allowance as at Prahran (£250 + £50) but with an additional annual allowance of £50 'for a horse'.[13] Where he lived at this time is not clear; the bank's new branch had 40 bedrooms directly above it, and it was noted at the laying of the foundation stone of the new building that 'it was becoming fashionable all the world over to live at hotels, as thereby a host of domestic annoyances were escaped.'[14] It is possible that Irvine took a room directly above the branch. If he did indeed spend his new £50 allowance on a horse, stabling would have been provided behind the hotel.

The year 1886 was a busy one for Irvine's rowing interests. Turning 39 in April, he retired from competitive rowing but threw himself ever more into committee work and leadership positions. Just the Saturday before

"A STERLING OARSMAN AND HARD WORKER"   135

commencing as St Kilda branch manager, Irvine had been present at a special meeting of the VRA to plan the 1886 Melbourne Regatta. Over 100 members attended the meeting at Edwards' Boatshed. Irvine moved that the two complimentary regatta tickets usually given to all members of the VRA be discontinued. Such was his persuasive way of speaking that the motion, which could have been very unpopular, was successfully passed.[15] A week later, another VRA meeting, this time held at Young and Jackson's Hotel, saw Irvine nominated as a judge in the forthcoming Melbourne Regatta, to be held on 20 February.[16] On 13 February, he was named as one of a four-man committee to choose the Victorian representatives of the 1886 intercolonial competition against New South Wales.[17]

The 1886 Melbourne Regatta was held on Saturday 20 February, on the Saltwater River (Maribyrnong) course:

> The committee of the Victorian Rowing Association were extremely unfortunate in the weather which they were inflicted with on Saturday; a cold and squally day with almost continuous rain, preventing the public from patronising the course.[18]

The reporter from the *Australasian* considered that the 'racing was not of the first order, and does not call for particular mention.' The intermittent rain had the effect of driving the 1,500 or so spectators into a large marquee, erected on the reserve at the junction of the Yarra and Saltwater rivers. Here, they were entertained by an excellent band, which was preferable to the 'exposure outside.'[19] Very few people watched the races – particularly the last one of the day, which was rowed in a maelstrom of wind and rain.

Throughout 1886, Irvine took on more umpiring and judging roles at various amateur competitions, helping to develop the skills of younger men coming up through the ranks. Now that he was no longer rowing competitively, he began to enter the ranks of illustrious past champions; the Tamar Rowing Club recognised him as a former member of renown in its 1886 annual report, the first of its members to be an intercolonial champion, and – surely the mark of a legendary past champion – he became a trivia topic in the newspapers. When 'J.R', a reader of the *Tasmanian* newspaper, queried how many times Irvine had competed in the Intercolonial Eight, the 'Answers to Correspondents' column confirmed that 'J.L. Irvine represented Victoria in the intercolonial Eight oared race four times.'[20]

The 1886 annual general meeting of the Melbourne Rowing Club was held on the evening of Friday 30 July at Young & Jackson's, in a room 'tastefully decorated with oars and the club's colours, [with] the trophies held or won by the club ... exhibited on the table, amidst a profusion of things of an edible nature.' About 50 members attended to celebrate the Club's wins over the past year, including: the Maiden Sculls at Warrnambool; the Maiden Four, Junior Sculls and Grand Challenge Briscoe Four at Melbourne; the Sunbury Challenge Cup at Ballarat; the Castlemaine Brewery Trophy at South Melbourne; and the Maiden Pair and Maiden Eight at the Upper Yarra Regatta. Attending only a few of these events as a senior member of the Club in 1885-86 would have obliged Irvine to make several trips around the colony. The Club was also celebrating the fact that three members of the Club had rowed in the 1886 Intercolonial Eight, defeating New South Wales in Sydney in late April. This would have been a proud achievement for Irvine, as a member of the Victorian selection committee. It is unlikely that he travelled to Sydney to watch the competition, but he would certainly have been present at a VRA supper for the New South Wales and Victorian crews at the Athenaeum in Collins Street on the evening of Saturday 24 April: 'tickets are 12s 6d., and it is expected that a large number of rowing men, both past and present, will be in attendance.'[21]

The MRC annual meeting in July also saw the election of office bearers for the 1886-87 rowing season. Irvine was elected club captain for the year, and the evening 'was pleasantly spent in the enjoyment of music and good cheer.'[22]

The following month, the Sandhurst Rowing Club committee decided to have framed photographs of former officers and prominent members hung in the boatshed.[23] They asked Irvine to send a photograph of himself. Unfortunately, these photos do not seem to have survived the intervening 130 years. Meanwhile, Irvine was elected treasurer of the St Kilda Cricket Club at their annual general meeting at the George Hotel on Friday 3 September. The Cricket Club committee congratulated themselves on the club's healthy finances and the improvements which they had made to the ground in the previous 12 months, including the erection of a 7 foot paling fence surrounding the ground (at a costs of £340). They had to admit that 'the past season had

"A STERLING OARSMAN AND HARD WORKER"   137

not been very successful from a cricket point of view,'[24] but at least the use of the cricket ground by the football teams had improved the club's receipts.

Irvine's committee work continued apace in October, when he chaired the annual meeting of the VRA at Young & Jackson's. The annual report was read, noting that works on the new Princes Bridge across the Yarra were:

> making rapid process, and in a short time the clubs on the banks of the Yarra must expect to be cut off from the water frontage for some time, whilst the stream is being widened; on the completion of this work a splendid rowing course will be created, and your committee look forward to rowing becoming much more popular than it can be expected to be on the present narrow and circuitous river.

The widening of the river required the building of coffer dams along the course of the riverbank, to hold back the water while the banks behind the dam were excavated; hence, the blocking of the boatsheds from the riverfront.

The meeting also expressed sincere sorrow in 'narrating the heavy misfortunes which have lately befallen one of our well-known and popular boatbuilders, Mr. W.T. Greenland.' Greenland's shed was on the southern bank of the Yarra, near to Edwards'. It was removed from the riverbank to make way for work on the new bridge in April 1885. His replacement shed, erected at:

> considerable cost, was burnt to the ground, and immediately after his replacing the old with a new building, the latter was rendered useless through the upheaval of the earth caused by the embankment made to connect the new bridge with the St Kilda Road. A movement is, we believe, shortly to be set on foot to assist Mr Greenland to retrieve his heavy losses, and your association is to be asked, and will doubtless render its willing assistance.[25]

The AGM elected Irvine to the Association's management committee for another year. The following week, on the evening of Friday 8 October, he was present at the year's first committee meeting. The committee resolved to open the 1886-87 rowing season with a regatta at Albert Park Lake on the Prince of Wales' birthday, 9 November. Usually, the venue for the season's opening

Albert Park Lake, around the time that it was the venue for the 1886 VRA regatta.

regatta was the upper course of the Yarra, but work on the new Princes Bridge and river widening works made access to the river difficult, if not impossible. A new venue was required. The Saltwater River was dismissed out of hand:

> It is not a straight course, and it cannot be denied that much depends on luck in getting a good position to start from. That it is the worst of all places to hold a regatta, from the public point of view, is beyond question, for the balance sheets of the association will ...[show]... that the public will not patronise a regatta held at Footscray.[26]

Ever the enthusiastic committee member, Irvine was nominated to the regatta organising committee. 'Really handsome prizes' for several of the races were presented to the organising committee: 'The prize for the Maiden sculling race is a beautiful mounted emu egg on blackwood stand, value £8 6s., and the entrance fee for the race will be 10s.'[27]

Public excitement around the Prince of Wales' birthday Regatta built throughout the month of October. The *Leader* announced that the 'full day's sport' would include not just Maiden Sculls, Maiden Pairs, Maiden Clinker Four, Eight Oar race and a procession of clubs in full club colours, but also scratch eights and water sports, 'including walking on the water, a tub race and walking the greasy boom.' The full program would 'tax the energies of the [organising] sub-committee to get through ...[but]... It is an innovation to open the season by such a meeting, and on so large a scale.'[28] The same reporter, 'Outrigger,' commented that Irvine had been named cox of an eight-oared crew to compete in a married vs single race, but it was going to have to carry an additional 12 pounds' weight to make up for the heavier weight of his rival 'steersman' in the married men's crew, G.E. Upward.

The Prince of Wales' birthday holiday, on Tuesday 9 November, dawned with 'delightful weather,' and the 'city all day long presented a lively and festive aspect, in which were the amplest evidence of a comfortable and prosperous population holiday-keeping.' Public buildings and offices in the city were hung with bunting, as were many of the ships in the Bay. Holiday attractions included marine excursions on bay steamers, a procession of Friendly Societies through the main streets of the city, a St Andrew's Gala fete at the Friendly Societies' Garden (now Olympic Park), and an 'Oriental Fair' at the Warehouseman's Cricket Ground at St Kilda Junction. The Botanical and Zoological Gardens were thronged, and the beaches of St Kilda and Brighton were crowded. Ten thousand people turned out to watch a match between the Victorian 11 and a visiting English team at the Melbourne Cricket Ground, and 8,000 attended a program of racing at Flemington. 'The day's events were happily unattended, either in town or country, by any serious casualty.'

Given the competition from other amusements on the day, the VRA's regatta was marked by a 'very small' attendance of spectators, 'although the lake may be described as having been fairly alive with the flotilla of sailing and pleasure boats that skimmed about throughout the day.' The day was fine, with a light south-easterly breeze rippling the water and helping to make the rowing pace a little faster than usual.

The various events on the program were 'splendidly contested, and aroused great excitement amongst those present.' The 'great struggle' between the married and single oarsmen was eagerly anticipated, with 'the veteran strokes R.D. Booth and S.H. Gowdie, having picked their crews from the best-known oarsmen of the metropolis. The single men started off strong favourites, but proved no match for the married men, who jumped away from the start and won by a length.' The single men were not helped by a small yacht in their way and the 'stroke side catching a crab [to fall backwards by missing a stroke].'[29] The day's rowing concluded with a social evening at Young & Jackson's, where the prizes were presented to the winners. So successful was Albert Park Lake as a regatta venue that it was suggested as the location for future regattas.

The 1886 Regatta was a high point in Irvine's career with the VRA. Just three months later, at a meeting of the VRA committee at Young & Jackson's on 7 February 1887, Irvine tendered his resignation from the committee, citing 'business engagements.' The committee accepted his resignation and thanked him for 'the valuable services he has rendered to rowing in the past.'[30] A report in the *Sportsman* referred to him as 'one of the oldest and most enthusiastic supports of rowing in this colony.'[31] Rowing was a young man's game indeed! Irvine was still two months off his 40th birthday. He was, however, still in demand for his judging and umpiring skills; the same week, he was appointed as a referee at the Richmond Rowing Regatta, held on the upper Yarra on the afternoon of Saturday 12 February. He then went on to umpire at the Upper Yarra Regatta, held in April.[32]

Irvine's long interest in football, dating back to the days of the friendly matches on Launceston's Windmill Hill in the 1860s, continued. In June, he hosted a dinner for the visiting Adelaide football team who had defeated St Kilda at the Warehouseman's ground on the afternoon of Thursday 1 June. The evening, at Clement's Café in Swanston Street, 'passed very pleasantly, for after the dinner, songs, recitations and speeches tinged with humour, were rendered.'[33]

Further socialising took place in mid-July, when he joined with other 'oarsman of days gone by'[34] at a social on the evening of Monday 18 July at Young & Jackson's. The guest of honour was P.J. Clark, one of the founders of the Sydney Rowing Club; he had recently returned from a trip to Britain, where he 'gathered some useful information for Australian oarsmen in regard to sending a representative crew to England and America. He is sanguine that a representative Australian crew could more than hold its own in English waters.'[35]

September 1887 saw Irvine returned as treasurer of the St Kilda Cricket Club at the club's annual general meeting – held, again, at the George Hotel on the afternoon of 6 September – and also chairing the 25th AGM of the Melbourne Rowing Club. That year, 1886–87, had been the MRC's most unsuccessful; the only victory was that of F. Edwards in the Maiden Sculls at the Upper Yarra Regatta, held back in April. The lack of success was laid squarely at the feet of the 'apathy of the members.'[36] Complaints were made regarding the carelessness of members in allowing subscriptions to fall into arrears. The annual balance sheet showed receipts of £367 and expenses of £432, indicating a debt of £65. Notwithstanding the generally gloomy tone of the meeting, Irvine was elected club captain for 1887–88.

The following month, October, Irvine probably attended an auction at the rooms of C.J. & T Ham, auctioneers, at 45 Swanston Street, in company with his brother-in-law Harvey Patterson. Since marrying Irvine's sister Kate in 1878, Harvey had been concentrating his efforts on his pastoral properties in the Riverina district of southern New South Wales, *Corona* and *Menamurtree*. In 1885, however, he paid £1,800 for one twenty-eighth share of the newly formed Broken Hill Proprietary Company Ltd when it was floated, becoming a founding director of the new company. Harvey and Kate seem to have kept

Harvey and Kate Patterson's *Inverleith*, in Acland Street, St Kilda.

a house in St Kilda since at least 1881, and their first child, Corona, was born there. Now, with Harvey's new position and a growing family of two daughters and two sons, they required a larger property. While casting around for a suitable house in his local area, he spoke to his brother-in-law John, who suggested that he look at an 'elegant mansion' in Acland Street, St Kilda.

Inverleith, described as a 'family mansion with about three acres of land,' was situated on the corner of Acland and Church (now Eildon) Streets, in the heart of St Kilda, only a block from the Upper Esplanade and about five minutes' walk down the hill from Irvine's branch of the Bank of Australasia. The house Harvey and Kate inspected was described as having two spacious drawing rooms, a boudoir, dining room, breakfast room, billiard room, two 'best' bedrooms with a dressing room apiece, and a further four bedrooms, a bathroom (with 'hot and cold'), a W.C., kitchen, scullery, pantry, laundry, store-room and two servants' bedrooms. The outbuildings included stabling for four horses with a hayloft and double coach house, a harness room and a groom's room; a four-roomed gardener's cottage; a cowshed; a large external cellar; a fernery; a fowl house; a drying yard and a pond. The grounds, 'comprising about 3½ acres, are laid out in garden[s], well stocked with choice trees and plants, shrubbery, lucerne paddock and small grass paddock. Water laid to all parts of the ground.'[37] The auctioneers were at pains to point out that the house was near the residences of J.L. Currie and Sir Robert Molesworth, a prominent squatter and a Supreme Court judge.

The house had been built by John Mullen, inspector and general manager of the Union Bank, and was 'a large two-storey rendered brick house in the mid-Victorian Italianate style with a symmetrical front having projecting bays at either end of a central loggia with verandah above and a hipped slate roof with bracketed eaves.'[38]

How much Harvey paid for *Inverleith* is unknown. As soon as they moved in, they began an extensive program of renovations, culminating in the building of an extravagant 'Moorish'-style ballroom able to host 300 guests. The Pattersons were now at home to the social elite of Melbourne and entertained on a sumptuous scale. Irvine became a regular visitor to his sister's house, mixing with her distinguished guests and the cream of Melbourne society. It was just as well that he had entrée to the world of high society; events which were to unfold in the new year of 1888 would require him to call in many favours.

THE MYSTERY OF THE HANDSOME MAN

Swanston Street taken in the late 1890s. Young and Jackson's Princes Bridge Hotel is on the left hand side of the image. The room where rowing club and VRA socials were held takes up most of the first floor, inlcuding the double window on the corner.

CHAPTER 8

'I could hardly see. I felt exhausted - very much so.'

The first weeks of the new year of 1888 were noted for being 'unusually cool and pleasant' for the Australian summer, but Saturday 11 February saw a rapid change come through: 'During the forenoon the heat became intense, the temperature increasing as the day advanced.'[1] A hot northerly wind blew up as Melburnians went about their regular Saturday business, working in offices, shopping or attending the official opening of the new State School in High Street, Prahran, or the laying of the foundation stone of the new Wesleyan Sunday School in Fitzroy Street, St Kilda. Irvine, along with another 3,000 people, made his way to Albert Park Lake for the VRA's annual Melbourne Regatta. The lake presented 'a very picturesque appearance,' although the wind made the water quite choppy and 'greatly increased the labours of the oarsmen' who completed a programme of 13 races.

A large marquee and refreshment booth was set up at the northern end of the lake, which was also set aside as the Ladies' reserve ('which was well patronised'). The South Melbourne Brass Band played popular musical selections 'to wile away the intervals between the races, which, though timed to start at very brief intervals, occasionally dragged considerably, an unusual difficulty arising through the dearth of coxswains.' The races started at the southern end of the lake, so the crews rowed every race into a strong headwind. The difficult conditions led many to consider that the racing didn't come up to the usual high standards of the Melbourne clubs. Annoyance was also expressed at a number of illegal gamblers who infiltrated the members' enclosure and 'who, carrying on their usual sharp practices, very narrowly escaped a lynching. The Committee were very desirous of turning them all out of the ground, but they were informed they had no power to do so.'[2]

However, the regatta crowd had a good day. Around 4pm, the races having finished, Irvine walked home to St Kilda to prepare for the prize giving ceremony at a 'social' to be held at Young and Jackson's. Dressed for the evening, he crossed Fitzroy Street to the St Kilda station and took the train to Flinders Street. He then crossed the road to Young & Jackson's, entering the hotel at 8pm.

About 80 rowing club members attended the social. In the intervals between toasts, speeches and songs, the orders for the day's trophies were handed out to the winning crews, along with trophies for a few other races which had taken place in the previous couple of months. Irvine took part in the usual singalongs and toasts but drank moderately, having only two glasses of Chablis during the course of the evening. By 11pm, not wanting to miss the last train home to St Kilda, Irvine made his farewells and left. The evening was warm, with 'little breeze to temper the oppressiveness of the atmosphere,'[3] and the hotel's upper room, where the social was held, had been uncomfortably warm. Leaving the hotel, Irvine decided to cool down by walking across the river to the South Melbourne railway station to catch the St Kilda train home.

A couple of blocks away, another group of young men had spent the sultry evening hanging around the corner of Little Collins and Russell Streets, looking for entertainment or trouble. Eighteen-year-old labourer, George Gossip, and 27-year-old John Thompson, a sometime sailor and gentleman's servant, started out by watching the crowds heading to the city's theatres or to the Eastern Market; the market would be open until midnight, offering an array of cheap stalls selling all manner of things, and entertainers such as palm readers, phrenologists and buskers. George's younger brother, 14-year-old Harold, a printer employed in a Little Bourke Street printing works, joined them, along with another mate, 18-year-old labourer John Reardon. The four wandered through the city streets. By 11pm, they were on the corner of Flinders and Swanston streets, outside Young & Jackson's, just as Irvine was leaving the rowing social.

While Thompson and the Gossip brothers hung back, Reardon approached Irvine, asking him for a match. Irvine's initial impression of Reardon, who was dressed in a dark suit, was that he looked 'respectable,' and he gave him 'five or six' matches. Reardon didn't light up a smoke, perhaps thereby signalling to Irvine that the request for a match was merely a conversation opener. (By

Top: George Gossip and John Holmes. Bottom: John Reardon and John Murray.

this time, 'have you got a light' was already a recognised way of striking up conversation between two men who might be interested in each other). Irvine offered Reardon a cigarette, but he declined, saying that they fell to bits in his mouth; he preferred his pipe. But he did not light his pipe either.[4]

Falling into step, the pair walked together along Flinders Street to the Falls Bridge, followed at a short distance by Thompson and the Gossips. Crossing the Falls Bridge, Reardon noted that it was 25 minutes to 12 o'clock, and Irvine said that he should get a cab to the South Melbourne station in order to catch the last train. Reardon reassured him, saying: 'there's plenty of time, if we step it out.'

At the southern end of the Falls Bridge, they walked under the railway viaduct which ran over the roadway and towards the junction of Moray Street

North and Maffra Street. Reardon started back towards the shadows of the viaduct, saying he had to 'ease myself – come with me.' Irvine said, 'No fear – I'll wait for you.'⁵ When Irvine refused to accompany him under the viaduct, Reardon then walked a little way along Moray Street North and turned up a dark sideway a little further along the street. Irvine hung back at the top of Moray Street North, saying that he would wait for Reardon.

While he was waiting for Reardon, Thompson and the Gossips overtook Irvine and passed him, turning left from the bridge approach, down Maffra Street. Harold Gossip later recalled Thompson saying that Irvine was a 'pouffter'⁶ and deserved a hiding. The three walked down Maffra Street until it joined City Road, then turned right and walked along the road towards the Main Point Hotel at the junction of City Road, Sandridge Road and Moray Street. Thompson and George told Harold to stop on the corner outside the pub, where a crowd was standing drinking on the footpath. The two older lads then crossed the junction towards the Castlemaine Hotel, on the corner of Moray Street North and City Road, to wait for Reardon and Irvine.

Meanwhile, back at the bridge end junction of Moray Street North and Maffra Street, Irvine decided to leave Reardon to his own devices, and walked down Moray. Reardon caught up with Irvine a little way down the street, and they walked as far as the Castlemaine Hotel, opposite the Main Point. There Reardon said, 'come home with me – I live in Byrne street, just around the corner.' Irvine said that he preferred to head home and would walk down Sandridge Road to the station. They crossed Moray Street and got a little way down Sandridge Road before Reardon asked for another match. Irvine said, 'I've already given you some matches.' 'I threw them away,' said Reardon. Irvine gave him another match. Reardon tried to light his pipe, but it wouldn't light; 'it's stuffed,'⁷ said Reardon.

At that, Reardon grabbed Irvine's hand, placed it on the fly of his trousers, and called out 'Look here lads; this man is taking hold of my person.' At that, Thompson and George Gossip materialised out of the shadows and seized Irvine by the arms and punched him in the face several times. One of them grabbed him around the waist from behind, and Reardon grabbed Irvine's watch chain, which broke as Irvine pulled himself free. The watch stayed in the pocket of Irvine's overcoat.

'I COULD HARDLY SEE. I FELT EXHAUSTED - VERY MUCH SO.' 151

Looking toward South Melbourne from the tower of the Melbourne Town Hall in the 1880s, Young and Jackson's Princes Bridge Hotel can be seen clearly in the centre of this photograph, on the corner of Swanston and Flinders Streets. Opposite the hotel are the long sheds of the Flinders Street Railway Station. Reardon and Irvine left Young and Jacksons and walked along Flinders Street and crossed Queens Bridge (the bridge downstream from the diagonal railway bridge) heading into South Melbourne.

'I COULD HARDLY SEE. I FELT EXHAUSTED - VERY MUCH SO.'

Having crossed Queens Bridge, Reardon and Irvine walked under the railway viaduct (where Reardon said he had to ease himself) and then walked down Moray Street, which runs south along the side of the railway line. The rest of the gang, having overtaken Reardon and Irvine, headed down Moray Street, which leads away from the viaduct diagonally to the right. Everything on the large triangular block to the right of Maffra Street is now buried beneath Melbourne's Southbank development.

Free of his attackers, Irvine ran back towards the crowd outside the Main Point Hotel, shouting 'save me, save me; they've tried to rob me.' The gang caught up with him, grabbed him by the arms and punched him again. One of the crowd, South Melbourne Market trader Uttrick Todd, who was on his way home to North Melbourne, said 'What's up?' Thompson punched Irvine again, and Reardon said, 'He tried to fuck a boy.' 'With that,' said Todd later, 'I left them to do as they pleased,'[8] and he turned away and continued on his way home.

With Irvine secured again, the gang then started pushing him along Sandridge Road in the direction of the school. As they frogmarched him along, Thompson yelled out: 'This man attempted to take liberties with Reardon.' 'It's a lie!' shouted Irvine.

Irvine remembered that he and Reardon had passed a police constable while they were walking down Moray Street. He decided to make another break for it and to head in the copper's direction. He struggled free of the gang and ran towards the Castlemaine Brewery. They caught up with him, tripped him onto the footpath in front of the Brewery and kicked him in the face. As they dragged him to his feet, tearing off his necktie and ripping his shirt and undershirt, Irvine called out for help, and one of the gang said, 'choke the bugger.' Someone got Irvine in a chokehold and placed their hand over his mouth. He was having trouble breathing, but he bit the hand covering his mouth. With a roar, his attacker released the stranglehold and, able to breathe again, Irvine broke free for a third time. Running along Sandridge Road, 'bleeding profusely' and with his clothes torn, Irvine recalled: 'I could hardly see. I felt exhausted – very much so.'

Constables Thomas O'Toole and Richard Jose, alerted to the commotion, ran up to Irvine, calmed him down and took him back along the street to face his attackers. Thompson repeated his accusation that Irvine had groped Reardon. Irvine denied it, saying: 'these men have set on me and attempted to assault and rob me.'[9] Thompson and George Gossip said that they knew Irvine 'to be a notorious man for this offence. They had been on the watch for him and could not catch him til now.'[10]

O'Toole and Jose arrested Irvine. The group walked 20 minutes to the South Melbourne watchhouse in Daly Street, at the rear of the Town Hall, accompanied by a large crowd. O'Toole and Irvine were in front, with Jose and Thompson, Reardon and George Gossip following behind. On the way,

'I COULD HARDLY SEE. I FELT EXHAUSTED - VERY MUCH SO.'   155

Irvine overheard Thompson say to Reardon: 'you'll have to go on the with case Jack. Say that you were making water and that this man came up and put his arm round your neck and placed your person in his mouth.' Irvine turned to the Constable O'Toole and said: 'it's a deliberate lie. There's no truth in it.' Reardon took the opportunity during the walk to the watchhouse of slipping Harold Gossip an envelope he had taken from Irvine, containing some tickets for the social and two half-crowns.

When they arrived at the watchhouse, all six men gave their conflicting statements to the police. When he gave his name and address, the police refused to believe that Irvine was who he said he was: 'They thought I was using an alias.' Although it was several years since he retired from competitive rowing and seven years since his last intercolonial race, Irvine's name was still well known enough for the police to disbelieve that they had such an illustrious sporting personality in their charge room.

Thompson, sizing Irvine up, said to the police constables, 'I think this man has done this sort of thing before. We've known of him, but we haven't been able to find him out before.'

During the struggle, Irvine had lost 30/- in silver, two small keys, an envelope with 10 tickets for the social, two half-crown coins which he had been paid for some of the social tickets, his season's pass railway ticket, reading glasses and his cigarettes. When accused of theft, George Gossip just looked at the cops and said, 'search us then.'[11]

With Irvine in the lock-up for the night, the police let the youths go, two constables walking with them back up Sandridge Road as far as the Brewery. Bidding them good night, the police left the four, who headed for their respective homes. Reardon asked Harold Gossip for the envelope that he had given him earlier. Opening it and finding it full of tickets for the rowing social and the money that Irvine had been paid for them, Reardon gave the tickets back to Harold, together with half a crown. Harold said 'These [the tickets] are no good to me,' but he hung on to them anyway. Reardon kept the other half-crown and gave Thompson some of the 30/- in silver lifted from Irvine.

The following morning, Sunday, with both eyes blackened, Irvine was bailed from the South Melbourne lock-up to appear before the South Melbourne Magistrates' Court on the following Wednesday. He headed home to St Kilda. The day's weather matched his mood; the hot sultry day was developing into a stormy evening. Dark and brooding rain clouds started gathering in the late afternoon, and vivid flashes of forked lightning lit the sky amid loud peals of thunder. A ferocious thunderstorm broke at half-past eight, and the city was drenched in torrential rain. Lightning lit up the night sky:

> Some of the thunder claps were startling, and seemed to crack overhead within a range not altogether agreeable to reflect upon. The [Melbourne] Telephone Exchange was quite unworkable during the whole of the evening, the lightning playing over the switchboard, and rendering it unsafe for the operators to enter the room.[12]

The storm raged for several hours before passing, just before midnight.

The same evening, just before the storm broke, Harold Gossip met his brother, Reardon, and Thompson in Little Collins Street around 8pm. The three older lads told Harold that he'd 'better keep out of this and have nothing to do with it.'[13]

The news of Irvine's ordeal was broken to the Melbourne public by the afternoon *Herald* newspaper on Monday: 'At a late hour on Saturday night, the South Melbourne police arrested Mr Irvine, manager of the Bank of Australasia, at St Kilda, on a very serious charge.' The police were apparently 'reticent' to discuss the matter with the reporter from the *Herald*, but it was strongly suspected by the paper that 'there is every reason to believe that the accused will be charged with indecent assault.' The *Herald* went on to say that Irvine was 'beaten by two men friends of the man who preferred the charge against him, and that the latter was unwilling to sign the charge, but was persuaded to do so by the two men.'[14] It was noted that Irvine strongly denied the charge and maintained that he was the victim of a robbery.

The following morning, Tuesday 14 February, the news made it into various Melbourne papers and was reported as far afield as Bairnsdale, Castlemaine, Colac and Sydney. While the *Bairnsdale Advertiser* and the *Colac Herald* both reported only that Irvine, manager of the Bank of Australia [*sic*], had been arrested on a 'serious charge,'[15] believed to be indecent assault, and the *Mount Alexander Mail* merely reprinted word-for-word the report in the previous afternoon's *Herald*,[16] the *Australian* in Sydney noted that the reticence of the police was due to them 'preserving secrecy in order to facilitate a further arrest in connection with the case.'[17] What could it mean?

Because the charge against him was an extremely serious one, carrying a maximum penalty of 10 years' imprisonment, Irvine spent Monday and Tuesday calling in a number of favours and securing the best legal representation he could. David Gaunson, a brilliant solicitor with a high public profile who had (unsuccessfully) represented the bushranger Ned Kelly at his trial for murder in 1880, agreed to take on Irvine's case. A year older than Irvine, Gaunson was described as 'endowed with a musical voice, good presence, fine flow of language, great quickness of mind, readiness to retort and a good deal of industry, ability and humour.' A fellow lawyer, parliamentarian Alfred Deakin, said that he was only disqualified from marked political and professional success by his 'utter instability, egregious egotism, want of consistency and violence of temper.' Gaunson had a reputation for defending the underdog; not only did he act as Ned Kelly's defence counsel, but he was also legal adviser to notorious Melbourne brothel owner Madam Brussels, to the Licensed Victuallers' Association and to the railway trades union. In later life, as a member of parliament, he was to be accused of accepting money from businessmen in order to push their private interests in parliament. He was also later to represent the shady financier and illegal gambling racketeer John Wren. Gaunson boasted that: 'he had cheated Pentridge [Prison] of more deserving tenants than any other practitioner in Victoria.'[18]

Six Justices of the Peace made up the bench of the South Melbourne Magistrates' Court which met in the courthouse in Daly Street, at the rear of the grand South Melbourne Town Hall. The courthouse shared premises with the police station; it was here that Irvine had been held in the watchhouse cells the previous Saturday night. Joseph Stead chaired the magistrates' bench, which also comprised Messrs Thistlethwaite, Glover, Jones and White and Dr Stewart.

The bench sat for several hours, during which time Gaunson thoroughly cross-examined the gang and presented a 'voluminous' amount of evidence, alleging that Gossip, Thompson and Reardon were a 'gang of river thieves.'[19] The gang's allegations against Irvine crumbled under a ferocious grilling from Gaunson, who singled out Gossip as having twice previously 'made charges of a similar nature in connection with persons whom it was alleged he had tried to rob.' Gaunson said that, on previous occasions, the victims 'would submit to any robbery and violence rather than be confronted with such diabolical charges.' In this case, however, his client, 'being an athlete', had successfully resisted 'the onslaught of Riordan [sic] and his confederates, defended his watch and property ... [Irvine] deserved credit as being perhaps the only man who would have faced such a revolting charge in order to bring this gang of miscreants to justice.'[20]

It was not until 7:15 that evening that Irvine, described as a 'gentlemanly looking man'[21] of 38 (although actually nearly 41), rose to make a statement to the bench, but Stead motioned for him to sit down, saying that it was not necessary for Irvine to defend himself, because 'they believed the whole affair to be a conspiracy.'[22] While Irvine 'may have been foolish in mixing himself up in any way with such creatures as his prosecutors,'[23] there were no grounds whatsoever for the serious accusations brought against him. Irvine was discharged by the bench and walked from the court 'without a stain on his character.'[24] The bench's statement was met with loud applause in the courtroom.

Stead continued by saying that he and his fellow magistrates 'considered that the story of the prosecutor [Reardon] and his witnesses was a concocted one, and that they had sought to make Mr Irvine the victim of a horrible conspiracy.'[25] Sensation in the courtroom continued when Detectives Harry Cawsey and Edward O'Donnell rose and revealed that they had brought with them William Tinkler, a groom employed by popular physician Dr Foster of St Vincent's Place, South Melbourne, and 19-year-old labourer John Holmes, a rather thuggish young man. Introducing the two to the court, Cawsey and O'Donnell stated that Tinkler had been assaulted and robbed by two men on the night of the 6 February, and his attackers had threatened that they would claim that he had made an indecent advance to them if he went to the police. In recent days, Tinkler had read of Irvine's case in the papers and, thinking that his experience mirrored that of Irvine, had approached the police with his story.

Tinkler stated that he had been standing opposite the Theatre Royal in Bourke Street on the night of 6 February when George Gossip, whom he identified in the courtroom, came up and asked him for a match. They got talking, and Tinkler took Gossip into a hotel for a drink. They decided to walk home together to South Melbourne. While walking along City Road, they were approached by another man, and Gossip accused Tinkler of having committed

Harry Cawsey

an indecent assault on him. The two then set on Tinkler, bashed him and took his watch and chain.²⁶

In court, Tinkler pointed at Holmes and confirmed that he was the other man who had bashed him, threatened him and relieved him of his watch and chain, worth £3. Reardon, Gossip and Thompson were immediately arrested on a charge of having assaulted and robbed Irvine, and Gossip and Holmes were charged with having robbed Tinkler. All four were conveyed to the cells forthwith to await further developments.

Such sensational showmanship was very much in Detective Cawsey's repertoire. Described as 'a fine lump of a fellow,'²⁷ Cawsey was renowned for 'great astuteness and a relentless pertinacity in following up the slenderest clue.'²⁸ Thirty-four years of age when he arrested Reardon and co., he was born in Werribee and joined the police force in 1874 at the age of 20. Apparently, 'from the very jump his conduct called forth the warm commendation of his superior officers.' He transferred to the detective branch in 1883. Something of a star, Cawsey 'figured prominently before the public'²⁹ and featured in a number of high-profile investigations in the 1880s, particularly a couple of well-publicised bank robberies and jewellery thefts, a notably gruesome murder in 1886 when a Coburg mother and her three adult daughters were found guilty of murdering their eight-year-old daughter/sister, and the 'Glenhuntly Outrage' of December 1887, when the stationmaster of Glenhuntly railway station was assaulted with an iron bar and left for dead in a robbery-gone-wrong. Such high-profile cases put Cawsey's name in front of the public on a regular basis, and he was known for his somewhat theatrical flourishes in presenting evidence in court; the public loved his exploits and looked forward to his court appearances as a species of high drama.

The sensational revelations of Cawsey and the skilful legal defence of Gaunson allowed Irvine to walk free from the court. He had much to be grateful for; he had faced a serious charge and had been exonerated. But, as a respectable member of the middle classes, friend to Melbourne's political and social elite, and a well-known former sporting champion, he had always hoped – indeed, expected – that his word would be believed over that of a gang of young 'river thieves.'

Who were the river thieves?

John Radcliffe Thompson, the oldest of the gang by nearly a decade, also went by the name Thomas Graham. Born in Scotland in 1861, he was 5 feet 7 inches in height, of a 'stout square build'[30] and with fair hair that was inclined to curl. In 1888, he wore a small, fair moustache of the type becoming popular among young men at the time. Although his occupation was given as a sailor, he had also been employed as a servant by the Sydney-based Shakespearean actor, theatre manager and theatrical impresario George Rignold.

John Reardon, born in Victoria in 1870, was 5 feet 7 inches tall, with a fresh complexion, 'sandy' hair and blue eyes. Like almost all young Victorians of his generation, he could read and write (compulsory State education having been introduced in Victoria in 1872). His father, also John Reardon, was a printer employed by the *Age* newspaper. John Jr's occupation was given as 'labourer,' although he had worked at the *Age* with his father for three and a half years. Both Reardons lived at 3 Byrne Street, South Melbourne.[31]

George and Harold Gossip had been born in England (in 1871 and 1874) and emigrated to Victoria in January 1883 in company with their mother Alina (or Ellen, or Helen, depending on which official source you check) and sisters

Helen (aged 10) and Mabel (aged 4). Their father, George Gossip, had already emigrated to Australia. By 1888, he was working as an 'editor of a newspaper in Sydney,'[32] while Alina Gossip supported the rest of the family by giving piano lessons in Melbourne. The Gossips lived at the St Kilda Road end of Bright Street, South Melbourne, just near the southern approach of the new Princes Bridge (and a stone's throw from the boatsheds on the southern bank of the Yarra). Byrne Street, the Reardons' family home, was only a block away, further down Bright Street. George, a good-looking lad, had a fresh complexion, brown hair and brown eyes. He had a small tattoo of an anchor on his lower left arm – traditionally a symbol of hope and salvation, long popular with sailors; it is possible that his friendship with the older Thompson, a seaman, had influenced his choice of tattoo.

John Holmes was a native of London, born in 1869. He arrived in Melbourne on board the *Leicester Castle* the same year as the Gossips arrived, 1883. Again described as a labourer (a useful, catch-all term for any unskilled nineteenth century working class man), he was also 5 feet 7 inches, with grey eyes and 'light' coloured hair, of a reddish hue, giving rise to his nickname 'Ginger.' It was noted that he 'walked lame'[33] and, having no family in Australia, often slept at the Reardon family's house in Byrne Street. Holmes had a petty criminal record for a number of small thefts and gambling offences, having served a total of nine weeks for five offences since January 1886.

They all lived near each other in a small tangle of streets near the southern bank of the Yarra, a district of factories, foundries, timber yards, corner shops, a great many small hotels and single-storeyed terrace houses, wedged between St Kilda Road and what is now known as Queens Bridge Street (then Moray Street North). The neighbourhood was bounded to the north by the river and to the south by Sandridge/City Road and dominated by the Castlemaine Brewery (with its onsite hotel, the Castlemaine) and the impressive new South Melbourne State School, both on City Road. City Road ran down to a junction of six streets (City Road, Hanna Street, Moray Street, Sandridge Road, Hanna Street North and Moray Street North) dominated by the South Melbourne Post Office and three hotels (the Castlemaine, the Trades Hall and the Main Point).

The whole area has now been submerged under the Southbank complex and a slew of skyscrapers, and very few streets survive from 1888. Those that remain have changed their names in the intervening years; Southbank Boulevard follows the line of Maffra Street, Riverside Quay is the route of the old Bright Street, and Byrne Street, where the Reardons lived at number 3, is now buried under the 91-storeyed Eureka Tower, Melbourne's tallest building. The only buildings in the area to survive from the night when the gang set upon Irvine are the South Melbourne State School and a couple of larger warehouses. Down at the junction of City Road and Sandridge Road, everything has been swept away except the Main Point Hotel, and even that is a rebuild from 1903. The junction is now overshadowed by the Kings Way overpass and is completely unrecognisable.

With the exception of the Catholic Reardon, all members of the 'river thieves' were nominal members of the Church of England. Apart from Holmes, none of the gang had been in trouble with the police previously. Reardon and the Gossips were from families who could be described as members of the respectable working class; all were literate, apparently gainfully employed, and came from a closely-knit local neighbourhood. However, only a couple of days after Irvine was released and the gang locked up, the Port Melbourne *Standard* employed a word guaranteed to strike fear into the hearts of middle-class Melbourne; Reardon was described as 'a lad of the larrikin type.'[34]

The labelling of Reardon and the rest of the gang as larrikins tapped into middle-class fears of the existence of a class of unruly, working class youth: semi-literate, antagonistic towards authority, violent, sexually promiscuous and given to various types of vicious criminality. The term 'was used as a handy way for journalists and the authorities to label any apparently lowborn young person who spent time in the streets and engaged in uncouth behaviour ... Much like the labelling of certain youth as Aborigines or Muslims or simply 'hoons' today, this branding of poor juveniles as larrikins contributed to a spike in police prosecutions'[35] from the 1870s onwards. Most of the police prosecutions were for offences against public order – drunkenness, swearing and unruly behaviour. The so-called 'boy nuisance,' which apparently threatened to rapidly extend all over the colony from the early 1870s, coalesced into the 'larrikin menace' – 'young ruffians ... who infest different quarters of the city after nightfall.'[36] Larrikinism was one of the main social anxieties of late nineteenth-century Australia, an affront to public decency and a well-run society.

If Reardon, Thompson, Holmes and the Gossips were tarred as larrikins, the law would likely fall heavily on them, in order to make an example of them. Detectives Cawsey and O'Donnell dug more deeply into the robberies of Irvine and William Tickler. While doing so, they were approached by plain-clothes Constable Thomas Fleming, who knew John Reardon and George Gossip and remembered them as having been involved in the assault of an elderly man, Donald McRae, on the night of 26 January.

Although not yet officially marked as 'Australia Day', 26 January had been declared a public holiday to mark the centenary of British settlement at Sydney Cove. The day had been filled with a number of public observances, sporting events, race meetings, bay excursions and a grand Caledonian Sports Day at the Melbourne Cricket Ground. It was to the MCG that McRae, a warder at the Melbourne Gaol in Russell Street, went. He had an enjoyable day at the sports and admitted indulging in whisky, brandy and ale 'more than he had ought.' Leaving the Cricket Ground, he made his way back into town and was approached by George Gossip on the corner of Swanston and Little Collins streets. Gossip asked McRae for a match and then, according to Gossip, McRae said to him, 'You're a fine boy' and invited him for a drink at the Cathedral Hotel in Swanston Street. After finishing one glass of beer, the two walked down Swanston Street, across Princes Bridge, and then turned into City Road. Unknown to McRae, they were being tailed by Harold Gossip, John Reardon and another lad, 17-year-old John Murray. According to George Gossip, it had been previously arranged that if one of the gang 'picked up any person,'[37] the rest would follow.

A little way down on the southern side of City Road was a timber yard with a number of large piles of logs stacked and awaiting the sawmill. Gossip and McRae, who was still rather the worse for drink, went behind one of the piles, where Gossip alleged that McRae groped Gossip's 'person.'[38] At that point, Reardon, Murray and Harold Gossip appeared and started bashing McRae, trying to choke him and breaking his watch chain in an attempt to steal his watch (which was worth £13 – a lot more than that of servant William Tickler).

The gang was interrupted by Ellen and William Morcom, who lived nearby and who were walking home after watching a fireworks show on the banks of the Yarra. Ellen cried out: 'My God, another robbery' and grabbed a stick and approached the group. William went round another way behind the group and grabbed Harold Gossip by the collar. Ellen Morcom cried out: 'Stop! Reardon, I know you!'[39] and the gang scattered. Harold, in the grip of William Morcom, yelled out that McRae was a 'pouffter.' Ellen, shaking her head, then accompanied McRae back towards Princes Bridge, looking for a policeman, but whether she was aiming to help the victim of a robbery or put a 'pouffter' in charge isn't sure. George Gossip doubled back to the scene of the crime, to find William Morcom still holding his younger brother. 'Let him go,' said George and Morcom released the lad, who ran off. George then headed for home.[40]

At the bridge, Ellen and McRae met Constable John McGowan. McRae told McGowan that he had been robbed and gave McGowan the remaining piece of his watch chain; the rest of the chain and the watch had been taken by Reardon. Ellen Morcom confirmed the identities of Reardon and George Gossip, and McGowan then found two other constables, John William Stokes and George Scott, who knew where the Gossips lived and decided to pay George a house call.

It was midnight when they arrived at the Gossips' house in Bright Street, to find George Gossip standing outside his house. Stokes said to Gossip, 'What's this you've got yourself into this evening?' and Gossip replied, 'Oh, it is only a pouffter. I met him in Swanston Street and he asked me to have a drink. He took me into the Cathedral Hotel and gave me one.' He described how they had walked down to City Road, where McRae had apparently 'put his arms around my waist and tried to bottle me.' The term to bottle someone referred to having anal sex and came from rhyming slang bottle and glass = arse.[41]

Gossip admitted that he, Reardon and Murray had given McRae a good thrashing, which he deserved, being a 'dirty old man,'[42] but they had not robbed him. 'If he's lost anything it must be where the scuffle took place.'[43] Stokes and Scott asked Gossip where Reardon lived, and Gossip agreed to show them. He took them around the corner to Byrne Street, where they found Reardon knocking on the window of his father's house, having been locked out for the night. The four then went back to the timber yard in City Road, where, by the light of matches, they found McRae's watch. Stokes said that, at that point, he came to the conclusion that McRae had been assaulted and not robbed. Both coppers considered that McRae, as a 'dirty old man', had received his just deserts at the hands of the lads. They let Gossip and Reardon go home. Unbeknownst to Stokes and Scott, Gossip had the watch in his pocket the

'I COULD HARDLY SEE. I FELT EXHAUSTED - VERY MUCH SO.' 165

whole time he was talking to the police outside his house; when they returned to the timber yard, he simply dropped it on the ground for Stokes to find.

A little over two weeks later, when Gossip and Reardon were arrested and in the court room at South Melbourne for the robbery and assault of William Tinkler, they were recognised as McRae's attackers as well. They may well have been responsible for a fourth robbery in the South Melbourne area; when Ellen Morcom cried out, 'My God, another robbery', it was because she was aware of a similar attack on the same piece of ground on the night of Sunday 22 January.

Reardon, George Gossip and Murray finally fronted South Melbourne Police Court on Wednesday 29 February, charged with the assault and robbery of Donald McRae on 26 January; Gossip and Holmes were charged with the assault and robbery of William Tinkler on 6 February; and Gossip, Reardon and Thompson were charged with the assault and robbery of John Irvine on 11 February. If the gang were responsible for a fourth attack on 22 January, the victim never came forward. The hearings took up the greater part of the day, at the end of which the five were remanded in custody to appear before Justice Williams at the Supreme Court on Thursday 15 March. Irvine was in court that day to give evidence pertaining to his case, and Mr Thistlethwaite, one of the magistrates, said that the bench wished to 'express great sympathy for Mr Irvine, who had been placed in a very awkward position. They hoped that the stigma raised would not interfere with his character for future life.'[44]

While the 'river thieves' awaited their trial, public sympathy for Irvine was growing. The St Kilda *Telegraph* of 10 March noted that a suggestion 'as to entertaining Mr Irvine at a social gathering has already been taken up by a number of influential residents who intend entertaining that gentleman at an early date.'[45]

The March 1888 Criminal Sittings of the Supreme Court opened at 10am on Thursday 15 March before Mr Justice Hartley Williams. Sixteen cases were due to be heard in this session, a range of assaults, burglaries, conspiracies, arson, shop-breaking and:

> George Gossip and John Holmes, robbery
> John Murray, George Gossip and John Reardon, robbery in company
> John Reardon, John R. Thompson and George Gossip, robbery in company.[46]

Hartley Williams was an unorthodox judge of the Supreme Court. Victorian-born, he was the son of a judge and Oxford educated. Called to the Bar in London in 1867, at the age of 23, he returned to Victoria later the same year and began an 'extensive and successful'[47] common law practice. Appointed to succeed Sir Redmond Barry as a judge of the Supreme Court on Barry's death in 1881; at 37, he was the youngest judge in Victoria's history. He was 'well known and respected for the common sense of his summings-up and judgements ... and showed considerable aptitude in the work of the Criminal Court.' He held unusual views on religion and politics, having declared in 1884 that England would one day become a republic, advocating federation of the Australian colonies and the establishment of an Australian republic, and publishing a pamphlet in 1885 entitled *Religion without Superstition* – which drew the ire of the established churches. He was a keen cyclist, cricketer, athlete, boxer and, like Irvine, rower. He was renowned as being the scourge of the city's larrikin element, having presided over many cases where he passed heavy sentences on young men for antisocial offences. One of his supporters said:

> Williams has force enough and can strike hard blows. His sentences recorded in the newspapers, and recorded on the backs of the brutal pests of society whom he has sentenced to long terms of hard labor and the lash, bear witness to this trait of character. There is no need to apologise for this severity either. It is needed. There ought to be more of it. We are nursing and cherishing gangs of larrikins and encouraging them in the commission of brutal crimes by inflicting upon them sentences that only make them laugh.[48]

When the 'river thieves' (or – as the group was now more commonly known – 'The South Melbourne Conspirators') case came to court, Alina Gossip pleaded that her son George had been without a father's control for several years, but that, while he was in respectable employment, he had brought his money home to supplement the income she earned by giving piano lessons. He had been laid off for a couple of months, but his former employers had given him a good character for honesty and hard work. In reply, Mr Justice Williams only commented that Mrs Gossip had better look after her other son, Harold: 'If he had his deserts [sic], he would be in the dock too.' Harold, however, had turned Queen's Evidence in order to escape prosecution.

In his defence, Reardon stated that Irvine was guilty of the offence of which he had accused him, and 'even if it cost him more, he would persist in the assertion.' He declared that Gossip was the main instigator of the scheme. Holmes and Murray also agreed that Gossip had been the brains behind what had become known as 'The South Melbourne Conspiracy.'

Deciding at that point that he could no longer brazen it out, Gossip changed his original plea of 'not guilty' and pleaded guilty to robbing McRae, Tinkler and Irvine. Reardon and Thompson pleaded not guilty to robbing Irvine; the jury took only a short time to find Reardon guilty and Thompson not guilty. Reardon was remanded for sentencing, and Thompson was discharged. Reardon was then also found guilty of robbing McRae; Holmes was found guilty of robbing Tinkler; and Murray was found guilty of robbing McRae. Justice Williams expressed his inability to 'fathom the process of reasoning by which the jury,' who had found Reardon guilty of the assault and robbery of Irvine, managed to find Thompson not guilty of the same offence.

Williams went on to say that the attacks which the gang had committed were of a particular level of 'gravity and [of an extremely] serious nature.' The gang were 'violent, brutal, cowardly, and loathsome' and their conspiracy particularly 'vile.' Becoming well and truly fired up, Williams continued:

> It is abundantly clear that you and others, who are not now before the court [including, apparently, Harold Gossip], have for some time past habitually combined together for the diabolical purpose of making charges of the commission of a foul and abominable offence upon the person of some one of your gang against, in most cases, perfectly innocent persons ... [You] conspired to assault and rob by night in gangs, members of the community returning to their homes. To shield yourself from prosecution for so serious a crime you ... have further combined and conspired to accuse your victim of having committed or attempted to commit a foul, abominable and unnatural offence ... knowing full well the improbability ... of your victim setting the law in motion ... [in case] he might expose himself to the risk of having to face a hideous charge against himself.

Williams finished his remarks by stating that the gang members were:

> a danger to the person, to the reputation, to the property of every member of this community ... I must pass such sentences upon you as will ring in the ears of the rest of your confederates, and of those who might otherwise feel tempted to endeavour to plunder and rob by the employment of similar means.[49]

They were remanded for sentencing on 19 March, the following Monday.

When the court reconvened, Williams sentenced Gossip to 18 years' hard labour and two whippings of 10 lashes each with the cat-of-nine-tails; Reardon, 20 years; Holmes, 10 years; and Murray, 10 years' hard labour. Reardon, Holmes and Murray were also to receive three whippings of 15 lashes each and to spend the first four days of the last 12 months of their sentences in solitary confinement. The four were removed from the court, to spend another five days at the Melbourne Gaol (was McRae their warder?) before being transferred to Pentridge Prison on 26 March.

Pentridge, on the outskirts of Melbourne's northern suburbs, was Victoria's largest maximum security gaol. Established in 1850 and rebuilt of the local volcanic bluestone in the late 1850s and 1860s, it was a dark fortress overlooking the main road to Sydney. Conditions were harsh, the labour to which the prisoners were put was backbreaking, and the inmates were punished for the slightest infractions. Melbourne's respectable classes were firmly of the opinion that it was a fitting place for the gang. As the gang members began their lengthy terms, newspaper articles as far afield as Western Australia, Queensland and Tasmania exulted in the 'Repression of Larrikinism' that Justice Williams' severe sentences represented.

As it turned out, none of the gang members served their full sentences. George Gossip served 4½ years of his original 18 year term. John Reardon served 7½ years of 20 years. John Murray served 7½ years of his 10 year sentence. John Holmes survived only 18 months in prison, dying on 12 September 1889, aged 20. Gossip, Reardon, and Murray, following their releases from prison, appear never to have come to the attention of police again.

There is no doubt that the 'South Melbourne Conspirators' chose their marks well. Larrikins had long been associated with street robbery, and groups of larrikins had been convicted for 'robbery in company' in the past. In July 1875, a group of four larrikins, 'repulsive looking individuals,'[50] had cornered labourer William Dodson in a dark allotment behind St James' School in Collins Street. Two of the gang kept sentry, while the other two slit the waistband of his trousers and removed £4 from Dodson's money pocket. Although reports of the Dodson robbery have no sexual overtones, some aspects of the gang's modus operandi are the same as the later South Melbourne Conspiracy: one of the gang approached Dodson in a hotel bar and started chatting to him. Dodson stood him a drink and then led him 'as he thought, in a friendly way'[51] to a dark and lonely spot, where the gang overpowered him. Setting apart the vaguely sexual act of slitting Dodson's trousers, it is interesting to note that one of the gang was 18-year-old James Nesbitt – later to be the offsider, partner and probably lover of Australia's 'gay' bushranger, Andrew Scott, alias Captain Moonlite.[52]

The 1880s were a time when the public was becoming aware of the 'homosexual' as a type, following a number of well-publicised scandals in London, Dublin and also Australia. Melissa Bellanta notes in her book *Larrikins* that the larrikin groups of the inner cities of Melbourne, Sydney and Brisbane shared social space with homosexual networks and possibly overlapped at particular points in time. Bellanta believes that some larrikins must have felt a degree of anxiety about 'hard-to-articulate feelings about same-sex acts' and their feelings for their mates; the friction which the larrikins felt about sharing their social space with homosexuals 'may well have enticed male larrikins to make trouble for known homosexuals.'[53]

George Gossip appears to have taken this knowledge of homosexuality, and perhaps something of his own innate nature, a step further by developing a 'badger game' (an extortion scheme in which a victim is tricked into a compromising position in order to make them vulnerable to blackmail or, in this case, robbery) which enabled him and his mates to prey on men whom they believed to be homosexual. Justice Williams, in his summing up of the case, acknowledged that Gossip and the rest of the South Melbourne Conspirators were very well aware of the existence of homosexuals in Melbourne, knowing that their victims might 'be prone to ... [be entrapped] into the commission of such an offence' and for that reason elected one of the gang to act as a 'decoy'[54] to lure their victim into the gang's clutches.

The use of the good-looking Gossip as the bait in two of the three cases; the well-rehearsed approach to the mark, asking for a match by way of striking up conversation; the marshalling of the target to the gang's home territory of South Melbourne; the luring of the victim into a dark and isolated place, using the excuse of having a piss; the tailing of the pair by the rest of the gang, who would act as witnesses when the decoy made his accusation of having had an indecent approach made to him; all these factors point to a well thought out and polished modus operandi.

However, in order to make the scheme work, the gang had to find a potential victim who was likely to take their bait. It is probable that the gang members approached many other men on the streets, but were rebuffed. The gang also wanted a victim who could be enticed to their familiar territory in South Melbourne, or who was heading there anyway. All three victims were snared in the city's central streets, and all three attacks took place in the same few streets in South Melbourne, where the gang knew the dark laneways, isolated timber yards and empty lots from which they could make a quick getaway home once they'd finished their attack. If a decoy approached a potential mark who was heading in a direction other than South Melbourne, the gang would have cut the conversation short and looked around for another victim who was heading their way.

Gossip and his mates knew that, having threatened their victims with allegations of indecent assault, they were unlikely to be reported to the police for their robberies. It was only when they attacked Irvine in a relatively public place, attracting the attention of onlookers, that their plan began to unravel. And it was the fact that they had robbed Irvine that initially brought the law down on them. No one was concerned about a gang of lads beating up a 'pouffter' – not the police, and not the crowd in the street on the night of Irvine's attack. When initially questioned by Constable Stokes about the bashing of McRae, Gossip airily remarked, 'Oh, it is only a pouffter.' The fact that McRae's watch was recovered from the scene of the beating, after being planted by Gossip, meant that the police were dealing with a bashing rather than a theft. Further, it was the bashing of a poofter, which the police and the public considered perfectly justifiable: remember Uttrick Todd's comment when Reardon said that the gang was bashing Irvine because 'he tried to fuck a boy' – 'I left them to do as they pleased.' A dozen or so years into the future, in 1901, when the Russell Street police were asked to investigate the use of public lavatories as places of homosexual resort, the investigating sergeant reported:

> I am convinced the complaint is very much exaggerated. It exists to a limited extent, and has done so for years. [However], if they do at any time make filthy or indecent overtures to any man, [it is because] they believe him similarly inclined, but should they make a mistake the man insulted never thinks of giving any of them in charge [having them arrested], but sometimes gives the offender a *well-deserved* [my emphasis] blow or kick instead, of which the recipient never complains.'[55]

McRae, Tinkler and Irvine denied that they had made improper advances to Gossip or Reardon; but they would say that, wouldn't they? Admitting that they had done anything improper or had attempted to do so would have left them open to possible prosecution for indecent assault, with its attendant possible gaol time, social disgrace and loss of employment, home and family. Far better to deny everything.

Did anything actually happen between the three victims and the lads? All three had allowed themselves to be 'picked up' (as Gossip said) in the street by a young lad, and all had willingly gone with Gossip or Reardon. Gossip stated that McRae had called him 'a fine boy' and had bought him a drink. Likewise, Tinkler had liked Gossip well enough, on an acquaintance of only a few minutes, to buy him a drink. Although Irvine protested that, when Reardon tried to lure him into a dark alley on the pretext of having a piss, he had said 'No fear!' we only have Irvine's word for that; in court, Reardon maintained that Irvine was indeed guilty of the offence of which Reardon had accused him. It came down to the authorities accepting the word of a prison warder, a groom employed by a fashionable doctor, and a well-connected bank manager and former sporting hero, against that of a group of larrikins from the gritty streets of South Melbourne. Middle-class Melbourne was unnerved by the case and the thought that any respectable member of society could find themselves facing the threat of blackmail. Society at large was both pleased and relieved that Williams threw the book at them.

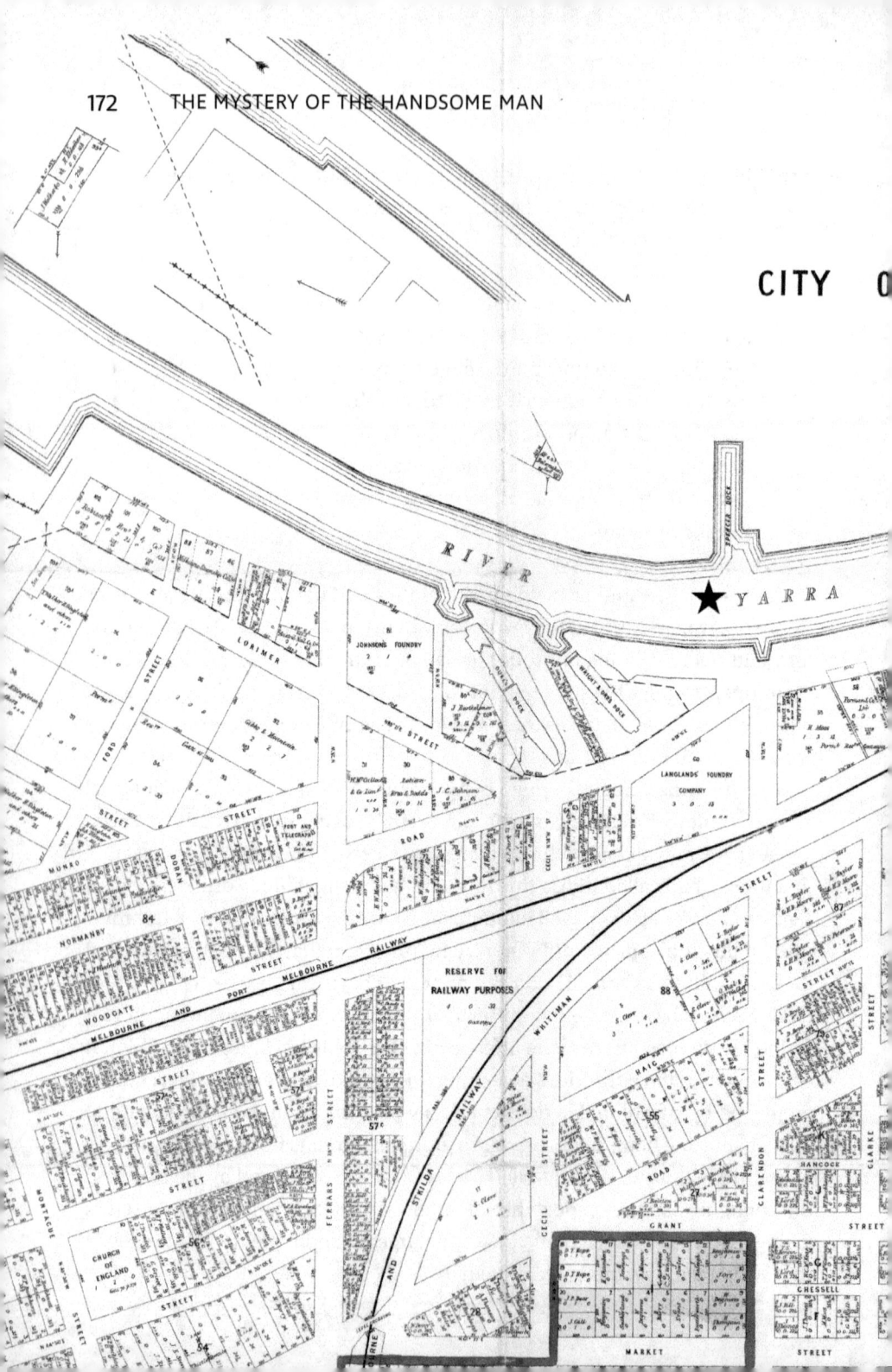

'I COULD HARDLY SEE. I FELT EXHAUSTED - VERY MUCH SO.' 173

This map of South Melbourne shows the South Melbourne Conspirators' stamping ground where all their attacks took place in the area bounded by Moray Street, City Road, and the Yarra River.

With the South Melbourne Conspirators now in gaol, Irvine was entertained to a testimonial meeting at Scott's Hotel in Collins Street, Melbourne, on the afternoon of Wednesday 28 March. About 30 prominent Melbourne citizens gathered 'for the purpose of showing their unabated esteem' for Irvine. Among those gathered at Scott's, one of Melbourne's leading hotels, were Sir James MacBain (President of the Legislative Council), J.B. Patterson MLA, Irvine's barrister David Gaunson, Cr F. Wimpole (former Mayor of St Kilda) and senior executive staff of the Bank of Australasia, including John Sawers (superintendent) and M.P. Blundell (general manager).

In presenting Irvine with a purse of sovereigns which he could use to cover the costs of his legal defence, Sir James MacBain 'assured the recipient that he still retained the entire respect and esteem of his many friends.' Irvine responded 'briefly, but feelingly.' Several speeches followed, each one testimony to the confidence that the Bank of Australasia, the people of St Kilda and various other groups and individuals had. J.B. Patterson said, 'referring to Mr Irvine's painful trial ... that he had never [met Irvine] before, and attended merely for the purpose of sympathising with him in a trial which might be the experience of any gentleman at any time.' The gathering was reported in both the St Kilda *Telegraph* and in the *Age*. It was hoped that, '[a]lthough there is no person who has for a moment doubted Mr Irvine's probity, the gathering will have the effect of silencing any evil disposed person for all time.'[56]

A further testimonial was a 'complimentary social' given for Irvine on the evening of Monday 21 May 'as a mark of sympathy for him in connection with the recent foul charges that were made against him'. It was said that

> there was a fair muster of rowing men present [and] the Sandhurst Rowing club sent a telegram expressing sympathy, and confidence in their old captain Mr Irvine. Mr Irvine spoke under great feeling and thanked those present for their kindness to him in the fearful agony he had had to undergo.[57]

The evening was spent in toasts and songs, rather like the evening of 11 February which had seen the whole saga of the 'South Melbourne Conspiracy' begin, four months earlier.

CHAPTER 9
'Your obliged servant J.L. Irvine'

Following the unwanted excitement of the South Melbourne Conspiracy, Irvine's life settled back into its usual routines. The remaining months of the 1880s were filled with banking business, family matters and committee work. There were also some momentous events of public interest.

On Wednesday 1 August 1888, Irvine joined the immense crowds who lined the city streets to watch the procession marking the opening of Victoria's Centennial Exhibition:

> The city was early astir preparing for the procession. There was plenty to see, and the people flocked in from all quarters to see it. The trams and trains and cabs came loaded, and ran back empty to bring more loads to the great show – the national procession, in which the military and naval forces, the friendly societies, and the trades unions were to take part. The national procession was the sight for the great mass of sight-seers. Only a privileged few could witness the opening ceremony [10,000 people had assembled inside the Exhibition Buildings in Carlton Gardens], but all could see the soldiers and the sailors, the waving banners, the nodding plumes, and the insignia of the different guilds.

The *Argus* reported that, by 10am, two hours before the procession was due to begin, the crowds were lined many deep along the steps of the Treasury Building and Parliament House in Spring Street, the streets were packed, and the cable trams were forced to a stop by the crush of people in the roadways.

Faces in the crowd: Wednesday 1 August 1888, two men in the crowd in Collins Street watch the parade for the opening of the International Exhibition.
Perhaps the one on the right is Irvine?

'The windows, the parapets, the roofs, the scaffolding, and the trees all along the street were black with gazers.'[1] The procession marched along the length of Collins Street before turning left into Spring Street, opposite the Treasury Building, and then headed north towards the Exhibition Building in Carlton Gardens. The Governor of Victoria, Sir Henry Loch, and the vice-regal party led the way, followed by representatives from all walks of Victorian life. It presented a wonderful spectacle.

The Exhibition was held to celebrate the centenary of British settlement of the Australian continent. By rights, New South Wales should have had the honour of mounting an exhibition; the centenary was theirs, after all. However, wealthy, pushy Victoria, 'knowing that New South Wales lacked an Exhibition Building and had left it too late to organize an Exhibition as part of its centennial celebrations, brought off a prestige-building coup with the utmost tact, and also persuaded itself that it was carrying out a major essay in colonial good will.'[2] The Exhibition Buildings in Carlton Gardens, built for the International Exhibition of 1880, were a fitting venue for a display of the produce and manufactures of the world. Exhibits came not only from the Australian colonies and New Zealand, but also from Britain, France, Germany, Italy, Austria-Hungary, the United States, Fiji, Scandinavia, Canada, India, Ceylon, Belgium, Russia and Spain; and the list went on. The Exhibition received more than 2,000,000 visits during the six months it was opened, and '[e]arnest clerks and artisans agreed that it was a "free education worth years of school."' The crowds thrilled to Edison's phonograph, the brilliant electric light which lit the building at night and a working tram imported from the United States. Some were shocked by the nude paintings in the French Court, while others appreciated works by Constable, Turner, Millais and Holman Hunt, lent for the Exhibition by British galleries.

A full musical festival, held in conjunction with the Exhibition, featured more than 260 concerts during the course of the Exhibition's run. Reports said that 11,000 people attended every Saturday to hear symphonic and choral works performed by an orchestra consisting of 15 musicians imported from Britain, augmented with local performers and a choir of 708 local singers. Melbourne had never heard anything like it, and still has not, to this day.

Irvine's mother Jemima was still living in Patterson Street, St Kilda. As a respected collector of plants and other biological specimens, she had been invited to contribute several displays to the Victorian Herbarium. The *Leader* reported:

> A good many examples of dried flowers, sea weeds, and similar things are shown, by far the most important being by Mrs J.F. Irvine, St Kilda, who exhibits specimens of plants, eggs, &c. from Western Australia; unfortunately for students the specimens are not named, but they are of very beautiful subjects; neither are they pressed or mounted but shown in bunches. The Rhodanths and many of the shrubs are exceedingly handsome.[3]

Whether Jemima had travelled to Western Australia for her specimens is not clear; she was known to carry on an extensive correspondence with other collectors throughout Australasia, so it is possible that the specimens could have been sent to her by a member of her network.

The extended Irvine family was now centred on St Kilda: Jemima lived with 27-year-old Nellie at Patterson Street, West Beach; Kate and Harvey Patterson lived at *Inverleith* in Acland Street; Florence and Toppy Longmore lived somewhere nearby (perhaps even with Jemima and Nellie); and John lived at the Bank of Australasia branch at the George Hotel Buildings in Fitzroy Street. Jemima had four of her eight surviving children living within a 15-minute walk. Dick Irvine was still in Launceston, looking after Irvine and McEachern; Charles was with the Adelaide Steamship Company and had married in Western Australia in 1886; and Claude was managing one of Harvey Patterson's cattle stations, *Corona*, in outback New South Wales. Daughter Jemima Adams was possibly still in New Zealand, but she was to move to Victoria sometime before the 1890s.

Like the rest of the upper-middle classes and society, those of the Irvine family living in Melbourne would have found their time taken up with the Exhibition and functions associated with it – a 'ceaseless routine'[4] of concerts, lectures, balls, banquets, parties and receptions. The Centennial Exhibition was the wonder of the age. However, in late September, scandal struck!

Around 8:45pm on the evening of Saturday 29 September, two policemen patrolling the promenades at the Exhibition Building noticed a young woman, accompanied by an older woman, strolling through the crowds. The young woman was 'behaving in a very imprudent manner', casting sideways glances at the men around her and attracting rather a crowd of admiring gentlemen. Thinking that the brazen woman was a prostitute trawling for business in the confines of the Exhibition, the policemen kept the pair under surveillance for around 20 minutes before approaching them. They asked the younger woman to accompany them to the Exhibition's police office. The young woman declined, and the senior of the two policemen, Detective Sexton, gripped her arm and started to pull her along with him. In her struggles, her hat and wig were knocked off, revealing her to be a young man!

Immediately, the crowd surrounding the police and the young man became violent: 'Kill the bugger', they cried.[5] A large crowd, estimated at about 1,000 people, quickly gathered and made 'determined attempts to seize the personator, so that they might wreak summary vengeance on him.'[6] It was with difficulty that the police managed to escort the man from the Exhibition. At the city watchhouse, he revealed himself to be 21-year-old Gordon Lawrence, a sometime actor, most recently a manservant in the house of Dr Henry of Brunswick. During his interrogation by police, Lawrence admitted that he was a 'sodomite and had practiced that vocation in New South Wales and Victoria.' The following day, police searched Lawrence's room at 274 George Street, Fitzroy and found articles of women's clothing which were identified as belonging to the wife of his former employer, Dr Henry. They also found indecent photographs and 'a number of bottles of Medicines and Syringes ... used by Sodomites.'[7] His landlady, Mrs Broughton, the older woman who had accompanied him to the Exhibition, said that he had been living at her house for the past six weeks and that she had no idea that he was a man. Lawrence was charged with insulting behaviour and vagrancy and held over to appear in court on Monday 1 October.

His appearance in the city court caused a sensation. He was dressed in a red skirt and a close fitting jacket of blue, striped with white;

> the outlines of his figure wonderfully resembled those of a woman, and the deception was still further increased by a flaxen wig, surmounted by a jaunty hat. The costume was, perhaps, a trifle loud; but even in the nervousness of the moment the prisoner displayed no awkwardness in his women's garments, which, indeed, he wore with the unconscious ease of a person long accustomed to their use. As he leant easily upon the bar, his eyes modestly downcast, and one silk-gauntleted hand fingering with the imitation diamond cross, which rose and fell perceptibly at his breast, there was nothing whatever to betray his sex. In every look, in every motion, in every line of his figure, he was a woman.[8]

It was reported that 'the evidence was decidedly of an unpleasant character'[9] and that Lawrence was one of a gang of men in Sydney who were known for committing 'horrid and disgusting'[10] offences – that is, they were homosexuals. Lawrence was quickly found guilty of vagrancy, of being an idle person with no means of support, and was sentenced to six months' imprisonment. On hearing the sentence, he gave a shriek and fainted, although it was later claimed that, as he was taken up from the floor, he was seen to wink at those men nearest him. 'A few minutes later he had divested himself of the borrowed plumage, and stood revealed as a sallow faced and unpleasant looking young man of rather vulgar type.'[11]

The revelation that a sodomite, one of a gang of such men, had been promenading at the Exhibition among the decent citizens of the metropolis was an outrage worthy of heavy reportage in the press. Although the facts of this scandal, Melbourne's second homosexual outrage within little more than six months, were not the same as those of the South Melbourne Conspiracy, and the feminine Lawrence was not the manly type of young man that Irvine was interested in, he must have felt slightly threatened by the attention given to the case by the press. The newspapers of the first week of October would have made particularly uncomfortable reading, reminding Irvine, and perhaps others, of his own brush with scandal earlier in the year.

Irvine busied himself with work and the ever-constant committee responsibilities that took up much of his spare time. In September, he was elected to the committee of the Melbourne Rowing Club.[12] Several weeks later, he was present at the annual cricket match played by staff from the Bank of Australasia against the Bank of Victoria. The match took place at 10am on Friday 23 November on the St Kilda Cricket Ground, practically opposite the Bank of Australasia's St Kilda branch.[13] Irvine was there to watch the Bank of Victoria team win by five wickets and 77 runs.

The *Sportsman*'s cricket correspondent, 'Batsman,' singled out Irvine a week later when reporting on the St Kilda Cricket Club:

> There are few, if any grounds in the colony on which a game can be more thoroughly enjoyed than on that belonging to the St Kildaites. Beautifully situated it is. Being near enough to the sea to enable players to receive the benefit of its breezes, while they do not get the full force of the wind as on many other enclosures. The ground can be reached by either train or tram, though by taking the lastnamed [*sic*] one is enabled, by making a few steps only after alighting, to arrive on the turf. One day last week I had a look at what has been accomplished of late years in the way of improvements, and I was much pleased at what I saw.

'Batsman' was shown around the ground by the curator, Kearney, who assured him that the recent improvements to the ground and its facilities were the work of two men, Arthur Stooke, the Club's secretary, and J.L. Irvine, the Club's treasurer. The improvements included a 'good, substantial fence' around the whole ground, costing £400, and a 'useful and ornamental' fence around the actual playing ground, which cost £100. A new pavilion was planned, and lawn tennis courts had been laid out to the north side of the ground:

> No better courts can be found, and though they get any amount of wear and tear they show no signs of it. They cost about £160. A neat pavilion has been erected for those ladies and gentlemen using them, the buildings being replete with every convenience.[14]

The new year of 1889 saw Irvine's brother-in-law, Harvey Patterson, establish a 7,500 acre thoroughbred stud at Melton, on the flat grasslands to the north-west of Melbourne, Although Harvey was a keen horseman, with a love for racing, his horses 'proved to be disappointing.'[15] For a wealthy man like Harvey, horse breeding was merely a hobby, albeit an expensive one. However, in the heady days of 1889, with Melbourne entering the height of the Boom, he was not the only man with an expensive hobby. The late 1880s were:

> carnival days when the wealthy indulged themselves in luxurious excess. Balls, dinners, theatre parties, and other entertainments followed each other in weekly profusion ... At the fashionable balls, [Melbourne's most sought after bands] swung into the Lancers, Quadrilles, waltzes, polkas, Varsovianas and Schottisches.[16]

Fashionable Melburnians were excellent dancers; they had plenty of practice, because private dances were a weekly event in the ballrooms of Toorak, Brighton and Kew.

One of the most fashionable balls of the 1889 season was given by sister Kate at *Inverleith*, on Thursday 8 November. The new ballroom that Kate and Harvey had built after buying the house two years' earlier was now finished; in order to celebrate the occasion, Kate held a ball for 300 guests. It was reported that the new ballroom:

> Viewed from the outside it is pleasantly suggestive of a church, but inside the ecclesiastical aspect is lost, and a more secular appearance prevails. On Thursday night, when it was well filled with dancing folk, this appearance was also particularly nice.[17]

Supper was served in a large marquee in the grounds, which was 'superbly decorated'[18] with flowers and greenery. The floor was described as 'tantalisingly smooth and suitable for dancing upon,'[19] and the ball was counted a great success. The guests, who included J.L., the hostess' brother, danced until the early hours of the morning.

Other family members missed Kate's ball because they were already in Launceston to attend the wedding of Irvine's brother, Claude, two days earlier. Claude had travelled from *Corona* station, near Broken Hill, to marry Ella Gaunt. Under the heading, 'Fashionable Wedding', Launceston's *Colonist* newspaper reported:

> On Tuesday afternoon [6 November] the crowded condition of the thoroughfares in the vicinity of St John's church gave evidence that a more than commonly interesting event was about to take place. And when the doors of that edifice were thrown open at 3pm every available post of vantage from which a good view of the chancel might be obtained was quickly occupied by those who were anxious to see the wedding, which was that of Miss Ella Gaunt, and Mr Claude Irvine.

The church was prettily decorated with arum lilies, ferns, garlands of roses and white daisies. The bride's dress was described as 'perfect,' while the groom's mother, Jemima, was resplendent in a:

> very handsome trained gown of black merveilleux [a silk or silk/cotton fabric in a twill weave with a lustrous finish], the side panels and tablier being of heliotrope satin veiled in black lace, the sleeves

were slashed with heliotrope puffings, bonnet of black lace with heliotrope marabout feathers drooping over the brim.

Following the ceremony, the wedding guests were entertained at the bride's parents' house in Tamar Street, Launceston, where the 'very numerous, and some of them valuable'[20] wedding gifts were displayed. The young couple returned to the hot, dry, flat plains of outback *Corona*, a very different place to green and cool Launceston.

Back in St Kilda, the remainder of 1889 was taken up for Irvine with the construction of a new Bank of Australasia branch building in Grey Street. Architects Reed, Henderson and Smart were commissioned to design a double-storeyed red brick building with stucco details on a site on the corner of Grey and Jackson Streets, opposite, and further east along Grey Street than, the George Hotel. Irvine would have been able to see the new building, a fashionable example of what was then called the 'Queen Anne' style,[21] as it rose across the street; he must have looked forward to the time when he would be able to move into the eight-roomed residence which was to be provided for the branch manager on the first floor, above the banking chamber. Around the time that the building was ready for occupation early in 1890, the bank raised Irvine's salary by £100.

To celebrate, and perhaps to take a break from the upheaval of the transfer of the branch from the George Hotel to the new building, Irvine booked for an Easter Excursion cruise to Tasmania. Sailing from Melbourne on Thursday 3 April, the Tasmanian Steam Navigation Company's *Pateena* offered a sightseeing itinerary that would take in the east coast of Tasmania, Port Arthur and Hobart, before returning to Melbourne. The entire six-night trip on board 'the magnificent steamship ... fitted throughout with electric light, ... including victualling for the whole trip and sleeping accommodation,'[22] cost £6; expensive, but not prohibitive for a man on £300 per year.

> The *Pateena* tripped anchor, or more properly cast off from her moorings at Port Melbourne at 5 o'clock on Thursday afternoon, and passing the Heads, she encountered the inevitable roll in the 'rip,' whereby a few of her passengers were thrown temporarily into difficulties. But with morning, fortune smiled again, and from that

out [sic] a benignant providence watched over and prospered the humble efforts of every excursionist to enjoy himself.

The steamer's 150 passengers, of whom there were only about a dozen ladies, enjoyed good weather, with sunshine, smooth water 'and placid moonlight nights.'[23]

The first port of call was Maria Island, a former convict outpost off the east coast of Tasmania, which was reached late on Good Friday afternoon. Dinner was served on deck, with the 'bold contour of the mountain, forming as it were the backbone of the island'[24] as the background to the evening meal. Next morning, the excursionists took to the island's small steam tender to travel from the ship to the island:

> Daylight ... brought enchantment. The calm waters of the straits rippled upon a thin sand line, above which were stretches of the freshest and richest greenery. Occasional patches of white buildings gleamed against this background, and behind all rose the mountain, its side covered with a dense forest of gum trees.

The island's inhabitants were busily ridding themselves of the settlement's convict past. Very few vestiges of the convict buildings were left. There was, however, 'a spick and span new hotel, and a row of wooden cottages that remind one dismally of the speculative suburban builder.'[25] The *Pateena*'s passengers spent Easter Saturday morning either walking the island, looking for remnants of the convict past, or exclaiming over the new hotel's full-sized billiard table, elegant drawing room and supply of Cascade Lager. However, by lunch time, they had to be back on the ship, headed for their next stop, Port Arthur.

Port Arthur, four hours' sailing away, was reached late on Saturday afternoon. This was Irvine's birthplace, but it is unlikely that he would remember much of it; he had left in March 1851, just before his fourth birthday, and had not returned since. The excursionists set out to explore the settlement in the late afternoon and into the gathering twilight. They found the church ruined, although it was noted that 'the incumbent is seeking to raise money to rebuild it.' They also toured the Model Prison, which was now privately owned, and shivered at the misery contained within its walls: 'there arose [among the visitors] a consuming desire to wipe out every trace of the convict establishment from what is otherwise so fair a spot.'[26] The visitors left the Model Prison, some clutching souvenirs:

> a piece of plaster from the wall of a punishment cell, a rusty vessel picked up in the purlieus of the kitchen ... a fragment of iron from the peephole in a cell door, a splinter of wood from the worm-eaten pulpit in the prison chapel. The depredators entertained no conscientious scruples as to their right to these mementoes.

Getting all the excursionists back on the boat before dark was not an easy task. 'When locking up time came one or two ladies were still cautiously investigating the mysteries of the solitary confinement cells and enjoying that sensation popularly known as "the creeps" while another straggler was found in the pulpit of the prison chapel conducting a mock auction'!

Dinner was held on deck again, and the passengers swapped stories of their impressions of Port Arthur. Most agreed that it was a cursed place, although some thought that it would be worth reopening it as a prison for Melbourne's wrongdoers. 'But,' suggested another, 'suppose the Tasmanian Government wouldn't allow it?' 'Then annex Tasmania,' was the reply'! The thought that Victoria could annex Tasmania in order to open up a prison settlement brings home the truth that, in 1890, all the Australian colonies were indeed very separate places. 'Annexation' would come in the form of Federation in another decade's time.

The *Pateena* spent Saturday evening in the harbour at Port Arthur. Passengers were entertained by the ship's band, who presented a 'most enjoyable' musical evening in the ship's music room. Several of the passengers were also found to be first-class amateur talent. It can be assumed that Irvine was among this number; but was he this:

> baritone, who could sing ballads in a clear and powerful soprano, trilling and shaking with exquisite and astonishing effect. Under the *nom-de-theatre* of 'Madame Oyster Patti,' [a play on the name of Adelina Patti, an Italian opera diva who was in her mature prime in the 1870s and 1880s] this gentleman contributed greatly

to the amusement of the voyagers, possessing also as he did the gift of producing with his lips a perfect imitation of the banjo, and performing sundry other equally rare and valuable feats.

The weather continued fine the following morning. At 8am, the ship sailed for Hobart, arriving at 3 pm on the afternoon of Easter Sunday. Easter Monday was spent exploring the picturesque Tasmanian capital before the *Pateena* and her passengers sailed for Melbourne that evening, arriving back to the 'roar of the Melbourne streets' early on a 'murky, misty [Wednesday] morning, with a drizzling rain falling.'[27]

The whirlwind voyage of the *Pateena* was an example of Australia's infant tourism industry; by the 1880s, there were enough people with enough leisure time and expendable cash to be able to take trips for pleasure. The very wealthy, with plenty of money and time on their hands, would be able to spend the months necessary for a trip to Britain or Europe or, more rarely, somewhere like Fiji, Ceylon or California. However, for the professional middle classes, a trip to a seaside or country resort like Queenscliff, the Dandenong Ranges, Mount Macedon or Daylesford was as far afield as they were likely to go. A coastal excursion, like that of the *Pateena*, was a form of travel experience gaining in popularity. Interestingly, in the case of the *Pateena*, most of the 150 passengers were male and would have been mainly single, professional men, very much like Irvine himself. For a man of Irvine's interests, the informal male camaraderie of the *Pateena* would have been particularly pleasing, and he obviously enjoyed the whole experience – so much so that he started thinking about taking a longer voyage, perhaps to New Zealand.

Always the 'clubbable' and social type, Irvine found plenty to amuse himself in Melbourne. The bank was doing well in its new premises, he was enjoying the comfort of his new residence in the heart of fashionable St Kilda, and the Cricket Club and St Kilda's seabaths offered both exercise and male society. His well-connected sisters, Kate and Florence, could always be relied upon for diversion; private dances in the ballroom at *Inverleith* would have been a weekly occurrence, and Kate and Harvey Patterson held larger, more formal balls frequently to entertain Melbourne society. As a useful single man, and a more than passable dancer, Irvine was always in demand to make up numbers whenever there threatened to be too many ladies and a shortage of suitable partners. On a mid-winter's Wednesday evening in 1890, Irvine walked down the hill of Jackson Street to *Inverleith* to join 250 guests at another of Kate's balls. The Pattersons went to great efforts decorating the house and gardens:

> The verandahs were closed in, and draped with bunting. The pathway leading from the street to the hall door was covered in canvas, making a graceful shelter from the keen night air. The house decorations were exquisite, fairy lamps most effectively lighting up the drapings of art silks, and the abundant foliage which was tastefully disposed in every available corner.[28]

Kate, wearing black velvet and diamonds, received her guests in the drawing room before they entered the ballroom, where music was supplied by Melbourne's most sought after band, that of Herr Plock. Around midnight, refreshments were served in the supper room attached to the ballroom, and then dancing continued to 2am on Thursday morning. Pity the poor bank manager who had to be at work the next day!

In 1890, it seemed that the Boom would last forever. Melbourne was the largest city in the southern hemisphere, with a population approaching half a million. The suburbs stretched out from the city for up to 10 miles in some directions, and new suburban subdivisions were being surveyed and sold speculatively every week. The shops and emporia of the city were filled with merchandise and desirable goods from all over the world, and the city's workforce travelled from their suburban homes to work in city offices, shops and factories in modern trains and trams. Most of the population, no matter their income or class, had access to entertainment supplied by theatres, sporting matches, numerous parks, seaside resort suburbs and the nearby cool mountains. Public institutions, such as the Public Library, the National Art Gallery and Museum, the University, Working Man's College and Trades Hall, were well funded and well used by the public. All in all, Melbourne was an up-to-date city, offering almost all the conveniences of modern life – including trams, suburban railways, piped water and a gas supply for both street lighting and domestic use – although an underground sewerage system was still almost ten years away. Life was prosperous, comfortable and secure and seemed set to remain so.

In the first half of 1891, the first small signs that something was not right with the world appeared. Investment in new industrial, pastoral and mining ventures, particularly by British investors, fell slightly. The speculative building industry suffered a small slump, laying off building workers. Unemployment rose, and the public's financial confidence waivered. Rumours that banks had made unwise loans to speculators began to circulate; depositors, with their life savings in banks, began to get nervous.

Nineteenth-century banking was based on gold coin and bullion: 'every bank had to keep sufficient gold in its safe and vaults to pay, without prior notice, any customer who wished to withdraw a deposit or to cash a banknote.'[29] Paper money was not legal tender; it was merely a promise by the bank to pay the value of the note in gold. If too many nervous depositors descended on a bank at the same time, demanding their money in gold, banks ran the risk of not being able to meet their obligations. Such 'runs' had happened before, but usually the banks had been able to meet the demands, their calmness in the face of the depositors' panic had reassured the public, and things did not get out of hand.

In August 1891, the depositors of the Bank of Van Diemen's Land, established in the 1830s, became nervous and rushed the banks' branches throughout Tasmania. The bank failed; 'for the first time since the 1840s a large bank was rushed by panicking depositors and was bled to death.'[30]

Although this was concerning, the failure of the Bank of VDL was seen as an oddity, an isolated incident, of note mainly in Tasmania. Whether any of the Irvines had money invested in the bank is not known; given J.L.'s position in the Bank of Australasia, however, most of the extended family's accounts were probably held by that bank, which was known for its sensible business practices.

Representing St Kilda's banking institutions, Irvine attended a men-only dinner in honour of ex-Councillor John Barker at the Esplanade Hotel, St Kilda, on the evening of Tuesday 27 October. Barker, who had been a member of the St Kilda Town Council in the 1880s, had recently returned from 'adventurous travels'[31] in South Africa and was staying for a few weeks at the Esplanade Hotel. As a former Bank of Australasia man, he was possibly a friend of Irvine's; the two would certainly have mixed in the same St Kilda circles. Barker entertained several of St Kilda's leading lights at dinner, including the Mayor, five former mayors, the city Health Officer, a couple of Councillors, the manager of the Commercial Bank and the manager of the Bank of Australasia, 'Mr J.L. Irvine.' Fourteen men sat down to a 'merry gathering' in a private dining room of the seafront hotel: 'the *menu* was of the choicest, and its virtues were tested to the accompaniment of a display of wit and good-humoured banter, making the evening most harmonious and enjoyable.'[32] Several toasts were proposed, with Irvine responding to 'Our Financial Institutions.'

Around this time, another of Irvine's many interests becomes apparent: collecting paintings. In November 1891, Irvine lent three 'fine paintings of exceptional merit'[33] to the Tasmanian Exhibition's art show in Launceston. The Tasmanian Exhibition was the brainchild of Launceston Mayor Samuel Sutton and was launched as a 'trade fair, cultural exhibition and expression of community achievement.'[34] It opened on 25 November and ran for four months. Visitors were able to wonder at over 1,300 exhibits from all the Australian colonies, Britain, France, Germany, Austria-Hungary, Italy, Switzerland and the United States, displayed in the purpose-built Albert Hall and temporary annexes in Launceston's City Gardens. Irvine's brother Dick was a member of the organising committee, so it is not surprising that family members were approached to provide exhibits for the show.

Jemima exhibited several collections of specimens in the Exhibition, including a 'magnificent exhibit of shells and seaweeds,'[35] as well as a lap dog and blue bonnet parrot in the associated poultry and dog show.[36] So well received were the shells and seaweeds that Jemima entertained ideas of taking them to the World's Columbian Exposition, to be held in Chicago in 1893. She does not appear to have pursued this idea.

Two of the three paintings that Irvine exhibited in Launceston, *Sunset on the Buffalo Ranges* and *Mount Feathertop*, were the work of landscape artist Charles Rolando, a neighbour in Jackson Street, St Kilda. The third, *In the Shades* (Gippsland, Victoria), was the work of William Curtis, 'presumably a pupil of [Rolando].' *Sunset on the Buffalo Ranges* was awarded a first prize at the Exhibition, while the other two works received second awards. Following the conclusion of the Exhibition, in May 1892, Irvine lent all three works to the newly founded Victoria Museum and Art Gallery in Launceston.[37] Of the three paintings, only *Sunset in the Buffalo Ranges* seems to have survived.

In April 1892, shortly before the Launceston Exhibition closed, a second bank failed. The Bank of South Australia experienced a run on its accounts, fuelled by rumours of financial mismanagement. Two months later, a smaller Victorian bank, The New Oriental, closed its doors. Deposits were not guaranteed, and those who had their savings deposited in the banks were likely to lose everything. No wonder depositors were nervous.

The worsening economic situation led the Melbourne City Council to establish a relief fund for the unemployed and destitute. With no central system of social security, assistance to the unemployed, the elderly and the disabled was in the hands of the churches and benevolent charities – and occasionally, when things got really bad, *ad hoc* funds set up by local councils. The committee of the city's Central Relief Fund noticed in August 1892 that subscriptions to the Fund had dropped off somewhat, perhaps because of the public's belief that the Fund had plenty of money; that '£5,000 from the Floods Relief Fund had been hung up in some way.'[38] It might also be that the citizens of Melbourne were suffering from what might now be called 'charity fatigue', or that the numbers of people able to spare money to donate to the appeal had been reduced by their own financial hardships. In any case, J.L. donated 10/- to the Fund from his own resources.

Ten shillings would not go far towards offering relief on the scale that would soon become necessary as the financial crises deepened into a depression. By Christmas 1892, another small bank, the Federal, shut down. So far, the failed banks had been local, not operating throughout the continent and not in the top dozen of the colonies' banks. They had usually been considered a bad risk. To this point, all the big banks were safe, and many in the business world were optimistic that things would bounce back in the new year of 1893.

One of the most optimistic was Irvine. At Christmas 1892, after nearly 10 years with the Bank of Australasia and nearly 30 in the banking profession, he tendered his resignation to the bank. His plan was to strike out on his own as a legal and general manager for small gold mining companies. Recent gold finds in Western Australia had fuelled a modern gold rush, while small fields in the north-east of Victoria, around Beechworth, Bright and the Mitta Mitta River, continued to offer hope of decent finds. Someone had to act as manager on behalf of the proprietors of these small firms, and Irvine figured that he had the knowledge, ability and financial acumen to do so.

Tourists on board the *Taraweera* in Hall Arm, Doubtful Sound, New Zealand, c. 1893.

His resignation was due to take effect on 25 March 1893, after three months' notice. In the meantime, he planned to take some time off and take another cruise, this time to New Zealand. The Union Line of Steamers advertised that their ship *Tarawera* would sail from Melbourne on Wednesday 4 January to Dunedin, calling at the west coast sounds of New Zealand on the way. Special rates to New Zealand were available, because the ship was heading to Dunedin in order to take a series of excursions to the sounds from 18 January. The trip promised to be more than an ordinary sea voyage, offering as it did the opportunity to cruise the calm waters of the New Zealand fiords.

Leaving Melbourne on the afternoon of 4 January,[39] with 264 passengers,[40] the *Tarawera* passed Wilson's Promontory at 1:30am on 5 January and entered Milford Sound at 7:20am on Sunday 8 January. Two days were spent exploring the beauties of both Milford and George Sounds, before the ship moved on to Dunedin, docking there in Port Chalmers on the morning of Wednesday 11 January.[41]

Irvine spent a week in the beautiful, hilly city of Dunedin before sailing for Auckland on the *Wairarapa*, arriving there on 20 January. Another week was spent there before sailing for Sydney on the *Tekapo* on 28 January. One wonders whether Irvine spent time in Auckland visiting sites and people who knew his grandfather, David Burn, who had died there in 1875.

Arriving in Sydney on Thursday 3 February, Irvine spent a few days revisiting former haunts and acquaintances before taking the train back to Melbourne. He had been gone just over five weeks. He returned refreshed, ready to wind up his affairs at the bank, pack his furniture and belongings and vacate the manager's residence in Grey Street. Time was running short, so he did not travel to Launceston to attend the wedding of his youngest sister, Nellie, which was to take place on 1 March.

He was no doubt sent clippings from the Launceston papers which reported Nellie's wedding to Harry Hawley, 'son of Mr William Hawley, of Surrey, England' at Holy Trinity Anglican Church:

> The body of the church as well as the galleries were crowded with spectators, the event evidently exciting unusual interest. The building was tastefully and elaborately decorated for the occasion, the chief ornament being a bell hung over the steps leading to the altar, composed of white marguerite daisies and China asters.[42]

Among the family members who attended were Dick and Frances Irvine, Claude Irvine, Nellie's mother Jemima, and sisters Kate Patterson and Jemima Adams.

After the ceremony, the guests were entertained at Dick Irvine's home, *Lebrina*, in Patterson Street. Dick and Frances received the guests 'in the drawing room. Refreshments were served in the adjoining apartment, and the health of the bride and bridegroom was drunk in bumpers of champagne. The Italian band played on the lawn throughout the afternoon.'[43] Nellie and Harry left the party later in the afternoon by private steam yacht from the landing at the bottom of the garden: 'The happy couple were rowed to the vessel in one of the Marine Board's boats, manned by a crew of the guests, who were attired in yachting costume.'

In true nineteenth-century style, the dresses of the guests and the wedding gifts were described in detail in the press reports. Among the 'numerous and valuable' presents were silver egg cruets, Japanese fans, drawn linen pillow shams, bread forks, butter dishes, marmalade jars, sets of fish knives and forks, table linen, dish covers and everything else thought necessary (or not) in order to establish a well set up home. Cheques were also a featured wedding gift, including one from the bride's brother, 'Mrs [sic] J.L. Irvine.'[44]

Nellie was now 32, four years older than her new husband; she had been living with her mother Jemima all her life and, since growing up, had acted as her mother's companion and private secretary. This arrangement would change with her marriage. Because Nellie and Harry were moving to a property at Kingston, on the east coast of Tasmania, it was agreed that Jemima would now live with Dick and Frances at *Lebrina*. Although nearly 70, she was not expecting to settle into a quiet retirement; she was planning several extended plant collecting expeditions to Broken Hill and to Western Australia.

Back in Melbourne, Irvine was preparing to leave the Bank of Australasia, set up his office and find new living quarters. Giving up the manager's residence above the branch in Grey Street meant that he needed to either rent or buy a house – or to find some other alternative. In the end, he decided that boarding house life would suit him best: to take a suite of rooms, perhaps, and not to worry about employing staff to do the shopping, cooking, laundry or cleaning. The fashionable suburbs of Melbourne were full of roomy, comfortable boarding houses offering accommodation to professional men. There were plenty in St Kilda; but was it time, perhaps, to look for something nearer to the city and more convenient for work? East Melbourne, where he had once lived, looked very inviting. Where he lived for the first part of the 1890s is unclear; in the latter part of the decade, his address was *Talbot Lodge* on the corner of Grey and Powlett Streets in East Melbourne, just a block from the Fitzroy Gardens and a half-hour walk to the financial district of Collins Street. *Talbot Lodge* was a large, double-storey house, surrounded by wide verandahs and large grounds. It offered 'Pleasant Quarters for gentlemen; terms moderate.'[45]

Renting office accommodation in the city was another task that had to be undertaken; he settled on a space in the Mercantile Bank Chambers at 349 Collins Street. By the time he left the bank on 25 March, he was ready to take on his new role as legal and general manager, accountant and financial and commission agent, essentially offering legal, financial and administrative services to companies who were too small to employ full-time office staff.

No sooner had he set up business and moved into his freshly painted Collins Street office, than the Melbourne economy started to free-fall:

> Just before the Easter of 1893, people passing the head office of the [Commercial] bank in Collins Street began to notice that business seemed very brisk: people were entering and leaving in surprisingly large numbers. Customers of the bank, knowing that their own savings would be endangered if the bank ran out of gold, joined the queues at the great counters of polished wood. By withdrawing their deposits in gold they did not realize that they hastened the event which they feared – the closing of the bank.

Rumours spread that the bank was about to close, and those rumours begat more panic, then more rumours. On 5 April 1893, the worst happened: the Commercial Bank closed its doors.

If one large bank could fail, people asked, how safe were the others?

The streets and hotels and clubs and vestries were full of rumours. The new telephone wires that now linked the larger business houses within the city sagged under the weight of the gloomy news, gossip and rumours they carried.[46] Rumours were published in the newspapers, both in Melbourne and throughout the colony, spreading the disquiet. Depositors besieged their local branches, seeking their money, and suburban and country banks began begging their head offices in Melbourne for more gold so as to be able to honour depositors' demands. Some banks simply ran out of gold.

During April 1893, five banks closed. At the end of the month, the Victorian Government declared a five-day bank holiday, asking all banks to shut in order to put a stop to the runs on branches. 'The proclamation advertised to the world that Victoria was in a state of crisis: it did nothing specific to ease the crisis.' Only the Union and Australasia stayed open; they both had

INSIDE THE UNION BANK.
SCENES IN COLLINS-STREET ON BANK MONDAY.

April 1893: a run on the Union Bank's Collins Street head office.

the reputation of having been well managed and cautious during the giddy heights of the boom. It was said that, at the beginning of 1893, Australia had 22 banks that issued banknotes; by the end of autumn, over half had closed:

> In Victoria and in Queensland two thirds of all deposits were locked up in ... closed banks. In New South Wales more than half of all deposits were locked inside those banks which had closed. In Australia as a whole every second customer was debarred from a bank.

It was not the best time to start a new financial business. Appropriately, the first advertisement that Irvine placed for his new enterprise was to inform the public that he had been appointed trustee for William Frederick Dixon, of Hawthorn, who had been declared bankrupt:

> I, the undersigned, John Lempriere Irvine, of 349 Collins-street, Melbourne aforesaid, accountant, was APPOINTED to fill the office of TRUSTEE of the Estate of the said insolvent and such appointment has been duly confirmed. All persons having in their possession any of the effects of the said insolvent must deliver them to me, and all DEBTS due to the insolvent must be PAID to me. Creditors who have not proved their debts must forward their proofs to me, 349 Collins-street, Melbourne aforesaid. Dated this 11th day of May, 1893. JOHN L. IRVINE Trustee.[47]

Dixon was an early victim of a 'throbbing nervousness [which] hung over the country' by mid-1893:

> [T]housands of business transactions were postponed. Debts which fell due in the normal course of business could not be paid. People who had borrowed money from banks could not be sure when their loan might be recalled: they only knew that if it were recalled too soon they themselves would be ruined. The market in shares and real estate was groggy, and a buyer with ready cash could buy shares and land at bargain prices. But, all values being chaotic, what was a bargain price? Some investors who bought shares at bargain prices found later that the shares were worthless.[48]

Irvine made a quick trip back to Launceston in late May, sailing back to Melbourne on the *Pateena* on 29 May[49] and then got stuck back into the business of increasing his list of clients and putting his new business on a solid footing. Despite the poor financial outlook, business grew at a steady pace. In October, he advertised that he wanted to buy deposits in the failed Colonial, National and Commercial banks. Offering to buy deposits in failed or locked up banks at a knock-down price from customers who needed ready cash was a legitimate business venture in the nineteenth century. The purchaser of the deposits would then hope that the deposits would be returned to them at full, or nearly full, value.[50] The following month, he acted on behalf of a 'Gentleman, with capital, [who] is desirous of Purchasing PARTNERSHIP in established business'[51] and offered to lend money on freehold suburban and country land.[52]

A mention of his glory days on the river appeared in the press in October 1893. He was remembered in an article in the *Melbourne Punch* as a member of the first Intercolonial eight crew, 15 years previously: 'where did you ever see as fine an eight as those men since? I tell you they were the finest crew and had the finest stroke that ever rowed together in the colony.'[53] Such reminders in the papers of his former fame were useful in keeping his name before the public, developing his business networks and promoting his business.

In March 1894, he advertised for an experienced miner to join a party to prospect 'a splendid mine'[54] Mining was becoming more and more his staple business. Over the years from 1894 to 1897, his list of mining clients grew to include companies with names like the Black Lead Gold Mining Company of Talbot, Victoria; the Emily GMC of Coolgardie, Western Australia; the Barfold GMC; the Morning Star GMC; the Glen Patrick Eversley GMC; and the Buffalo Hydraulic Gold Mining Company in the Victorian high country. Other clients included such diverse concerns as the Queenscliff Gas and Coke Company, which would hold its annual general meetings at Irvine's offices.

He joined an early, although short-lived, professional association, the Australian Institute of Legal Managers, in October 1894. The Institute had been formed in April 1894 with the aim of professionally accrediting legal managers:

> in order that companies might only be managed by duly qualified men, the diploma of membership being a guarantee of capacity, fitness and respectability; to regulate all matters in connection with legal management, to adopt rules for the guidance of mining companies, and to bring about the Amendment of the Companies Act 1890 by which only members of this institute shall be eligible for legal management.[55]

Hydraulic mining in the Mitta Mitta, 1890s.

Although starting off with high ambitions and plenty of enthusiasm, holding monthly meetings and accrediting managers as far afield as Western Australia, the Institute seems to have petered out in 1895.

The hot summer of 1894 saw Melbourne ringed by grassfires, one of which threatened Harvey Patterson's horse stud at Melton Park. Harvey was absent in Western Australia when the fire broke out in late November. Irvine, who was staying at the estate at the time, led the firefighting efforts. In a letter of thanks to the many locals who turned out to help fight the fire, published in the *Bacchus Marsh Express* several days later, Irvine 'beg[ged] to tender hearty thanks to all those persons who so kindly rendered much valuable assistance in subduing the fire.' Although 'a large portion' of the estate had been burned, the house and stud buildings were saved; 'had not [the help of the neighbours] been so willingly given, the effects of the fire must have been most disastrous to the property. Again, thanking you, one and all, in Mr Patterson's name and my own, I remain, your obliged servant J.L. Irvine'[56]

Shortly before the Melton Park fire, Irvine had moved his office to the Empire Buildings at 418 Collins Street. The Empire was a six-storeyed neo-Gothic building, located between William Street and Queen Street in the heart of the city's financial district. Built in 1889 at the height of the boom, the Empire boasted 'an elegant façade of freestone with numerous embellishments giv[ing] the passer by the idea that he is viewing the exterior of a huge bride's cake – with promise of good things within.' Those entering the building's foyer from Collins Street were impressed with a red and white marble staircase costing £2,500, leading to the upper floors, which were also serviced by 'luxuriously furnished and beautifully carved lifts.'[57] Each office was provided with burglar and fireproof saves. When opened, the building featured a basement café, 'The Arches,' which took its name from the arched undercroft of the building and was described as completely Parisian in style. In 1884, however, by the time Irvine moved in, rent would have been cheap because of the deepening depression:

> the heart of the city was ... almost as quiet as a cemetery. New skyscrapers stood like tall stucco headstones, and many headstones were blank. Some of the tall offices became boarding houses, and the new lodgers walked along the uncarpeted corridors, their footsteps echoing, to rooms which were furnished frugally and lit dimly. The owners of other skyscrapers let out the upper floors as residential rooms and the lower floors as offices, but even the cheap rents did not attract businessmen.[58]

Most of Irvine's business was done from the comfort of Collins Street, but in the winter of 1895 he travelled to Bright, in the Victorian high country, to visit a mining claim that one of his largest clients, The Buffalo Hydraulic Gold Mining Company, was setting up. Hydraulic mining consisted of blasting huge torrents of highly pressurised water at hillsides in order to wash out potentially gold-bearing soil, which was then washed in sluice boxes to reveal any nuggets left behind. Hydraulic mining was an expensive exercise, requiring significant investment in heavy machinery. It was also an environmental disaster, leaving whole hillsides denuded of vegetation and topsoil. A good example of the damage done can be viewed at the Pink Cliffs at Heathcote, Victoria; even after 120 years, the land has not recovered.

In the 1890s, Bright was an isolated, although thriving, gold town, the service centre for an extensive area of gold mining claims scattered through the rugged Victorian Alps. Reaching it from Melbourne required catching a train as far as Wangaratta and then changing to a branch line along the Ovens

Valley, which had been opened as far as Bright in October 1890. That such a trip was deemed necessary shows the importance of the Buffalo operation, set up on the banks of the Buckland River. The company was floated in August 1895, and a mining lease was granted in September.[59] Tenders were called on 19 October for 2,500 feet of wrought iron pipes and fittings for hydraulic sluicing.[60] In December, the company registered further claims for a dam, reservoir, bank sluicing claim and tail race.[61]

The Buffalo Hydraulic was officially opened with a banquet held at the mine, at Brookside, on the Buckland River, on Saturday 4 April 1896. 'Among the guests were the principal business and mining men of the district and a large gathering of the general public to the number of several hundred.' The day's activities were to include the ceremonial switching on of the giant hoses at midday, but many of the guests and other attendees were still arriving at the site at that time, so the ceremony was delayed to later in the afternoon. A large group toured the mine, water races and equipment and had the 'mysteries of the elevator, giant nozzle, cocoa matting, iron nipple, pressure per inch on the head pipes, and other items of useful information' explained to them. The tour was followed by a half-hour demonstration of the hoses and sluices in action. An outdoor lunch was served, which included 'the pleasing innovation of the ladies present being accommodated at the tables.' Mining lunches and other business functions were usually men-only affairs in the nineteenth century, and it is unlikely that many of the men present would have been overly confident in dealing with female guests at what would usually be a male preserve.

Following lunch, and a long list of speeches, toasts were made (including 'The Ladies'). Irvine's health was toasted, the chairman of the Company, A.A. McRae, stating:

> that the company were under many obligations to their manager. He was always ready to assist, and never spared himself in any way when he could do anything for the advantage of the company ... Mr Irvine in response said it was very gratifying to have his name mentioned and honoured in such an enthusiastic manner. At first he had his doubts about the working of the ground by hydraulic elevators, but that it could be had been proved ... The success of their claim should be of great benefit to the Bright district, for it will open

Queen Street skyscrapers: Prell's Building in the foreground and Norwich Union Chambers further down the street. Norwich Union Chambers became Irvine's office in 1897.

out vast fields of auriferous deposit, which by ordinary methods would not be payable. (Applause.)[62]

At the end of the proceedings, James Bray, photographer of Beechworth, took several photographs of the party assembled at the mine. Unfortunately, these do not appear to have survived.

Despite the high hopes of April, Irvine was back in Bright in June, only two months later, to consult with the Buffalo's manager regarding the working of the mine. The winter of 1896 was an unusually dry season, and the shortage of water was causing problems operating the giant sluicing hose and the wash boxes. The dryness of the season was a foretaste of what would come to be known as the Federation Drought, a run of dry years which would last from 1896 to 1903. The drought is considered to have been Australia's worst drought since European settlement, ruining farmers from Queensland to South Australia. It ended 'squatter-dominated pastoralism in [the eastern colonies], as bank foreclosures and the resumption of leases led to the partition of large stations for more intensive settlement and agricultural use.'[63] Irvine's brother-in-law Harvey Patterson was sufficiently wealthy and diversified in his investments into other industries, including mining, to manage to ride out both the depression and the drought. He continued to employ Irvine's brother Claude as a station manager throughout the 1890s.

While in Bright, Irvine also attended the Bright Mining Warden's Court to defend an application for a mining lease which he and the mining manager of the Mt Buffalo Hydraulic had lodged. Irvine and Davidson had applied for a lease on 50 acres, which they later reduced to 30, but another miner, Bell, had pegged out and registered a portion of their ground. The Warden found in favour of Bell, and Irvine and Davidson agreed to the excision of Bell's small claim to their lease, provided that they were allowed an access easement across it.[64]

Travelling back to Melbourne in order to interview a mining manager for the newly-established Glen Patrick Eversley Gold Mining Company, based near Elmhurst in the Grampians, west of Melbourne,[65] Irvine took the opportunity to attend the Melbourne vs North Melbourne football match at the Melbourne Cricket Ground on Saturday 18 July. The match was played in misting rain, on a 'greasy' field in front of a thin crowd of unenthusiastic observers who were more intent on discussing the latest news of the test cricket being played in Manchester than watching what was described as a match that was 'as dull as one could see for the greater part of the game' [Melbourne won 12-8 to 5-6]. A miserable day was made worse when Irvine had a gold scarf pin stolen by a pickpocket in the crowd. It was never recovered.[66]

August saw him once again in the Victorian Alps; his trips always seemed to happen in the middle of winter, battling low temperatures, rain and occasional snow, riding through inclement conditions to remote mining settlements or bumping along in coaches over roads so rough as to be almost non-existent in places. He visited several sites, including the Grasshopper Mine at Sandy Creek, near Kiewa, the site of a minor rush in 1854 but since mostly abandoned apart from fossickers.⁶⁷ While at Sandy Creek, he was given a number of samples of 'granitic rock, very highly mineralised, and showing gold freely.' He brought these to Melbourne, arriving back in late August and making them available for display to potential investors at his office. The *Argus* considered the specimens 'well worthy of inspection.'⁶⁸

January 1897 was spent on a summer holiday in Launceston. He arrived back in Melbourne on board the *Coogee* on 8 February before getting back to the business of annual meetings of the Buffalo, the Glen Patrick Eversley and the newly formed Barfold GMC. Another trip to Launceston, on board the *Pateena*⁶⁹ in mid-April, saw him at Dick's home at *Lebrina* for belated 50th birthday celebrations before heading back to Melbourne, where the Empire Buildings were up for sale. Because it was uncertain whether current leases would be continued by a new owner, Irvine decided to move offices once again, this time to Norwich Union Chambers at 34 Queen Street.

Norwich Union Chambers was one of three nearly identical nine or 10-storey skyscrapers built in 1888 for F.W. Prell. Designed by architect F.W. White and built by David Mitchell (father of Melbourne's famous diva, Dame Nellie Melba), it stood on the south-eastern corner of Queen Street and Flinders Lane. The other two Prell buildings were Broken Hill Chambers (where Harvey Patterson had his offices) on the south-western corner of Queen Street and Flinders Lane and Prell's Buildings at 54–70 Queen Street, on the south-eastern corner of Queen and Collins Streets. The Norwich Union stood nine storeys above Queen Street and offered 140 offices, serviced by three lifts 'guaranteed to run at the rate of 500ft per minute, which is considerably above the speed of those now in use.'⁷⁰

The pace of business increased through the winter and spring of 1897. New clients signing up included the Southern Leads Gold Mining Company of Rutherglen, and every busy working day was filled with the business of financial administration, coordinating tenders and interviewing prospective staff. Irvine's life was good; business was booming, despite the depression and the drought. His home life at the supremely comfortable *Talbot Lodge* was calm and peaceful, and no doubt his evening walk home through the darkened Fitzroy Gardens offered some interesting diversions.

However, as the end of September 1897 approached, everything was about to go wrong.

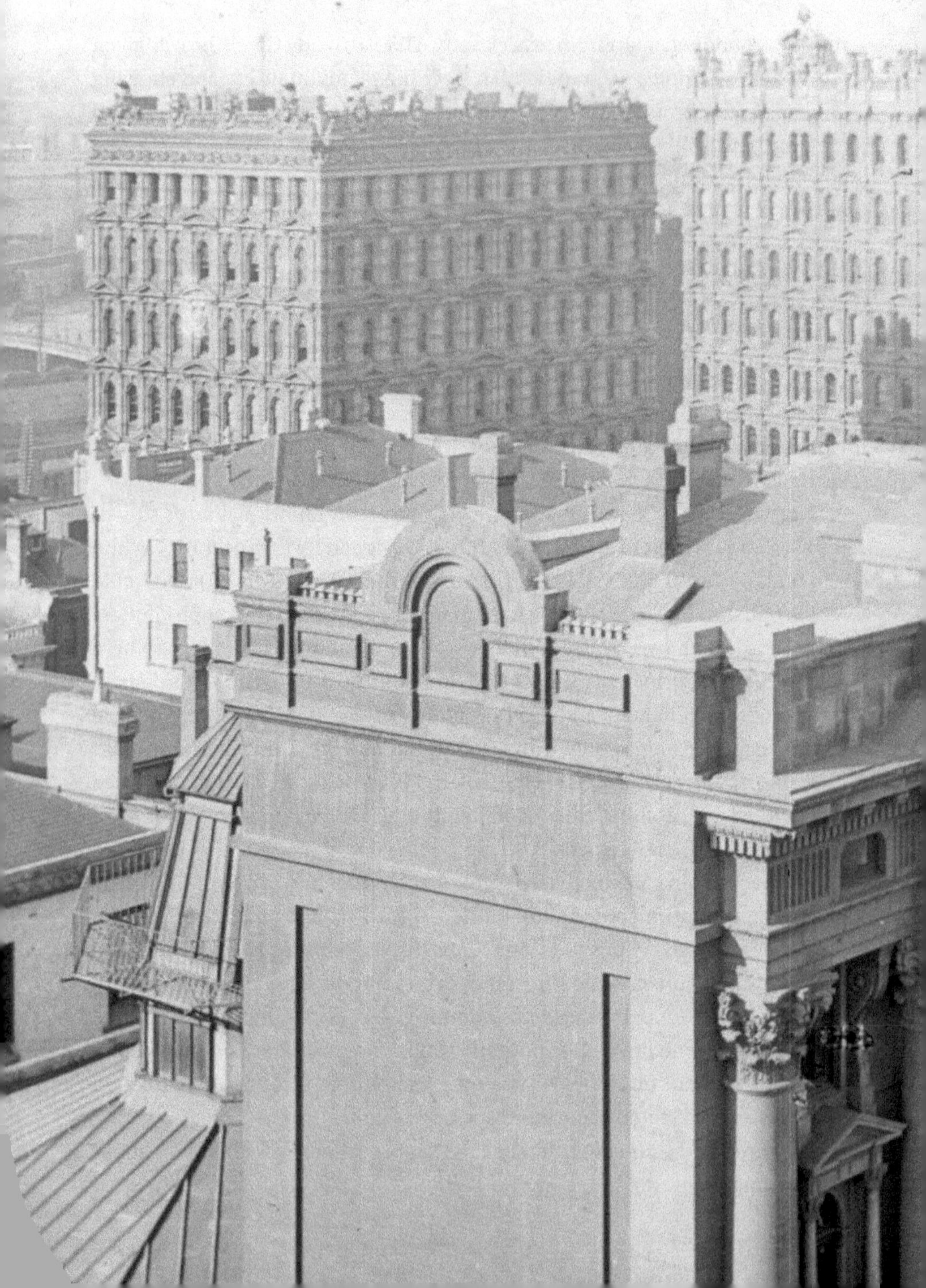

The commercial heart of Melbourne in the late 1880s. Looking southwest from Collins Street one can see the Norwich Union Chambers on the left, then Broken Hill Chambers, and then the rear of Prell's Building; three great skyscrapers built in the last years of Melbourne's great Boom of the 1880s. These new buildings of the late 1880s dwarf the Union Bank's building (with the two arched towers in the right hand bottom corner) which was one of the tallest buildings in Collins Street when built just ten years earlier.

CHAPTER 10
'An Unfortunate Gentleman'

This is where we came in: the evening of Monday 27 September 1897. Irvine had gone to Carlton for some reason. It was not in his usual orbit; home was in East Melbourne, and work was in lower Queen Street in the city. Carlton was a good 40-minute walk from home and half-an-hour from the Norwich Union Buildings. What was he doing there? Was he catching up with friends, or doing some business? Was he out for an innocent evening stroll, or had he gone there with another, less pure, aim in mind?

In any case, by 8:30pm, he was walking along Grattan Street opposite the main gates of the university when he saw Ernest Smith and his mate standing outside the Bowling Club. Approaching the two, Irvine apparently looked squarely at Smith and asked, 'Hallo, are you working?'

From that point, everything unravelled. Smith's mate walked off; Irvine made his 'improper proposal' and offer of three shillings; Smith knocked him back and walked off; Irvine followed him, caught him and groped Smith's crotch. Smith broke away and ran off to find the nearest policeman, on the beat in Leicester Street. Irvine was apprehended, charged, and spent the night in the Carlton watchhouse.

We saw in Chapter 1 that, when the case came to court on Thursday 7 October, the Carlton magistrates were not particularly impressed by Smith, with his criminal record for perjury and his far-fetched stories of being accosted by lads who threatened to kill him if he said anything about Irvine. They quickly came to the conclusion that the working class Smith was an unreliable witness, out to besmirch the reputation of a respectable member of the establishment. The case was dismissed, and, had it not been reported in the press, that would have been an end to it.

The story made a short item in the *Age* on the morning of Friday 8 October, noting that the 'bench dismissed the case without calling for a defence.'[1] It was also reported briefly by the *Ballarat Star* under the headline 'A False Charge.'[2] Nothing noteworthy there. However, the story was also reported by the *Bendigo Independent*, which published the details of the case in greater detail that same morning. After including Smith's wild stories of being threatened, the *Independent* concluded its article with the bald statement: 'The bench without any comment dismissed the complaint.'[3] So far, so good. But the *Independent* chose to run the story under the banner headline 'An Unfortunate Gentleman: Twice Arrested on Shameful Allegations' and above another article, entitled 'A Previous Experience,' which detailed Irvine's brush with the South Melbourne Conspirators back in 1888. The second article, which referred to Irvine as a 'well known rowing man', outlined the South Melbourne case in some detail: Irvine's bashing and the theft of his watch and money, the accusations by the South Melbourne gang that Irvine had attempted 'an abominable crime on one of the party,'[4] the subsequent magistrate's hearing, Irvine's acquittal, and the gang's eventual convictions for the robberies of Irvine, Tinkler and McRae.

By the afternoon of the same day, the *Independent*'s dual stories were picked up by the Melbourne evening paper, the *Herald*, which published the two stories under the headlines 'Was He 'Insulting'?: The Bench Say No: Disgusting Statements: Not Sustained' and 'A Previous Experience.'[5] The similarities of the two cases outlined by the *Independent* and the *Herald*, and their relatively sensational headlines, raised the eyebrows of readers and, no doubt, gave rise to much innuendo and gossip on the streets, pubs and offices of Melbourne. As the old saying goes, 'mud sticks.'

But why did the *Bendigo Independent* publish the two stories together? Who would remember the nine-year-old case of the South Melbourne Conspiracy? By this stage, it was long dead and forgotten, and the conspirators had been released several years previously, long before their 20-year gaol terms were due to expire. It was old news. Who cared to bring it up?

It is interesting that the newspaper which put together the two cases involving allegations of indecency against Irvine was a Bendigo newspaper. It has to be recalled that, when Irvine lived in the central Victorian city in the early 1880s, he had ruffled a few feathers and made a few enemies. Remember those letters to the *Bendigo Advertiser* back in 1883, when the Bendigo Rowing Club accused him of being bombastic and of being the cause of discord between the Bendigo and the Sandhurst Rowing Clubs? Remember the embarrassing fall-out from the Electric Light Festival of October 1882, when he was accused of defrauding the public and of alienating public land by fencing off Lake Weeroona and charging access to the public? Remember, too, the accusations that he had taken the glory which rightfully belonged to other men for training crews. Clearly, Irvine had made enemies in Bendigo, enemies with long memories who took the opportunity to cause trouble by digging up the past scandal of the South Melbourne Conspiracy and making sure that the newspaper-reading public could put two and two together to come up with some quite juicy, and damaging, gossip.

The publication of the juxtaposed articles in the *Bendigo Independent* and, more damagingly, in the Melbourne *Herald*, dealt Irvine's reputation a fatal blow. Although both the 1888 case and this recent one had been dismissed, and he had never been charged in either case, the fact that he had now twice been accused of behaviour which, in nineteenth-century eyes, was of the very worst type exacted a heavy price. In the week following Irvine's appearance at the Carlton Court House, his very successful business crashed. His entire client list distanced themselves from him, taking their business away and publicly recording in the pages of Melbourne's leading morning newspapers that they wanted nothing to do with him. The advertisement that the Buffalo Hydraulic placed in the *Age* was representative:

> The Buffalo Hydraulic Sluicing Company No Liability, Brookside, near Porepunkah – Notice is hereby given that the registered office of the above company is situate [*sic*] at Broken Hill-chambers, 31 Queen-street, Melbourne, and that Mr James Prince Cameron has been appointed Legal Manager, vice Mr John L. Irvine, resigned.
>
> A.A. McCrea and William Bruce (Directors), J. Prince Cameron, Manager
>
> Melbourne, 7th October 1897.[6]

The business that Irvine had developed so successfully, against the backdrop of the worst economic depression to hit the Australian colonies, vanished within seven days. He was the subject of gossip and rumour. Rooms would have fallen silent when he entered them, and he would have been ostracised at *Talbot Lodge* and avoided in Queen and Collins Streets.

The question is, did he really do it? Did he really make advances to Reardon in 1888 and Smith in 1897? One of the difficulties of using court records as historical evidence is that everyone is trying to make themselves look as innocent as possible. Witness statements are, at best, a polished version of the truth, and at worst, outright lies.

While it is an obvious truth that the South Melbourne Conspirators were a gang of thieves and blackmailers, they did know how to pick their targets. They were able to recognise men who would not report them to the police; men who perhaps felt guilty enough about their own proclivities and characters to be uncomfortable reporting that they had (perhaps falsely) been accused of behaving indecently. The only reason that Irvine's case came to public attention was that they were effectively caught in the act by the police; if the police had not been involved, maybe Irvine would have just taken the beating, then limped home, bathed his wounds and tried to forget the whole thing.

The fact that Ernest Smith willingly went to the police and accused Irvine of making an improper advance to him is interesting. Smith already had a criminal record; he was no friend of the police and would have been wary of them. He had nothing to gain by reporting Irvine to the police. He was not trying to blackmail Irvine or gain any other kind of advantage. What reason did he have to lie about Irvine's actions? Why would he go to the police with false allegations of having been propositioned, groped and assaulted? He would have known that no one would believe him, a working class lad with a shady past, if he did go to the police with a made-up story. As it turns out, when he got to court, no one did believe him; his wild stories of standover tactics, death threats and the mysterious piece of paper he was forced to sign soon convinced the magistrates that he was a fantasist. But were his wild claims perhaps the desperate attempt of a scared, uneducated youth to hold the attention of a group of men who were completely disinclined to give him any kind of a fair hearing right from the start? If that is the case, and if we leave aside the wild stories Smith told in court, did he tell the truth to the policeman on the night of 27 September? On balance, I think that he did.

If we accept that Smith was telling the truth – that Irvine did proposition him, chase him and grope him – the calm way in which Irvine made the first approach speaks of a man who was confident in making sexual contacts on the street. 'Hallo, are you working?' was a question long asked by men seeking prostitutes. The way in which Irvine offered Smith three shillings suggests a man who was familiar with the way to make these sorts of transactions. This was not the first time that Irvine had done this; usually, however, the deal probably went a lot more smoothly, and the police had never been involved. On the night of 27 September, it was Irvine's bad luck to approach the wrong person; he might have thought that Smith looked like a working boy, but he was horribly mistaken.

Male prostitution in nineteenth-century Melbourne was a hidden world of which practically nothing is known today. There were no prosecutions or convictions of male prostitutes for being prostitutes, and only vague indirect references exist about the possibility that there were men working in the sex trade. Indeed, male prostitution, as such, did not exist as an offence; anyone working as a male prostitute would have been prosecuted for the standard offences of sodomy, attempted sodomy or indecent assault on a male person. Whether or not money changed hands was immaterial; it was the acts themselves that were illegal. There was the case of John Wilson in Fitzroy in 1863: he was definitely working as a prostitute, but was dressed as a woman and presenting himself as a woman. He managed to get away with his masquerade, thanks in great part to always keeping his clothes on during the act, and the nineteenth-century male's general unfamiliarity with the female body. The police who arrested Gordon Lawrence at the Exhibition in 1888 initially thought that he was a female prostitute; once he was unmasked, they were at a loss as to what his motives for cross-dressing were, but there was some thought that he might be on the game. Court cases often refer to small amounts of money or gifts changing hands for sexual favours, particularly when the case involved an older man and a younger lad, but these appear to be one-offs rather than evidence of an organised or structured male sex trade. In fact, Irvine's throw-away enquiry to Smith happens to be one of the strongest pieces of evidence that someone, at least, knew that there were young men to be had for hire on the streets of the metropolis.

'AN UNFORTUNATE GENTLEMAN' 211

With his life, business and reputation in tatters, Irvine shut down his office, moved out of *Talbot Lodge* and appears to have left Melbourne. He headed home to Launceston, where his family was still talking to him; how he explained the situation to them, and what they made of it, is anyone's guess. What he did with himself, how he would earn a living, what he would do for money, is a mystery. But the mystery would deepen further.

On the afternoon of Wednesday 30 November 1898, just over 13 months after the events of that evening in Carlton, the Mayoress of Launceston, Mrs S.J. Sutton, held an 'at home' at the Albert Hall in Launceston's City Park, the scene of the 1891 Launceston Exhibition. The hall:

> had been arranged as a drawing-room, with wicker furniture, including numbers of pretty wicker and bamboo tables, flower stands, screens, settees and chairs. Rugs and squares of Japanese matting were laid here and there about the floor, and assisted much in relieving that bareness that is inevitable in a large hall.[7]

In the centre of the hall, surrounded by 'a profusion of flowers', the Mayoress and the Mayor greeted their guests, who were then treated to a programme of instrumental and vocal music while enjoying an afternoon tea of strawberries and cream, fruit salad, cream cakes and sandwiches. The guests were drawn from the cream of Launceston and Tasmanian society. Among them were Mr and Mrs R.F. Irvine (Dick and Frances), Mr and Mrs C.R. Irvine (Claude and Ella) and Mr J.L. Irvine.

Having enjoyed the music and the afternoon tea, the guests gathered their wraps, coats, handbags and other belongings and streamed out into the late afternoon sun, J.L. and his brothers and their wives among them. It was to be the last official sighting of John Lempriere Irvine.

CHAPTER 11
Falling off the Face of the Earth

What happened next? We have no clue. He walked out of Albert Hall and appears to have fallen off the face of the earth. There are no official records relating to him in Australian sources after that day, and no newspaper references can definitely be pinned to him. He simply vanished after that Wednesday afternoon in November 1898.

It is particularly odd that a well-known figure from a prominent family, with a well-documented life, could vanish like this. Irvine's life up to the age of 50 is a particularly public one; his family background, his sporting achievements, his professional life, his willingness to join clubs and societies, and even his brushes with scandal and the underworld, meant that he was constantly in the newspapers from the age of 14, when he achieved the second-place prize for the 1861 school year at the Reverend Kane's School at Rostella. His family's social prominence in Launceston and Melbourne society meant that his extended family's lives and activities were well reported and well documented – his great-grandmother's land and financial dealings, his grandfather's journalism and play-writing, his father's government and commercial life and his mother's work as a collector and exhibitor. Most of his siblings had socially prominent lives or successful business careers which left behind plenty of traces. Records of the family abound, in newspapers, public libraries, university archive collections and public records offices. Several of the family have entries in the *Australian Dictionary of Biography*. These are members of the establishment. These are people of note. How, then, did one of them disappear so completely?

The most likely answer is that he wanted to vanish; that he engineered his own disappearance. The social disgrace fostered by the *Bendigo Independent*'s

Albert Hall

reporting of the Carlton case, along with the destruction of his business, gave Irvine very good reasons for avoiding the public eye and getting right away from gossip, innuendo and sideways glances. He would always be that 'unfortunate gentleman – twice arrested on shameful allegations.'

In the late nineteenth century, it would have been very easy to make yourself disappear and to create a new life. All that would be necessary would be to travel to another colony, either by train or in steerage in a coastal steamer, so as not to appear on any published passenger lists. Then, step off the train or boat in, say, Sydney or Brisbane and book lodgings under a new name. A new bank account could be opened without the stringent proof of identity now required. Even travelling overseas was not an insurmountable obstacle; British subjects living in Australia (white Australians, that is; Indigenous Australians were not counted as citizens) did not require passports until the first Commonwealth passports were issued in 1912.

Even if Irvine had remained in Australia and died away from his family, the details on his death registration would only be what the person reporting his death knew about him. A boarding house keeper who knew him as 'Mr Irvine' (or worse, as 'Mr Smith' perhaps) but did not know where he came from could not give much information to the registrar. His death would be almost impossible to trace.

It is possible that he spent the first half of 1899 in Launceston and returned to the mainland on the *Coogee* on 7 July 1899. There is a 'Mr Irvine' in the passenger list published in the Launceston Examiner. However, as he usually styled himself 'J.L. Irvine', we cannot be certain that it is John. After that, the already faint scent goes completely cold.

He took no further part in business affairs. Two mining leases which he had taken out in his own name in the Buckland goldfield were ruled to have been abandoned and declared void in February 1902.[1]

During the first decade of the new century, Irvine's name appeared a couple of times in newspaper articles reminiscing about the glory days of the intercolonial eights back in the late 1870s. By this stage, no one was sure whether he was alive or dead or what had happened to him. In May 1905, the *Sydney Morning Herald* listed the crews of the first Intercolonial eight of 1878 and noted that, of the Victorian crew, R. Ward and Bill Tuckett were dead, but not, apparently, Irvine.[2] By 1912, an article marking the 38th anniversary of the first Intercolonial eight-oared race noted that Irvine and Tuckett died 'quite a long while ago [Tuckett had died in 1885], but it is believed the [rest of the crew] are alive, and well.'[3]

By the 40th anniversary of the eight-oared interstate championship (which would have been the 45th anniversary, but for the fact that the race was not held during the years of the Great War) in March 1921, Irvine was little more than a name in a list of old-time rowers of whom no one appeared to know anything. However, Jack Latham, an old rower from Launceston, that year revived memories of Irvine, remembering when 'Jack' Irvine was presented with a 'pair of crossed miniature silver skulls [sic] as the winner of the champion sculling race, at a performance given by Launceston amateurs.' This would have been back in the '60s. Latham remembered Jack Irvine as 'a "hail fellow well met", and liked by everyone especially in aquatic circles. He was a splendid rower in an outrigger and a fine stamp of a man.' Latham wasn't sure what happened to Irvine, but 'If I mistake not, I fancy he is living in Melbourne or Sydney at present.'[4] He was not; there is no record of John

Lempriere Irvine in either Sydney or Melbourne in 1921, or anywhere else in Australia at that time or after.

Latham's uncertainty over Irvine's whereabouts is interesting. As an old Launceston rower, Latham would almost certainly have known J.L.'s brother Dick, who was still living in Launceston and who had kept up his connections with local rowing clubs. Surely Dick knew whether his brother was dead or alive and, if he was alive, where he was living? It is very possible that Dick did not know. If he did, he may not have wanted to stir up memories of a brother with an unseemly reputation. A search of the Launceston papers for the weeks following Latham's article turns up no additional information or corrections to the old rower's reminiscences.

There are other John Irvines in the newspapers, but they do not appear to be J.L. They were homeopathic chemists, or married with many children, or arrested for sly grogging, or were arrested in NSW for forgery; none of the reported facts about their lives match up with J.L. In the first decade of the twentieth century, there was a popular amateur singer from Bendigo called J.L. Irvine. Very confusingly, around the turn of the century, there was an interstate rower from Adelaide called J.L. Irvine; an engineer by training, he had represented South Australia in intercolonial championships in 1899 and into the new century, before suffering an accident at work which left him a paraplegic for the last five years of his life. He died in Birkenhead, South Australia, in January 1907, aged 33.[5]

What Irvine's family made of his apparent disappearance is unknown. Did they know where he was and what had happened to him? If they did, they made no mention of it in the sources that have survived. Irvine's mother, Jemima, kept a copious scrapbook which focused on the activities of her family, friends and acquaintances, as well as acting as a repository for pieces of interesting information, trivia and humorous items that appealed to her. Now kept in the Launceston Municipal Library, the scrapbook charts the births, weddings, deaths and careers of her children and grandchildren from the 1880s. In the early part of the book, there are several articles celebrating J.L.'s rowing achievements; in the 1890s, references to him peter out. Interestingly, a number of articles in the latter part of the book have been neatly razored out, leaving mysterious holes in some pages. Jemima is unlikely to have defaced her own scrapbook, so it is possible that one of her children or grandchildren

Jemina Irvine's scrapbook, in the collection of the Launceston Public Library.

is responsible for the missing articles. It is unlikely that we will ever know what is missing. Were they articles relating J.L.? Was someone in the family looking to get rid of an embarrassing uncle or great-uncle?

Jemima Irvine maintained her scrapbook until the time of the Great War and continued to collect plant specimens, shells and other objects of general interest almost to the end of her life. In April 1919, she celebrated her 98th birthday at her daughter Nellie's home, *Ingleside*, Evandale, where she was living, and:

[she] was the recipient during the day of visits from her family and friends, also numerous letters and telegrams of congratulations and good wishes. Although she has attained so great an age, Mrs Irvine is in full possession of all her faculties, though somewhat frail in general health. Her recollections of the early days of the colony are very vivid and she takes a lively interest in present day doings.[6]

Jemima Irvine died three months later, on Thursday 17 July 1919; 'a highly esteemed … cultured and very intelligent lady [with] a host of friends in both in the South and the North' of Tasmania.[7]

Of the remainder of Irvine's siblings, Dick survived his mother by only two years, dying in September 1921 at the age of 76. His obituary noted that, in addition to being the managing director of Irvine and McEachern, he had been a sharebroker, legal manager, and secretary of the Launceston Stock Exchange until resigning in 1919 because of failing health. He was a commissioner of the Northern Fisheries Association and a member of the Launceston Hospital Board. The death of his son, Dr Charles Irvine, in the Spanish flu epidemic of 1919 'was a great blow to him.'[8] Dick was survived by two of his three children, May and John, and his wife Frances, who died in 1923.[9]

Kate and Harvey Patterson left Australia for Europe in 1898 with their three children, Corona (aged 17), Raymond (aged 14), and Hazel (aged 12). One of the reasons for the trip was to place Raymond into boarding school at Harrow.[10] Harvey returned to Australia shortly thereafter, leaving Kate, Corona and Hazel in Europe. Kate and Harvey appear to have been estranged when Kate died (seemingly of liver failure) at 48 in the German resort town of Wiesbaden in 1902. She was nursed to the end by her two daughters, 21 year-old Corona and 16 year-old Hazel; according to a member of the Patterson family who visited Kate and the girls in Wiesbaden in February 1902, the task of looking after their mother was 'too much responsibility for the two girls to have all on their shoulders.'[11]

Kate was buried in Wiesbaden, and Harvey remarried in 1913. *Inverleith* had been given up as a family home and rented out when the family left for Europe in 1898. The new tenant operated the house as an exclusive, although rather bohemian, boarding house until Harvey eventually sold the property in 1920. The gardens of *Inverleith* were then subdivided for flats in 1927, while the house remained as a boarding house, slipping further down the social scale. Kate's ballroom was demolished in 1958, although the house itself lasted until the 1960s.[12] By that time, Harvey was long gone, having left Australia to settle in England in 1926. He died at 83 in Wimbledon, London, in May 1931.

Charles and Claude Irvine, J.L.'s younger brothers, both ended up in Western Australia. After a long career in the Adelaide Steamship Company, Charles was appointed Chief Harbour Master for Western Australia in 1902. He retired to a country property at Kelmscott, W.A. in 1917. He died at 65 in July 1922, survived by his wife Flora and their two children.[13] Claude Irvine, having managed properties in New South Wales for his brother-in-law Harvey Patterson, moved to Western Australia and ran cattle stations in the Onslow District in the Pilbara. He and his wife, Ella, had four children, a daughter and three sons, one of whom was killed at Gallipoli. Claude retired from station management in 1929 and died aged 73 at Karrakatta, Western Australia, in July 1934.[14]

Sisters Florence Longden and Jemima Adams slipped from public view. When Toppy Longden died suddenly in Mexico City in December 1924, it was his sister and brother who inserted a death notice in the *Argus*, rather than Florence.[15]

Claude Irvine's twin sister Nellie, who had married Harry Hawley in 1893, was left a widow five years later when Harry died at the age of 33. Harry had been managing the Scone Estate, near Perth, Tasmania, when he was stricken with typhoid in April 1898. He died after an illness of three weeks, leaving Nellie a widow with a two-year-old daughter and pregnant with a son who would be born in September, five months after his father's death. Harry's funeral left from *Lebrina*, Dick Irvine's house, where Nellie and Harry's wedding reception had been held just a few years previously.[16]

Nellie and her children moved to *Ingleside*, in the village of Evandale just south of Launceston, and were joined by her mother Jemima. Known for her charitable work in the district, Nellie founded the Evandale Benevolent Society and was secretary of the local Red Cross Society. After her mother's death, she moved to Launceston, but failing health in her later years saw her move to her daughter's house at Longford. She died, aged 72, in September 1933.[17]

Although the deaths of his mother and most of his siblings were recorded in respectful obituaries in newspapers as far afield as Tasmania, Victoria,

Jemima Irvine aged 80.

New South Wales and Western Australia, J.L. Irvine's death was not noted in any Australian newspaper – like his sisters, Jemima and Florence. When and where he died is unknown, but I am certain that he did not die in Australia under his own name. Where he went after leaving the Albert Hall is a mystery. The story of his active, well-documented life just stops in November 1898.

I have researched Irvine's life for several years, amassing facts, following leads and pursuing clues. At first, the research was easy; his was a life so rich in documentary sources that he was easy to follow. His great-grandmother's letters regarding his birth, numerous newspaper references to his sporting career and involvement in community activities, his employment records held in the ANZ Bank archives, even some of his trophies and belongings such as paintings that he owned – all are still in existence. Most of the bank buildings he worked in still stand, as do many of the public buildings, hotels and streetscapes that he knew, making it easy to visualise his surroundings in life. Although only one photograph of him exists [from his mother's album], and the only other images of him are line drawings in newspaper supplements from the 1870s and 1880s, there are rich visual clues to his world: photographs of people he knew, streets, parks and places that he frequented, and boats and holiday spots that he visited. It was so easy for me to follow Irvine's trail and see his world.

And then, it stopped. At the age of 50, he vanished. There are no further sightings. Although there is no record of him leaving Australia under his own name, it is possible that he went overseas. Numerous places would have been attractive to an Australian at the time, particularly the United Kingdom or other parts of the Empire within easy reach of Australia: New Zealand, the Pacific Islands, South Africa; perhaps the west coast of the United States, or Canada; possibly Europe. No one knows, and we shall probably never know. Irvine's life ends with a question mark, symptomatic of a spectacular fall from grace at the hands of public opinion. His is definitely a lost nineteenth-century life.

AFTERWORD

I discovered John Lempriere Irvine by accident, searching the National Library of Australia's digitised newspaper archive, Trove, for nineteenth-century reports of male-to-male sexual encounters and relationships. Doing so involves using a range of terms and phrases which were in vogue then and not now, and avoiding using current terminology which was not used in the nineteenth century. So, rather than searching for 'homosexual' and 'homosexuality' (which were not used in Australian newspapers until the early twentieth century), I was using 'unnatural offence,' 'disgusting practices,' 'heinous offence,' 'serious charge,' 'peculiarly disgusting,' etc.

These terms led me to the reports of Irvine's bashing and robbery at the hands of the South Melbourne Conspirators in March 1888. Because the conspirators were tried for robbery, the case had not previously been noticed for its homosexual content in research that I and others had done in Victorian court records. Here was an interesting new case: a larrikin gang using the threat of exposing respectable members of the public to blackmail and humiliation by claiming that they had made improper advances to them. However, a little more searching of Trove soon brought to light the second case of Irvine being accused of making improper advances to another man, in Carlton in 1897. That led to the realisation that the second scandal had ruined his business and his life, and that I was dealing with a nineteenth-century homo-inclined man.

The plot thickened as I began to explore Irvine's life, discovering him to be a sporting champion and a member of a socially elite family. These facts, combined with his propensity to get involved with clubs, societies, choirs and other social activities in every town his employers transferred him to, meant that his was an extensively documented life. The addition of family correspondence, scrapbooks, employment records and photographs, held in public collections in Tasmania, Victoria and New South Wales, meant that I was able to track his life on almost a month-by-month basis over 50 years. This level of documentation of a relatively ordinary person's life over 120 years ago is unusual. It is usually only possible if the individual kept a diary, and Irvine did not. The detailed record of his life is made all the more unusual by the fact that he was a single man, a man who never married and left no descendants to remember him.

However, the trail went dead after he attended the Mayoress' afternoon reception in 1889, which in itself is telling; that a member of a well-known and well-connected family, a sporting figure, a great joiner-of-clubs, a businessman, could disappear without a trace, is unusual. The only way it could have happened is if the individual concerned *wanted* to disappear.

Irvine's life is a great piece of social history. Born in the convict period at one of the most brutal of Australia's penal settlements, he lived into the age of electricity and city offices with lifts. He saw the advent of modern city life in Australia, changing attitudes to women, periods of boom and economic depression. He was an early adopter of trends (rollerskating) and technology (the telephone). He mixed with the social elite of Melbourne during the boom of the 1880s, and he saw regional society develop. Reading his life story allows us to see how one man lived his life against this changing background.

His life also gives some insight into how a man who was attracted to those of his own sex could navigate a successful life in the nineteenth century. Little is known of the lives of homosexual men in colonial Australia. Usually, the stories of homosexual men come to light in connection with criminal prosecutions; their sexual and emotional lives are recorded in legal documents and witness statements, always in a negative light. The sexual lives of homosexual men who avoided brushes with the law and managed to live successful lives left fewer traces. Often, any evidence they may have created themselves, in letters, diaries and photograph albums, was destroyed, either by themselves or by family members who were 'straightening up' their life story. Historians of homosexual lives, therefore, become very adept at reading between the

AFTERWORD

lines of the past, seeing clues and making connections hidden in plain sight. So it is with Irvine. That he was involved with two homosexual scandals was a matter of public record, but other clues also pointed to a gay life story: the fact that he never married; where he chose to live, and their proximity to known beats; his involvement with homosocial sporting and social activities; and the comfort he felt in mixing with younger men. Even his polished and practised way of approaching Ernest Smith on the street in 1897 points to Irvine having had a familiarity with homosexual tactics.

He may not have been a member of any nascent homosexual subculture in Melbourne or elsewhere at the time – if, indeed, any existed – but he obviously knew how to attract sexual contacts and the necessary codes of behaviour. Barring the run-in with the South Melbourne Conspirators in 1888, he managed to live a successful homosexual life, right up until he approached Ernest Smith in September 1897.

In researching Irvine's life, I am indebted to a great many people and institutions. Particular thanks are due to:

- the National Library of Australia's Trove database, for bringing Irvine's story to light in the first place and then providing over 130 years of press reportage of Irvine's life and those of his family
- the Launceston Library, who hold Jemima Irvine's scrapbook, correspondence between Jacobina Burn and Jemima Irvine and a wealth of other family material
- the State Library of New South Wales, for their assistance with delving through an extensive collection of rowing memorabilia
- Graham Willett, for his enthusiasm for this project and for acting as one of my first readers
- John Waugh, for his assistance with navigating the court records relating to the South Melbourne Conspiracy
- Alex Bayley, for an enjoyable afternoon of touring historical queer Ballarat
- Terry Rankin, historian of the Banks Rowing Club (Melbourne), for his work in digging out Irvine from the BRC archives
- D. Lasky-Davison, of the ANZ Banking Archives, for allowing me access to Irvine's employment records with the Union Bank and Bank of Australasia

- staff in the reading room at the Public Records Office, Melbourne, for their never-failing help in navigating court records and police gazettes
- staff in the Special Collections reading room at the Baillieu Library, University of Melbourne, who hold the Patterson family archives
- John McCullagh, private collector, who generously took most of a day to show me Jemima Irvine's wonderful collection of objects of interest
- and Peter, for putting up with J.L. Irvine for the past five years.

ENDNOTES

NOTE ON SPELLING

In the late nineteenth century what we would now call American spelling was very common in the Australian colonies: 'color', rather than 'colour'; 'organize' rather than 'organise' and so on. This has been retained in all quotations from the period.

CHAPTER 1

1   'An Unfortunate Gentleman', *Bendigo Independent*, 8 October 1897, p. 4.
2   'Advertising', *Argus*, 8 October 1897, p.3; 'Advertising', *Argus*, 9 October 1897, p.7; 'Advertising', *Argus*, 14 October 1897, p.3.

CHAPTER 2

1   N. Chick, *Tasmanian Family and Community Reconstitution: With a case study of some estates and families of Bothwell, Hamilton and Ouse*, Ph.D. diss., University of Tasmania 2006, p. 225; D. Burn, 'Obituary Mrs Jacobina Burn', *Daily Southern Cross*, 4 March 1851, n.p.
2   Chick, *Tasmanian Family*, p. 225.
3   L. Sussex, *Blockbuster: Fergus Hume and the Mystery of a Hansom Cab*, Melbourne, Text Publishing Australia, 2015, p. 17.
4   J. Boyce, *Van Diemen's Land*, Melbourne, Black Ink, 2014, pp. 158–159.
5   Lachlan Macquarie, 'Journal of a Voyage and Tour of Inspection to Van Diemen's Land 1821', www.mq.edu.au/macquarie-archive/lema/1821/.
6   D. Burn, 'Obituary Mrs Jacobina Burn'.
7   Chick, *Tasmanian Family*, p. 212.
8   G. Morris, 'Irvine family history notes by Gill Morris', Family History Files, Launceston Municipal Library.
9   Chick, *Tasmanian Family*, p. 212.
10 Burn, 'Obituary Mrs Jacobina Burn'.
11 'The Black Line' National Museum of Australia [website], www.nma.gov.au/defining-moments/resources/the-black-line, accessed 12 June 2018.
12 Burn, 'Obituary Mrs Jacobina Burn'.
13 Morris, 'Irvine family history notes'.

14   D. Borchardt, 'David Burn (1799-1875)', *Australian Dictionary of Biography*, Melbourne University Press.
15   Morris, 'Irvine family history notes'.
16   Burn, 'Obituary Mrs Jacobina Burn'.
17   Chick, *Tasmanian Family*, p.223.
18   D. Borchardt 'David Burn (1799-1875)'.
19   Jacobina Burn, letter to Jemima Burn, 17 October 1836. Launceston Public Library [hereinafter LPL].
20   Jacobina Burn, letter to Jemima Burn, 15 April 1842, LPL
21   K. Von Stieglitz, *Six Pioneer Women of Tasmania*, Hobart, Country Women's Association, 1956, p. 10.
22   'General News', *Courier*, 30 September 1842, p. 3.
23   'Charles Irvine and Jemima Burn', marriage certificate, 22 Jun. 1843. Registration number 1843/650. Tasmanian Registry of Births, Deaths and Marriage [hereinafter TRBDM].
24   Jacobina Burn, letter to Jemima Irvine, 1 May 1844, LPL.
25   'Birth notices', *Colonial Times*, 2 April 1844, p. 2.
26   Jacobina Burn, letter to Charles Irvine, 16 May 1845, LPL.
27   G. Ritchie, 'Cascades Probation Station', On the Convict Trail [website] 1 January 2014, ontheconvicttrail.blogspot.com/2014/01/cascades-probation-station.html, accessed 8 May 2019.
28   Jacobina Burn, letter to Jemima Irvine, 1 May 1845, LPL.
29   F. Hooper, 'Charles O'Hara Booth (1800-1851)', *Australian Dictionary of Biography*.
30   M. Weidenhofer, *Port Arthur: a place of misery*, Melbourne, Oxford University Press, 1981, p. 57.
31   Von Stieglitz, *Six Pioneer Women*, p. 10.
32   Weidenhofer, *Port Arthur*, p. 58. Sexually, the only act which was punishable by law was sodomy, or the attempt to commit sodomy. This had been illegal since the reign of Henry VIII, but was rarely prosecuted and difficult to prove, unless the participants were caught in the act. It was not until 1885 that all sexual contact between men was criminalised as 'Gross Indecency' in Britain. The various Australian colonies were much slower to adopt similar legislation; Victoria only introducing the offence to the statute books in 1919. Non-conforming sexual identities could, however, be prosecuted as other offences, including vagrancy, public nuisance, and insulting behaviour.
33   Von Stieglitz, *Six Pioneer Women*, p. 11.
34   Von Stieglitz, *Six Pioneer Women*, p. 10.
35   'General News', *Gazette*, 18 March 1846, p. 2.
36   'General News', *Hobarton Guardian*, 31 January 1849, p. 4.
37   'General News', *Courier*, 16 June 1847, p. 1.
38   'General News', *Launceston Examiner*, 17 March 1847, p. 3.
39   Jacobina Burn, letter to Jemima Irvine, 22 April 1847, LPL.
40   Jacobina Burn, letter to Jemima Irvine, 12 July 1847, LPL.
41   'George Irvine', birth certificate, 12 January 1849. Registration number 1849/638, TRBDM.
42   'Jemima Irvine', birth certificate, 27 October 1850. Registration number 1850/188, TRBDM.
43   'Launceston Gaol', press clipping, 7 March 1971, LPL.
44   Morris, 'Irvine Family History Notes'.
45   'Mervyn Irvine', death certificate, 29 March 1854. Registration number 1854/1307, TRBDM.
46   'Charles Hamilton Irvine', death certificate, 26 February 1855. Registration number 1855/1686, TRBDM.
47   Von Stieglitz, *Six Pioneer Women*, p. 5.
48   R. Hilder, 'Emu Bay to Launceston and Return' (unpublished manuscript), 1930s, LPL.
49   'Death of Mr C.J. Irvine', *Cornwall Chronicle*, 18 November 1863, p.3; 'Death of Mr C.J. Irvine', *Launceston Examiner*, 17 November 1863, p. 5.
50   'General News', *Cornwall Chronicle*, 18 November 1863, p. 4.
51   'General News', *Cornwall Chronicle*, 21 November 1863, p. 4.

ENDNOTES

CHAPTER 3

1. 'General News', *Launceston Examiner*, 26 December 1863, p. 2.
2. 'General News', *Cornwall Chronicle*, 21 December 1861, p. 5.
3. 'Interesting Reminiscences', *Advocate*, 26 June 1924, p. 6.
4. D. Adair, 'Two dots in the distance: Professional sculling as a mass spectacle in New South Wales', *Sporting Traditions* [online journal], 1992, academia.edu, p.1. accessed 15 June 2018.
5. 'Tamar Rowing Club', *Tasmanian*, 18 October 1879, p. 4.
6. 'Shipping', *Argus*, 6 July 1864, p. 4.
7. Union Bank employment register, ANZ Archives, Melbourne.
8. A. Seltzer and K. Simons, 'Salaries and career opportunities in the banking industry: Evidence from the personnel records of the Union Bank of Australia', *Explorations in Economic History*, 38, 2001, pp. 195–224.
9. 'John Irvine', entry in Union Bank Employment register, Series U/271/1, ANZ Group Archive.
10. For this and the following on the Regatta: 'General News', *Cornwall Chronicle*, 5 September 1866, p. 4; 3 November 1866, p. 7; 23 January 1867, p. 5.
11. Martin Crotty, '"Separate and distinct"? The manual labour question in nineteenth-century Victorian rowing', *The International Journal of the History of Sport*, vol. 15, no.2, pp. 152–163.
12. 'Tamar Regatta', *Launceston Examiner*, 30 January 1868, p. 5.
13. 'Tamar Regatta', *Cornwall Chronical*, 29 January 1868. p. 3.
14. 'Tamar Regatta 1870', *Launceston Examiner*, 3 February 1870, p. 2.
15. 'Tamar Regatta', *Cornwall Chronical*, 5 February 1870, p. 6.
16. 'Launceston Amateur Dramatic Club', *Cornwall Chronicle*, 30 July 1870, p. 10.
17. 'Launceston Amateur Dramatic Club', *Cornwall Chronicle*, 21 September 1870, p. 3.
18. 'Launceston Amateur Dramatic Club', *Cornwall Chronicle*, 14 September 1870, p. 3.
19. 'Launceston Amateur Dramatic Club', *Launceston Examiner*, 15 September 1870, p. 5.
20. 'Launceston Amateur Dramatic Club', *Cornwall Advertiser*, 21 October 1870, p. 2.
21. 'General News', *Launceston Examiner*, 27 October 1870, p. 2.
22. 'Northern Tasmanian Poultry Society', *Cornwall Chronicle*, 17 September 1870, p. 11.
23. 'Tamar Regatta', *Tasmanian*, 11 February 1871, p. 5.
24. 'Entertainment at the Invalid Depot', *Launceston Examiner*, 13 May 1871, p. 2.
25. Sussex, *Blockbuster*, p. 212.
26. 'Homoeroticism and Homosociality', Encyclopedia.com, www.encyclopedia.com/social-sciences/encyclopedias-almanacs-transcripts-and-maps/homoeroticism-and-homosociality, accessed 23 July 2018.
27. M. Popova, 'A photographic history of bromance 1840–1918', *Brainpickings*, 18 November 2010, www.brainpickings.org/2010/11/18/dear-friends/, accessed 4 January 2019.
28. 'The Scott Centenary Celebration', *Launceston Examiner*, 17 August 1871, p. 3.
29. 'Launceston Amateur Dramatic Club', *Launceston Examiner*, 23 September 1871, p. 5.
30. 'Launceston Amateur Dramatic Club', *Cornwall Advertiser*, 1 December 1871, p. 2.
31. 'Miscellaneous', *Tasmanian*, 4 May 1872, p. 11.
32. 'Launceston Amateur Dramatic Club', *Tasmanian*, 9 November 1872, p. 11.
33. 'Tamar Regatta for 1873', *Cornwall Chronicle*, 14 February 1873, p. 2.
34. 'General News', *Cornwall Chronicle*, 7 May 1873, p. 2.
35. 'Northern Tasmanian Poultry Society Annual Show', *Weekly Examiner*, 13 September 1873, p. 2.
36. 'Choral Union', *Weekly Examiner*, 27 September 1873, p. 16.
37. 'Tamar Regatta', *Launceston Examiner*, 10 January 1874, p. 2.
38. 'Regatta Meeting', *Tasmanian*, 17 January 1874, p. 7.

CHAPTER 4

1. 'Shipping Intelligence', *Argus*, 18 February 1874, p. 4.
2. Victorian Heritage Database Report https://vhd.heritagecouncil.vic.gov.au/places/78/download-report

3 A. Trollope, *Australia and New Zealand*, Leipzig, Bernhard Tauchnitz, 1873, p. 46.
4 'News and Notes', *Ballarat Star* 13 April 1874, p. 2.
5 'News and Notes', *Ballarat Star* 27 April 1874, p. 2.
6 'Aquatics', *Ballarat Courier*, 14 May 1874, p. 4.
7 'News and Notes', *Ballarat Star*, 14 May 1874, p. 2.
8 Terry Banks (Melbourne Banks Rowing Club), email to Wayne Murdoch, 6 October 2016.
9 'News and Notes', *Ballarat Star*, 22 June 1874, p. 2.
10 'A New Musical Union', *Tasmanian*, 4 July 1874, p. 8.
11 'Ballarat Rowing Club', *Ballarat Star*, 6 August 1874 p. 2.
12 'Rowing Matches at Lake Wendouree', *Ballarat Star*, 21 September 1874, p. 2.
13 'City Council', *Ballarat Star*, 6 October 1874, p. 2; 'City Council', *Ballarat Courier*, 12 January 1875, p. 4.
14 Victoria Police Department, *Victoria Police Gazette*, Melbourne G.P.O., 8 December 1874, p. 259.
15 'Advertising', *Argus*, 21 October 1874, p. 12.
16 'News and Notes', *Ballarat Star*, 28 October 1870, p .2. 'Disgusting practices' could just refer to public urination in the laneway. Having visited the laneway in September 2019, I can say that it is still a dark spot and perfect for getting up to mischief. However, it also runs alongside the wall of the Ballarat prison and might have been a little too close to official oversight for comfort.
17 Trollope, *Australia and New Zealand*, p. 60.
18 'Geelong Regatta', *Ballarat Courier*, 17 March 1875, p. 3.
19 'Ballarat Regatta', *Ballarat Courier*, 29 March 1875, p. 2.
20 'Banks Challenge Cup', *Australasian*, 29 May 1875, p. 13.
21 'News and Notes', *Ballarat Star*, 24 June 1875, p. 2.
22 'General News', *Ballarat Courier*, 30 June 1875, p. 2.
23 'General News', *Ballarat Courier*, 2 July 1875, p. 2.
24 'General News', *Ballarat Courier*, 15 July 1875, p. 2.
25 'Town Talk', *Geelong Advertiser*, 15 July 1875, p. 2.
26 'General News', *Ballarat Courier*, 14 August 1875, p. 2.
27 'Football', *Hamilton Spectator*, 25 August 1875, p. 4.
28 'News and Notes', *Ballarat Star*, 4 September 1875, p. 2.

CHAPTER 5

1 R. Twopeny, *Town Life in Australia*, Sydney University Press, 1973, p. 2.
2 Trollope, *Australia and New Zealand*, p. 39.
3 Twopeny, *Town Life in Australia*, p. 5.
4 Twopeny, *Town Life in Australia*, p. 4.
5 Trollope, *Australia and New Zealand*, p. 43.
6 'Richard Francis Irvine and Frances Beatrice Lette', marriage registration, 23 November 1875. Registration number 1875/187, TRBDMs.
7 'Melbourne Annual Regatta', *Ballarat Star*, 10 April 1876, p. 4.
8 J. Lang, *Victorian Oarsmen: with a Rowing Register*, Melbourne, A.H. Massina & Coy, 1919, p. 43.
9 'Tasmanian Oarsmen in Victoria', *Tribune*, 21 March 1877, p. 2.
10 'Tamar Rowing Club 1877', *Daily Telegraph*, 10 November 1911, p. 7.
11 'Proposed Intercolonial Eight-Oared Match', *Australian Town and Country Journal*, 18 August 1877, p. 31.
12 'The Intercolonial Boat Race', *Daily Telegraph*, 7 March 1878, n.p.
13 'Aquatics', *Age*, 6 December 1877, p. 3.
14 'Aquatics', *Age*, 1 January 1878, p. 3.
15 'Aquatics – Rowing Notes', *Weekly Times*, 5 January 1878, p. 3.
16 'Rowing Notes', *Weekly Times*, 16 February 1878, p. 5.
17 'The Intercolonial Eight-Oar Race', *Argus*, 7 March 1878, p. 6.
18 'Intercolonial Boat Race', *Geelong Advertiser*, 7 March 1878, p. 3.
19 'General News', *Argus*, 7 March 1878, p. 5.

20 'The Intercolonial Eight-Oar Race', *Argus*, 7 March 1878, p. 6.
21 [item] 898: Intercolonial Eight Oar Race, www.noble.com.au/site/docs/cats/sale_88/A03.pdf, p. 79, accessed 12 September 2019.
22 'News of the Day', *Age*, 7 March 1878, p. 2.
23 'Rowing Notes', *Weekly Times*, 16 March 1878, p. 5.
24 'Board and Lodging', *Argus*, 2 November 1878, p. 12.
25 'Advertisements', *Argus*, 3 February 1881, p. 2.
26 'Criminal Assault in Fitzroy Gardens', *Herald*, 18 March 1876, p. 2.
27 'The Night Side of our Public Gardens', *Leader*, 29 January 1870, p. 11.
28 'Aquatics', *Leader*, 7 December 1878, p. 11.
29 Lang, *Victorian Oarsmen*, p. 44.
30 'Rowing Notes', *Australasian*, 10 May 1879, p. 13.
31 'The Intercolonial Eight-Oar Boat Race', *Illustrated Australian News*, 12 May 1879, p. 75.
32 This and following quotes: 'Intercolonial Eight-Oared Race', *Australasian*, 7 June 1879, p. 12.
33 'Rowing Notes', *Australasian*, 11 October 1879, p. 12.
34 'Union Bank, Collins-street', *Age*, 4 August 1879, p. 3.
35 'Rowing Notes', *Leader*, 27 September 1879, p. 12.
36 'Victorian Rowing Association', *Australasian*, 28 February 1880, p. 13.
37 'General News', *Argus*, 12 April 1880, p. 4.
38 'Union Bank', *Herald*, 8 May 1880, p. 3.
39 'The Union Bank', *Argus*, 29 May 1880, p. 9.
40 M. Crotty (1998) '"Separate and distinct"? The manual labour question in nineteenth-century Victorian rowing, *International Journal of the History of Sport*, 15:2, 152-163'
41 T. Rankin,' John Lempriere Irvine 1847 – (Date of death unknown): The Oarsman who Vanished', unpublished manuscript prepared for Banks Rowing Club, 2017.
42 'Rowing Notes', *Leader*, 8 January 1881, p. 13.
43 'Rowing Notes', *Australasian*, 15 January 1881, p. 12.
44 'Aquatic Notes', *Weekly Times*, 15 January 1881, p. 5.
45 'Rowing Notes', *Leader*, 22 January 1881, p. 11.
46 'Aquatic Notes', *Australasian*, 5 February 1881, p. 21.
47 'Rowing Notes', *Leader*, 5 February 1881, p. 11.
48 'Notes by Pinafore', *Australian Town and Country Journal*, 19 March 1881, p. 35.
49 'Annual Report of the Victorian Rowing Association', *Leader*, 17 September 1881, p. 12.
50 'Intercolonial Eight Oar Race,' *Sydney Mail and New South Wales Advertiser*, 16 April 1881, p. 628.
51 'Our Rowing Champions', *Geelong Advertiser*, 21 April 1881, p. 3.
52 Victoria Police Department, *Victoria Police Gazette*, Melbourne G.P.O., 7 September 1881, p. 36.
53 'Victorian Rowing Association', *Australasian*, 17 September 1881, p. 12.
54 'Banks Rowing Club', *Australasian*, 22 October 1881, p. 13.
55 T. Rankin, 'John Lempriere Irvine 1847 – (Date of death unknown)'.

CHAPTER 6

1 Trollope, *Australia and New Zealand*, p. 53.
2 'History of Bendigo Rowing Club', www.rowinghistory-aus.info/club-histories/bendigo/04-1.html, accessed 17 August 2019.
3 'Sandhurst Rowing Club's Regatta', *Bendigo Advertiser*, 1 December 1881, p. 2.
4 'The Sandhurst Rowing Club's Regatta', *Bendigo Advertiser*, 8 December 1881, p. 2.
5 'Competition for the Joseph Trophy', *Bendigo Advertiser*, 23 February 1882, p. 2.
6 'Rowing Notes', *Leader*, 25 February 1882, p. 13.
7 'Sandhurst Improvements', *Bendigo Advertiser*, 18 November 1872, p. 1.
8 'The Sandhurst Rowing Club at Geelong', *Bendigo Advertiser*, 16 March 1882, p. 2.
9 'Sandhurst Rowing Club', *Bendigo Advertiser*, 21 March 1882, p. 2.
10 'Sandhurst Football Club', *Bendigo Advertiser*, 29 March 1882, p. 2.

11   'General News', *Bendigo Advertiser*, 14 April 1882, p. 2.
12   'The Mayor's Ball', *Bendigo Advertiser*, 29 June 1882, p. 1.
13   'The Mayor's Ball', *Bendigo Advertiser*, 26 June 1882, p. 2.
14   'Sandhurst Telephone Exchange of the Crossly Telephone Company', *Bendigo Advertiser*, 8 September 1882, p. 2.
15   'Sandhurst Rowing Club', *Bendigo Advertiser*, 10 August 1882, p. 2.
16   'The Rowing Season', *Bendigo Advertiser*, 9 September 1882, p. 2.
17   'Opening of the Rowing Season', *Bendigo Advertiser*, 28 September 1882, p. 3.
18   'The Electric Light', *Bendigo Advertiser*, 23 October 1882, p. 2.
19   'The Illuminated Festival', *Bendigo Advertiser*, 26 October 1882, p. 2.
20   'The Electric Light Exhibition', *Bendigo Advertiser*, 27 October 1882, p. 2.
21   'Letters to the Editor', *Bendigo Advertiser*, 28 October 1882, p. 2.
22   'General News', *Bendigo Advertiser*, 7 November 1882, p. 2.
23   'Florence Irvine and Edward Wrixon Duncan Longden', marriage registration, 1 December 1882. Registration number 1882/4739. Victorian Registry of Births, Deaths and Marriages.
24   John Irvine, entry in Bank of Australasia Employment register, Series A/60/7, ANZ Group Archive, Melbourne.
25   'Football', *Bendigo Advertiser*, 11 April 1883, p. 3.
26   Articles about 'The Rowing Challenge' and the feud are from the *Bendigo Advertiser*, 21 April to 26 September 1883.
27   'Sandhurst Rowing Club', *Bendigo Advertiser*, 8 August 1883, p. 1.
28   'Sandhurst Rowing Club Regatta', *Bendigo Advertiser*, 15 November 1883, p. 3.
29   'Sandhurst Annual Regatta', *Bendigo Advertiser*, 22 November 1883, p. 3.
30   'Sandhurst Rowing Club Regatta', *Bendigo Advertiser*, 15 November 1883, p. 3.
31   Unidentified press cartoon, c. 1880s. State Library of New South Wales collection [Collection of newspaper cuttings and photographs on mainly Australian and English rowing and rowers, from the Davis Sporting Collection No. 2].
32   'Soirée Musicale', *Bendigo Advertiser*, 12 December 1883, p. 3.
33   'The Richmond Annual Regatta', *Age*, 17 December 1883, p. 6.
34   'Sandhurst Crew at the Richmond Regatta', *Bendigo Advertiser*, 19 December 1883, p. 1.
35   'Athletics and Aquatic Notes', *Bendigo Advertiser*, 19 December 1883, p. 1.
36   'Athletic and Aquatic Notes', *Bendigo Advertiser*, 9 January 1884, p. 1.
37   'Complimentary Banquet', *Bendigo Advertiser*, 25 January 1884, p. 2.
38   'Sporting Notes', *Bendigo Advertiser*, 3 April 1884, p. 3.
39   United Grand Lodge of England 1863-1887, 'Register of Contributions: Country and Foreign Lands, Supplement 1, Fols 312-628' on ancestry.com.
40   Sands & McDougall, *Melbourne Directory*, 1885.
41   'The Intercolonial Exhibition – Supplementary Awards', *Argus*, 28 April 1884, p. 6.
42   'John Irvine', entry in Bank of Australasia Employment register, Series A/60/7, ANZ Group Archive.
43   'Advertising', *Bendigo Advertiser*, 8 July 1884, p. 1.
44   'Hanlan's visit to Sandhurst', *Bendigo Advertiser*, 11 July 1884, p. 2.
45   'The Return Ball', *Bendigo Advertiser*, 23 July 1884, p. 3.
46   'Departure of Mr J.L. Irvine', *Bendigo Advertiser*, 23 July 1884, p. 2.
47   'John Irvine', entry in Bank of Australasia Employment register, Series A/60/7, ANZ Group Archive.

CHAPTER 7

1   'Clearances – December 5', *Sydney Morning Herald*, 6 December 1884, p. 12.
2   'Shipping News', *Tasmanian*, 27 December 1884, p. 20.
3   'Shipping', Launceston Examiner, 31 December 1884, p .2.
4   M. Cannon, *The Land Boomers*, Carlton, Melbourne University Press, 1966, p. 7.
5   'St Kilda Swimming Club', *Telegraph St Kilda, Prahran and South Yarra Guardian*, 31

ENDNOTES 231

      January 1885, p. 6.
6   'Barwon Rowing Club', *Geelong Advertiser*, 26 March 1885, p. 3.
7   'Rowing Notes', *Leader*, 28 March 1885, p. 22.
8   'Sporting Intelligence', *Argus*, 28 July 1885, p. 6.
9   'Rowing Notes', *Australasian*, 1 August 1885, p. 21.
10   'Deaths', *Argus*, 23 July 1885, p. 1.
11   'Rowing Notes', *Australasian*, 19 September 1885, p. 23.
12   'George Hotel, St Kilda', *Telegraph, St Kilda, Prahran and South Yarra Guardian*, 2 May 1885, p. 5.
13   'John Irvine', entry in Bank of Australasia Employment register, Series A/60/7, ANZ Group Archive.
14   'George Hotel, St Kilda', *Telegraph, St Kilda, Prahran and South Yarra Guardian*, 2 May 1885, p. 5.
15   'Aquatics', *Sportsman*, 27 January 1886, p. 6.
16   'Rowing Notes', *Australian Town and Country Journal*, 6 February 1886, p. 38.
17   'Rowing Notes', *Weekly Times*, 13 February 1886, p. 6.
18   'Aquatics', *Sportsman*, 24 February 1886, p. 6.
19   'Melbourne Annual Regatta', *Australasian*, 27 February 1886, p. 22.
20   'Answers to Correspondents', *Tasmanian*, 29 May 1886, p. 5.
21   Rowing Notes', *Leader*, 24 April 1886, p. 20.
22   'Aquatics', *Australasian*, 31 July 1886 p. 21.
23   'Athletic Notes', *Bendigo Advertiser*, 18 August 1886, p. 1.
24   'Cricket', *Argus*, 10 September 1886, p. 3.
25   'Victorian Rowing Association', *Argus*, 1 October 1886, p. 7.
26   'Rowing Notes', *Leader*, 6 November 1886, p. 22.
27   'Rowing Notes', *Leader*, 16 October 1886, p. 21.
28   'Rowing Notes', *Leader*, 23 October 1886, p. 20.
29   'Prince of Wales' Birthday', *Argus*, 10 November 1886, p. 5.
30   'Victorian Rowing Association', *Age*, 8 February 1887, p. 6.
31   'Aquatics', *Sportsman*, 9 February 1887, p. 8.
32   'Upper Yarra Amateur Regatta', *Argus*, 18 April 1887, p. 10.
33   'Adelaide V. St Kilda', *Australasian*, 4 June 1887, p. 22.
34   'Rowing Notes', *Australasian*, 23 July 1887, p. 22.
35   'News from Melbourne', *Evening News*, 19 July 1887, p. 6.
36   'Melbourne Rowing Club', *Australasian*, 24 September 1887, p. 21.
37   'Advertising', *Telegraph, St Kilda, Prahran and South Yarra Guardian*, 8 October 1887, p. 4.
38   St Kilda Historical Society, 'Inverleith', https://stkildahistory.org.au/our-collection/houses/acland-street/12-inverleith, accessed 12 September 2019.

CHAPTER 8

1   'News of the Day', *Age*, 13 February 1888, p. 4.
2   'Victorian Rowing Association Annual Regatta', *Argus*, 13 February 1888, p. 9.
3   'News of the Day', *Age*, 13 February 1888, p. 4.
4   Cigarettes were a rather fashionable habit in the 1880s and Irvine's use of them in 1888 marks him clearly as a fashionable man-about-town.
5   John Irvine, witness statement in PROV, VA 667 Office of the Victorian Government Solicitor, VPRS 30/P29 Criminal Trial Briefs, Unit 720, Item 14 The Queen v John Reardon, John R. Thompson and George Gossip.
6   Harold Gossip, witness statement in PROV, The Queen v John Reardon [et al].
7   John Irvine, witness statement in PROV, The Queen v John Reardon [et al].
8   Uttrick Todd, witness statement in PROV, The Queen v John Reardon [et al].
9   John Irvine, witness statement in PROV, The Queen v John Reardon [et al].
10   Thomas O'Toole, witness statement in PROV The Queen v John Reardon [et al].
11   John Irvine, witness statement in PROV, The Queen v John Reardon [et al].
12   'News of the Day', *Age*, 13 February 1888, p. 4.

13   Harold Gossip, witness statement in PROV, The Queen v John Reardon [et al].
14   'The Last Moment', *Herald*, 13 February 1888, p. 3.
15   'Latest Intelligence', *Bairnsdale Advertiser and Tambo and Omeo Chronicle*, 14 February 1888, p. 2; 'Serious Charge against a Bank Manager', *Colac Herald*, 14 February 1888, p. 3.
16   'Items of News', *Mount Alexander Mail*, 14 February 1888, p. 2.
17   'Arrest of a Bank Manager', *Australian*, 14 February 1888, p. 6.
18   G. Serle, 'David Gaunson', *Australian Dictionary of Biography*.
19   'The Day's Doings', *Herald*, 16 February 1888, p. 2.
20   'A Revolting Conspiracy', *Standard*, 18 February 1888, p. 2.
21   'Serious Charge Against a Bank Manager', *Leader*, 18 February 1888, p. 29.
22   'The Day's Doings', *Herald*, 16 February 1888, p. 2.
23   'Viewing the Body', *Bendigo Advertiser*, 17 February 1888, p. 2.
24   'Serious Charge Against a Bank Manager', *Age*, 16 February 1888, p. 5.
25   'A Revolting Conspiracy', *Standard*, 18 February 1888, p. 2.
26   'A Series of Assaults and Robberies', *Age*, 1 March 1888, p. 5.
27   'The D's', *Melbourne Punch*, 4 July 1889, p. 5.
28   'Ex-Superintendent's Death', *Age*, 14 June 1935, p. 10.
29   'The D's', *Melbourne Punch*, 4 July 1889, p. 5.
30   Victoria Police Department, *Victoria Police Gazette*, Melbourne G.P.O., 28 March 1888, p. 104.
31   'John Reardon', Prison Register (Prisoner number 22397), VPRS PROV, VA 1464 Penal and Gaols Branch, Chief Secretary's Department, VPRS 515 Register of Male Prisoners 1855-1947.
32   'George Gossip' Prison Register (Prisoner number 22398).
33   'John Holmes' Prison Register (Prisoner number 22399).
34   'A Revolting Conspiracy', *Standard*, 18 February 1888, p. 2.
35   M. Bellanta, *Larrikins: A History*, St Lucia, University of Queensland Press, 2012, p. xxi.
36   'General News', *Weekly Times*, 5 February 1870, p. 5.
37   George Gossip, witness statement in PROV, VA 667 Office of the Victorian Government Solicitor, VPRS 30/P29 Criminal Trial Briefs, Unit 720, Item 11, The Queen v Gossip: John Murray, George Gossip and John Reardon.
38   William McRae, witness statement in PROV, The Queen v Gossip, John Murray [et al].
39   Ellen Morcom, witness statement in PROV, The Queen v Gossip, John Murray [et al].
40   William Morcom, witness statement in in PROV, The Queen v Gossip, John Murray [et al].
41   John Stokes, witness statement in in PROV, The Queen v Gossip, John Murray [et al]. J. Green, *Crooked Talk: Five Hundred Years of the Language of Crime*, London, Random House, 2011, p. 335.
42   Harold Gossip, witness statement in PROV, The Queen v Gossip, John Murray [et al].
43   John Stokes, witness statement in PROV, The Queen v Gossip, John Murray [et al].
44   'A Series of Assaults and Robberies', *Age*, 1 March 1888, p. 5.
45   'Local News', *Telegraph, St Kilda, Prahran and South Yarra Guardian*, 10 March 1888, p. 5.
46   'Criminal Sittings for March', *Age*, 14 March 1888, p. 5.
47   R. Miller, 'Sir Hartley Williams (1843-1929)', *Australian Dictionary of Biography*.
48   'Pen and Ink Sketches of Prominent Persons', *Herald*, 26 July 1888, p. 5.
49   'The South Melbourne Conspirators', *Herald*, 19 March 1888, p. 3.
50   'Police Intelligence', *Age*, 13 July 1875, p. 4.
51   'Criminal Court', *Herald*, 16 July 1875, p. 3.
52   In his death cell letter, Moonlite said: 'Nesbitt and I were united by every tie which could bind human friendship. We were one in hopes, one in heart and soul and this unity lasted until he died in my arms. I long to join him where there shall be no more parting.' On Moonlite, see Paul Terry, *In Search of Captain Moonlite: The strange life and death of the notorious bushranger*, Sydney, Allen and Unwin, 2013.
53   Bellanta, *Larrikins*, p. 164.
54   'The South Melbourne Conspirators', *Herald*, 19 March 1888, p. 3.
55   PROV, Victoria Police Inwards Correspondence Files, VPRS 807/162, File P 8531, Cleal Re: Men frequenting public urinals.

ENDNOTES 233

56 'Sympathy with Mr J.L. Irvine', *Telegraph, St Kilda, Prahran and South Yarra Guardian*, 29 March 1888, p. 5.
57 'Rowing Notes – Melbourne Centennial Supplement', *Leader*, 26 May 1888, p. 22.

CHAPTER 9

1 'The Outdoor Procession', *Argus*, 2 August 1888, p. 3.
2 G. Serle, *The Rush to be Rich: A history of the colony of Victoria 1883–1889*, Carlton. Melbourne University Press, 1971, p. 285.
3 'Horticulture at the Exhibition', *Leader*, 18 August 1888, p. 14.
4 Serle, *The Rush to be Rich*, p. 286
5 S. Davies, 'Sexuality, Performance, and Spectatorship in Law: The case of Gordon Lawrence, Melbourne 1888', *Journal of the History of Sexuality*, vol.7, no.3 (January 1997), p. 391.
6 'Remarkable Imposture: A man disguised as a girl', *Weekly Times*, 6 October 1888, p. 6.
7 Detective Sexton's report, quoted in Davies, 'Sexuality', p. 395.
8 'A Man Personates a Woman in Melbourne', *South Australian Weekly Chronicle*, 6 October 1888, p. 11.
9 'Strange Scene at the Exhibition', *Leader*, 6 October 1888, p. 31.
10 'Vagrancy', *Colac Herald*, 2 October 1888, p. 3.
11 'Strange Scene at the Exhibition', *Leader*, 6 October 1888, p. 31.
12 'Rowing: Melbourne Rowing Club', *Age*, 22 September 1888 p. 11.
13 'Brief Mention', *Herald*, 22 November 1888, p. 6.
14 'Cricket – Cricket Jottings', *Sportsman*, 28 November 1888, p. 2.
15 D. Boadle, 'Daniel Whittle Harvey Patterson (1848–1931), *Australian Dictionary of Biography*.
16 Serle, *The Rush to be Rich*, p. 284.
17 'Social Notes', *Australasian*, 9 November 1889, p. 42.
18 'Social', *Melbourne Punch*, 7 November 1889, p. 11.
19 Social Notes', *Australasian*, 9 November 1889, p. 42.
20 'Fashionable Wedding', *The Colonist*, 9 November 1889, p. 13.
21 *City of Port Phillip Heritage Review*, Citation number 2115.
22 'Advertising', *Argus*, 24 March 1890, p. 1.
23 'A Holiday Cruise in the *Pateena*', *Argus*, 10 April 1890, p. 7.
24 'The *Pateena* Easter Trip', *Colonist*, 19 April 1890, p. 12.
25 'A Holiday Cruise in the *Pateena*', *Argus*, 10 April 1890, p. 7.
26 'The *Pateena* Easter Trip', *Colonist*, 19 April 1890, p. 12.
27 'A Holiday Cruise in the *Pateena*', *Argus*, 15 April 1890, p. 9.
28 'Society Chat', *Colonist*, 26 July 1890, p. 13.
29 G. Blainey, *A Land Half Won*, South Melbourne, MacMillan, 1980, p. 320.
30 Blainey, *A Land Half Won*, p. 321.
31 'A Travelled Victorian: Ex-Councillor John Barker of St Kilda: Roamings in South Africa', *Prahran Telegraph*, 31 October 1891, p. 3.
32 'Ex-Cr Barker Gives a Dinner: A Merry Gathering of Old Friends', *Prahran Telegraph*, 31 October 1891, p. 3.
33 'Victoria Museum and Art Gallery', *Launceston Examiner*, 3 May 1892, p. 3.
34 https://www.launcestonfamilyalbum.org.au/about, accessed 24 November 2019.
35 'Tasmanian Exhibition', *Tasmanian*, 27 February 1892, p. 28.
36 'Tasmanian Exhibition Show: Poultry and Dogs', *Launceston Examiner*, 2 April 1892, p. 5.
37 'Victoria Museum and Art Gallery', *Launceston Examiner*, 3 May 1892, p. 3.
38 'The Destitution and the Relief Fund', *Argus*, 19 August 1892, p. 3.
39 'Shipping Intelligence', *Age*, 5 January 1893, p. 4.
40 'Shipping', *Launceston Examiner*, 7 January 1893, p. 4.
41 'Shipping', *Evening Star*, 11 January 1893, n.p.
42 'Wedding Bells', *Launceston Examiner*, 2 March 1893, p. 5.
43 'Fashionable Wedding', *Daily Telegraph*, 2 March 1893, p. 3.

44 'Wedding Bells', *Launceston Examiner*, 2 March 1893, p.5.
45 'Advertising', *Argus*, 8 April 1892, p. 8.
46 Blainey, *A Land Half Won*, pp. 323, 325, 328.
47 'Advertising', *Age*, 12 May 1893, p. 8.
48 Blainey, *A Land Half Won*, p. 328.
49 'Shipping', *Mercury*, 30 May 1893, p. 8.
50 'Advertising', *Argus*, 21 October 1893, p. 3.
51 'Advertising', *Argus*, 15 November 1893, p. 1.
52 'Advertising', *Age*, 14 November 1893, p. 3.
53 'Sport and Play', *Melbourne Punch*, 12 October 1893, p. 11.
54 'Advertising', *Age*, 3 March 1893, p. 5.
55 'Institute of Legal Managers', *Age*, 17 April 1894, p. 6 .
56 'Grassfire', *Bacchus Marsh Express*, 8 December 1894, p. 3.
57 'Caffe Italia', *North Melbourne Advertiser*, 14 September 1889, p. 3.
58 Blainey, *A Land Half Won*, p. 333.
59 'Mining Notes', *Ovens and Murray Advertiser*, 28 September 1895, p. 6.
60 'Advertising', *Age*, 19 October 1895, p. 21.
61 D. Talbot, *Buckland Valley Goldfield*, Albury, NSW, Specialty Press, 2004, p. 196.
62 'New Departures in Alluvial Mining in the Bright District', *Ovens and Murray Advertiser*, 11 April 1895, p. 8.
63 'Federation Drought', www.nma.gov.au/defining-moments/resources/federation-drought, accessed 29 November 2019).
64 'Bright Warden's Court', *Ovens and Murray Advertiser*, 13 June 1896, p. 9.
65 'Advertising', *Age*, 8 July 1896, p. 8.
66 Victoria Police Department, *Victoria Police Gazette*, Melbourne G.P.O., 22 July 1896, p. 29.
67 R. Kelly, *Mitta Mining*, Mitta Mitta, Vic., Wombat Gully Productions, 2004, p. 5.
68 'Mining at the Mitta Mitta', *Argus*, 21 August 1896, p. 7.
69 'Shipping', *Launceston Examiner*, 17 April 1897, p. 8.
70 'New buildings in Melbourne', *Argus*, 14 June 1888, p. 5.

CHAPTER 10

1 'Police Intelligence: A Peculiar Case', *Age*, 8 October 1897, p. 6.
2 'A False Charge', *Ballarat Star*, 8 October 1897, p. 2.
3 'An Unfortunate Gentleman', *Bendigo Independent*, 8 October 1897, p. 4.
4 'A Previous Experience', *Bendigo Independent*, 8 October 1897, p. 4.
5 Was He 'Insulting?': The Bench Say No: Disgusting Statements: Not Sustained' and 'A Previous Experience', *Herald*, 8 October 1897, p. 4.
6 'Advertising', *Age*, 9 October 1897, p. 7.
7 'Mayoress's Reception', *Launceston Examiner*, 1 December 1898, p. 7.

CHAPTER 11

1 'Leases Declared Void', *Weekly Times*, 8 February 1902, p. 36.
2 'History of the Eight-Oar Championships', *Sydney Morning Herald*, 13 May 1905, p. 12
3 'Aquatics: Rowing and Sculling', *Sydney Mail and New South Wales Advertiser*, 6 March 1912, p. 54
4 'Presentation of a Trophy', *Examiner*, 9 February 1921, p. 8.
5 'Obituary', *Chronicle*, 26 January 1907, p. 40.
6 'Social Notes', *Daily Telegraph* (Launceston), 10 April 1919, p. 7.
7 'Personal', *Mercury*, 18 July 1919, p. 2
8 'Death of Mr R.F. Irvine', *Advocate*, 24 September 1921, p. 3.
9 'Launceston Family Album', www.launcestonfamilyalbum.org.au/detail/1030638/frances-beatrice-irvine, accessed 10 December 2019.

10 D. Boadle, 'Daniel Whittle Harvey Patterson (1848–1931), *Australian Dictionary of Biography*.
11 John Ettershank, letter to John Hunter Patterson, 20 February 1902, University of Melbourne Archives [Patterson family archives].
12 St Kilda Historical Society, 'Inverleith', https://stkildahistory.org.au/our-collection/houses/acland-street/12-inverleith, accessed 12 September 2019.
13 'Death of Captain Irvine', *Daily News*, 13 July 1922, p. 9.
14 'Mr C.R. Irvine's Death: Well-Known Station Manager's End', *Daily News*, 30 July 1934, p. 3.
15 'Family Notices', *Argus*, 10 February 1925, p. 1.
16 'Current Topics', *Launceston Examiner*, 30 April 1898, p. 9.
17 'About People', *Examiner*, 19 September 1933, p. 9.

PICTURE CREDITS

Every effort has been made to ensure all graphical material has been appropriately credited. If there are any errors please contact the publisher and these will be corrected.

ABBREVIATIONS

PROV: Public Record Office Victoria
SLV: State Library of Victoria

p. 2:	SLV Accession number: H2013.223/40
p. 3:	PROV: Register of Male Prisoners, 1896
pp. 4-5:	Photographer Charles Nettleton, SLV: Accession no: H96.160/1529
p. 8:	Photo taken from J.O. Randell, The Pastoral Pattersons: The history of Myles Patterson and his descendants, Queensberry Press, 1977, p. 40
p. 11:	Artist unknown.
p. 14:	Collection of the Queen Victoria Museum and Art Gallery, Launceston. QVM: 1987: P: 0997
pp. 32-33:	Launceston Public Library: Local History Collection
p. 38-39:	Launceston Public Library: Local History Collection
p. 40:	François Cogné, SLV: Accession no: H15456
p. 41:	Launceston Public Library: Local History Collection
p. 56:	William Bardwell, SLV: Accession no: H96.160/2717
pp. 58-59:	Photographer Fred Kruger, SLV Accession no: H39614/17
p. 61:	Ballarat Rowing Club, www.wbrc.com.au
p. 64:	SLV: Ballarat Directory 1875
pp. 66-67:	Illustrated Sydney News and New South Wales Agriculturalist and Grazier, 18 September 1875 p.20. Courtesy State Library of NSW
p. 78:	Illustrated Australian News, 12 May 1879 p.73, SLV: Accession no: IAN12/05/79/73
p. 82:	Illustrated Australian News, 20 March 1878 p.4,; SLV: Accession no: IAN20/03/78/44
p. 83:	Illustrated Australian News, 8 May 1880 p.69, SLV: Accession no: IAN08/05/80/69
pp. 84-85:	SLV: Accession no: H4512
pp. 88-89:	Illustrated Australian News, 20 February 1878 p.17, SLV: Accession no: IAN20/02/78/17

PICTURE CREDITS

p. 103:	Charles Nettleton, SLV: Accession no: H859
p. 107:	N.J. Caire, SLV: Accession no: H92.353/23
p. 108-109:	Robert Scott, SLV: Accession no: H96.160/1176
p. 132:	J W. Lindt, SLV: Accession no: H42622/49
p. 138:	Illus trated Australian News, 8 January 1887 p.13, SLV: Accession no: IAN08/01/87/13
p. 142:	Photographer unknown, SLV: Accession no: H87.91/16
pp. 144-145:	SLV: Accession no: H11751
p. 148:	PROV: Register of Male Prisoners, 1888
pp. 150-151:	Paterson Brothers, SLV: Accession no: H8012
pp. 152-153:	A. C Cooke, SLV: Accession no: H17929
p. 159:	Melbourne Punch, 4 July 1889 p.5. Courtesy National Library of Australia
pp. 172-173:	SLV: Cartographic material, File name vc000420-001
p. 176:	Charles Rudd, SLV: Accession no: H39357/200
p. 191:	Photographer unknown.
p. 195:	SLV: Accession no: IAN01/06/93/16b
p. 198:	SLV: Accession no: H2012.143/7a
p. 201:	J.W. Lindt, SLV: Accession no: H2001.60/31
pp. 204-205:	SLV: Accession no: H2013.223/22
p. 213:	Photographer unknown.
p. 216:	Photograph by the author of scrapbook in the collection of the Launceston Public Library: Local History Collection.
p. 219:	Collection of the Queen Victoria Museum and Art Gallery, Launceston. QVM:1987: P: 0935

Queer Oz Folk publishes Australian queer history, covering the period from the earliest days to the 21st century – a history of diverse sexes and genders and sexualities and of the lives organised around these. We publish with eye to quality, affordability and the widest possible audiences.

Series editor: Graham Willett

—— ALSO BY INTERVENTIONS ——

Radical Perth, Militant Fremantle
Edited by Charlie Fox, Alexis Vassiley,
Bobbie Oliver, and Lenore Layman

Radical Perth, Militant Fremantle tells 34 fascinating stories of radical moments In the cities' past, from as long ago as the 1890s and as recent as Occupy: the revolutionary theatre of the Workers Art Guild; the riot of unemployed workers outside the Treasury building; rock concerts inside St Georges Cathedral; bodgies and widgies cutting up the dance floor at the Scarborough Beach Snake Pit; the Point Peron women's peace camp, and many more.

ALSO BY INTERVENTIONS

Revolution is for us
The left and gay liberation in Australia
Liz Ross

'The homosexual is essential to the sexual revolution; there can be no revolution, no liberation, without us.'

Australia's Gay Liberation movement arose at a time when revolution was in the air and gays wanted to be part of it. It was the Left which had a theory and practice of revolution - Marxism. But it is often asserted that the Left was backward and even hostile, that Marxism had no tradition of dealing with sexual oppression. This book challenges those claims and shows that the Left - and the working class - was involved in the earliest gay rights movements and was integral to the new Gay Liberation Movement. It also refutes the claim that the Left has no intellectual tools to explain the oppression of women and gays. The book uncovers the rich history of the Left and Gay Liberation in Australia, an inspiration for activists today.

www.ingramcontent.com/pod-product-compliance
Lightning Source LLC
Chambersburg PA
CBHW070250010526
44107CB00056B/2415